Working Together with God to Shape the New Millennium
Opportunities and Limitations

Other titles in EMS Series

#1 *Scripture and Strategy: The Use of the Bible in Postmodern Church and Mission*, David J. Hesselgrave

#2 *Christianity and Religions: A Biblical Theology of World Religions*, Edward Rommen and Harold Netland, Editors

#3 *Spiritual Power and Missions: Raising the Issues*, Edward Rommen, Editor (out of print)

#4 *Missiology and the Social Sciences: Contributions, Cautions, and Conclusions*, Edward Rommen and Gary Corwin, Editors

#5 *The Holy Spirit and Mission Dynamics*, C. Douglas McConnell, Editor

#6 *Reaching the Resistant: Barriers and Bridges for Mission*, J. Dudley Woodberry, Editor

#7 *Teaching Them Obedience in All Things: Equipping for the 21st Century*, Edgar J. Elliston, Editor

Working Together with God to Shape the New Millennium
Opportunities and Limitations

Kenneth B. Mulholland
and Gary Corwin
Editors

Evangelical Missiological
Society Series #8

visit us at missionbooks.org

Working Together with God to Shape the New Millennium:
Opportunities & Limitations

Copyright 1999 by Evangelical Missiological Society
All Rights Reserved

No part of this book may be reproduced, stored in a retrieval system, or transmitted in any form or by any means—electronic, mechanical, photocopy, recording, or otherwise—without prior written permission from the publisher, except brief quotations used in connection with reviews in magazines or newspapers. For permission, email permissions@wclbooks.com. For corrections, email editor@wclbooks.com.

Published by William Carey Publishing (formerly William Carey Library)
10 W. Dry Creek Cir
Littleton, CO 80120 | www.missionbooks.org

William Carey Publishing is a ministry of Frontier Ventures
Pasadena, CA | www.frontierventures.org

ISBN: 978-1-64508-521-8 (paperback)

Printed Worldwide
27 26 25 24 23   2 3 4 5 6   IN

Library of Congress Cataloging-in-Publication Data on file with the publisher

Contents

Preface   7
Gary Corwin

Author Profiles   9

Biblical Foundations for the New Millennium
1. *What God is Doing to Shape the New Millennium*   14
   Henry Blackaby

Context of the New Millennium
2. *Setting the Scene for 2020: Shifting Missions into the Future Tense*   32
   Tom Sine

3. *Global Theological Challenges*   63
   T.V. Thomas

Working Together Theologically in the New Millennium
4. *Opportunities and Limitations*   82
   Charles Van Engen

   Response to Van Engen Regarding Opportunities and Limitations   123
   John H. Orme

5. *Working Together with Conciliar Groups*   132
   Charles Van Engen

6. *On the Theological Possibility of Orthodox/Evangelical Cooperation in Mission*   138
   Edward Rommen

7. *Theological Guidelines for Working Within a Roman Catholic Context*   144
   John Nyquist

   Response to Van Engen, Rommen, and Nyquist on the Possibilities of Working Together Theologically in a Wider Way   151
   James J. Stamoolis

Working Together Doxologically in the New Millennium

8. *Calling an Army of Artists* — 158
   Frank Fortunato

9. *Contextualized Worship and Arts in World Evangelization* — 162
   Byron Spradlin

10. *What's in the Middle? The Implications of Doxology for Missions in the Twenty-first Century* — 174
    Dave Hall

Working Together Strategically in the New Millennium

11. *Southern Baptists: Working Cooperatively to Reach the World* — 182
    Avery T. Willis Jr.

12. *Assembly of God Missions: Strategy on the Run* — 189
    Gary B. McGee

13. *AD2000 and Beyond: Toward a Conceptual Model* — 197
    Luis Bush

Leadership Needed for the New Millennium

14. *Challenging, Nurturing, and Forming Leaders for 2010* — 210
    Leighton Ford

Epilogue — 231
Kenneth B. Mulholland

Preface

Gary Corwin

The joint IFMA/EFMA/EMS Triennial Conference, held in Virginia Beach, Virginia, in September 1999, is the source for the articles and responses included in this volume. The authors represented are as varied and unique as the subjects upon which they write. Their contributions, however, coalesce around a challenging and highly important subject, though, as with any collection of conference articles, the reader should be reminded that the authors bring their own perspectives, styles of communication, and points of view.

The theme of that conference was "Working Together to Shape the New Millennium," a challenging task revolving around an incredibly ambitious purpose. While the theme served well to communicate the focus and aspirations of that Conference, it left some of us uneasy. This was primarily for two reasons. First, it seemed a bit presumptuous to suggest that a few hundred mission agency leaders and mission professors had it within their grasp to shape anything so grand as a new millennium. That was a problem with the question of "Who?"

The second reason/problem had to do with the question of "What?" Were we really there to shape a new millennium, with all the political, economic, social, moral, and religious images which that thought conjures up? Or was our purpose somewhat less grandiose, if no less noble—namely, to explore how to work more closely together with one another and others in this new millennium, so that we could work more closely with God in accomplishing all that He has in mind.

I have since reconciled my own concerns over these matters in the process of preparing this book for publication. The question of Who? and What? are both solved by making explicit in the book's title what is either explicit or implicit in all the articles which it contains. Namely, that it is God who does the work, and that we are privileged to be co-laborers together with Him in all that He is doing. Furthermore, as co-laborers with Him, we are of necessity also co-laborers with all others who belong to Him. Many of our articles focus explicitly on the opportunities and limitations related to that glorious fact.

The volume is organized into six sections, containing fourteen chapters (two of which also include responses), in addition to the preface and epilogue written by the editors:

(1) Biblical Foundations for the New Millennium describes both the ways and the means that God is already using to shape the new millennium, and what it takes to partner with Him;

(2) The Context of the New Millennium makes plain both the worldview and the global theological challenges which must be faced;

(3) Working Together Theologically explores the opportunities and limitations that evangelicals must consider in working together with others who are identified with the Conciliar Movement, Orthodox Churches, or the Roman Catholic Church;

(4) Working Together Doxologically highlights the centrality of worship to the missions enterprise, and the role of artists in enhancing it;

(5) Working Together Strategically provides both practical models and striking examples of how effective mission can be carried forward; and

(6) Leadership Needed for the New Millennium points the way forward in a heart-warming fashion for developing and mentoring the new generations of leaders that the task requires.

While the work of each author has undergone revision to achieve more of a print style than an oral one, the editors have endeavored to maintain the passion, perspectives and content of each one.

Shaping a new millennium is no mean task. In fact, it's not even a human one; though God for his own reasons, and out of His grace, invites us to join with Him in it. And working together is not always easy, even when we like each other. But this is the grand and glorious endeavor to which we are called, and we can take heart in knowing that even what is impossible with man, is possible with God.

Author Profiles

Henry Blackaby is the author of numerous books including the widely acclaimed, *Experiencing God*. He speaks widely and provides consultative leadership on prayer for revival and spiritual awakening.

Luis Bush was born in Argentina and served as International Director for the AD2000 and Beyond Movement until that group's recent planned sunset. He is a widely sought speaker and previously served as President of Partners International.

Gary Corwin is currently Associate Editor of EMQ, having also served as its Editor, and has been both Deputy Executive Director and an Executive Vice President of EMS. He has served with SIM in Ghana and as International Research and Education Coordinator, and is now a Special Representative.

Leighton Ford is a widely known evangelist and President of Leighton Ford Ministries, which specializes in developing young Christian leaders worldwide. He has written numerous books including *Sandy, A Heart for God*, and *Transforming Leadership*.

Frank Fortunato is the International Music Director for Operation Mobilization. He has also served as Coordinator of the AD2000 Movement Worship and Arts Network.

Dave Hall is founder of Worship to the Nations (WTN), a ministry of the international movement of PIONEERS which empowers worship-arts leaders to glorify God by serving existing PIONEERS teams, and by discipling worship-arts leaders among the unreached.

Gary B. McGee is Professor of Church History and Pentecostal Studies at the Assemblies of God Theological Seminary in Springfield, Missouri. He is an ordained minister and has consulted widely with the Division of Foreign Missions for The General Council of the Assemblies of God.

Kenneth B. Mulholland has a long history of leadership in the Evangelical Missiological Society, and currently serves as its President. He is Dean of the Columbia Biblical Seminary and School of Missions, having served previously as a missionary in Latin America.

John Nyquist is Associate Professor of Mission and Evangelism at Trinity Evangelical Divinity School, and also served for many years with Campus Crusade for Christ.

John Orme is Executive Director of the Interdenominational Foreign Missions Association (IFMA), and an adjunct professor of Moody Graduate School. He previously served as a missionary professor in Guatemala, and as a pastor in Michigan.

Edward Rommen has served as a missionary in Europe, and has taught at Trinity Evangelical Divinity School and Columbia International University. He is currently serving as Parish Priest at Holy Transfiguration Orthodox Church in Raleigh, N.C.

Tom Sine is an author, teacher, historian and international consultant in futures research for both Christian and secular organizations. He is author of the widely read *Mustard Seed Vs. McWorld*.

Byron Spradlin is the President of Artists in Christian Testimony, a mission board and nonprofit organization covering ministry for Christian artists in five countries and ten states.

James J. Stamoolis is Executive Director of the Theological Commission of the World Evangelical Fellowship. He previously served as Dean of the Graduate School at Wheaton College.

T.V. Thomas is the International Minister-at-Large for Every Home for Christ International, and Director of the Centre for Evangelism and World Mission in Regina, Saskatchewan. He is also the founding President of the Fellowship of Canadian Evangelists, and Vice President of the Academy for Evangelism in Theological Education.

Charles Van Engen is the Arthur F. Glasser Professor of Biblical Theology of Mission at the School of World Mission, Fuller Theological Seminary. He has also served previously as a missionary in Mexico and as the President of the Reformed Church of America. He is also the author of numerous books and articles.

Avery T. Willis is Senior Vice President of the International Mission Board of the Southern Baptist Convention, having served previously as a Southern Baptist missionary in Indonesia.

Biblical Foundations for the New Millennium

Chapter 1

What God is Doing to Shape the New Millennium

Henry Blackaby

If someone were to look at what you are doing and ask, "Why are you doing this" or "Why do you continue to do this"? What would your answer be? If God suddenly moved you in a dramatic way, and someone asked, "Why are you doing what you are doing" How would you answer them? I believe that Jesus provides us with the answer.

Let's look at two Scriptures, putting them into the context of our generation. The first is John 5:17, 19, 20, and is a foundation-centering piece. These passages tell us how Jesus responded to questions about what He was doing.

Jesus had mightily touched an individual. But there were those around who didn't understand and questioned Him. Jesus answered by telling them "It is my Father who is doing this." Suddenly it registers in us that what we do should not be what *we* are doing, but what *the Father* is doing through us.

If that is how Jesus functioned, it is also how you and I need to function. Jesus dwells within us, and He will not function in us differently from the way He Himself functioned in the days of His flesh. Verse 17 tells us what Jesus said when asked, "What in the world are you doing?" He answers by saying, my Father has been working right up until now and I have been working. Jesus draws a connection between the Father who is at work, and Jesus Himself who is at work. Now the words that follow are not idle ones. They are our life. They explain how Jesus knew what to do.

Do you ever sit in a planning meeting trying to figure out what to do? What your long-range goals should be? Jesus never did that. He approached it very differently. Again, when asked, "What are you doing?," he answered "My Father has been working right up until now and I have been working." It is interesting to note that it goes on to say they sought to kill him. You and I don't normally have that problem, but Jesus did. Jesus answered them saying, "Most assuredly." The King James Version says, "Verily, verily...." What does this mean? Jesus is saying that what he is about to tell them is exceedingly important. He is saying, if you don't hear anything else I have been saying, you had better hear what I am about to say. The NKJ says: "Most assuredly I say to you, the Son can do nothing of himself..." (i.e. on his own initiative) "...but what He sees the Father do, for whatever He does, the Son also does in like manner."

Jesus had just healed someone and was asked, "What are you doing?" His response was "my Father has been at work...." They could have interrupted and said, "We're not asking what your Father is doing, we're asking what you are doing." He would say, "You don't understand. I never do anything except what my Father is doing. I look to see what He is doing, and that's where I put my life."

Is that how you do your planning? Do you watch to see what the Father is doing and join him? The reason I am asking this is because you need to understand from Romans 8:28 that God's goal for you, and for your ministry, is to conform you to the image of his Son. He will not do anything different in you and me, or in guiding your organization, than He did in the days of his flesh. And He said the Son never took the initiative.

I am often asked, "Do you ever set goals?" That question comes straight out of the world. I answer, "No." "Why don't you?" they ask. I tell them, "I'm afraid I would reach them and never know what God really wanted to do."

Most of the time when we set goals, we set them so that we can achieve them—so we don't have to walk by faith to accomplish them. We set goals that we are reasonably sure we can reach. Jesus never set a goal that I know of. His goal was to do the will of the One who sent Him. And He was always watching to see where the Father was at work. It was his Father who was on a mission, and He had his Son in history to accomplish the next phase of that mission. Remember what the Scriptures say, "And God was in Christ reconciling the world to himself." So where Jesus saw the Father working, that's where He put his life. He let the Father complete his work through him.

The Father shows his children what He is doing, so that we can join Him. He never asks us to sit down and figure out how to work for Him or how to accomplish the Great Commission. He is completing the Great Commission. He is looking for those who understand his ways and the way He was with his Son. The Son never took the initiative. He did whatever He saw his Father doing, and joined Him. He put his life alongside what the Father was doing, and the Father completed His work through his Son.

In John 14, the disciples said, "Lord, if you could just show us the Father, that would be sufficient." What was Jesus' answer? "Have you been with me all this time and have you not known me? If you have known me you have known the Father." And He said, "If you don't believe me, at least believe for the works sake." The works were not his, they were the Father's. In verse 10 Jesus says, "The words I shared with you, they are not mine. It is my Father living out his life (or completing his work) through me."

Lord, did you not feed the multitudes? "No, my Father did," he said. "God simply used me to accomplish that." He says, "I didn't come to do my own will. I came to do the will of Him who sent me, and my Father is always with me, telling me what it is on his heart. The Father does anything I ask because I am doing it in accordance with what is on his heart. There is nothing in the heart of my Father that is not immediately in my own life fully. And when the Father sees that, there is nothing I need to accomplish that He is not fully and unreservedly responsive to in my life." So He said, "You have seen the Father when you have seen me."

Then Jesus turned to the disciples and said, "The same relationship I have with the Father and my Father has with me, that's the relationship that I want you to have with me." In John 17, He says, "Father, I pray for all those who will believe in me. I pray that they may be one in us, as you are in me and I am in you, and I will be in them." Then He adds that enormous moment, "Father, the glory that you have given to me I gave to them that they may have that union with me and therefore with you." And what is the reason? So the world may believe. The greatest single strategy I know for global evangelization is found right there. Evangelism is a by-product of a relationship with Jesus Christ. It is when He is fully in relationship with us that anything on the heart of our Lord—anything that He makes clear to us—prompts the answer "yes" without hesitation.

This is one of the most significant Scriptures when it comes to understanding how Jesus knew what to do. He said, "My Father has been working right up until now and I have been working." The Son does not take the initiative. Whatever He sees the Father doing, that is what the Son does. I am going to open up to you what I believe is the activity of the Father today, so that we can make some major adjustments in our lives. And I'll challenge you to release everything in you to get on board with what God is doing.

In John 15, Jesus talks about the vine and the branch. What is the first thing He says the vinedresser does? He prunes. What was successful last year, He is going to cut off. Don't fight to perpetuate it. Why does He deal with the most successful and fruitful part of your ministry? So that you can bear much more fruit. And if you don't let him deal with the successes of last year, then you are going to find out it isn't quite as successful this year as it was last year. Then we often try to explain it away, arguing that it was an unusual year, but that God has told us to keep on doing this until He comes.

That is not the way our Vinedresser works. He picks the most fruitful part of your ministry and cuts it off, or prunes it back. His purpose is to develop a much more fruitful ministry. Many of us, on the other hand, hold on to the most successful things we've done, seeking to perpetuate them. When things start to go down, we wonder why and try to compensate with more and more activity. John 15 is a wonderful lesson on how to let the Father complete a work in you, so He can bring maximum fruit from your life and ministry.

The second Scripture I want to touch on is 2 Corinthians 6, beginning at verse 1. It has so much in it about being ambassadors for Christ, the love of Christ controlling us, and always wanting to please Him. It reads, "We, then, as workers together with Him also plead with you not to receive the grace of God in vain, for He says, 'In an acceptable time...'" Some translations say, "In the time of God's favor..."

When God grants his favor, it is a special moment in history. One can go back and trace many moments of God's favor. The Reformation was such a moment. You can't explain it. In some of the darkest moments God granted his favor and said, "This is my moment." It turned the whole world upside down. It changed our world.

Another moment in history was when the Moravians met. Every

time I read the story of that great moment, I weep and ask, "Oh, God, would you do it again?" As that little group of individuals met around the Lord's table, what a moment it was! It changed the course of missions. I don't believe they expected that, but it was God's moment. And when God chose that moment, it changed the course of history. Not only did it change that group of individuals in a great and mighty revival; they began, in the power of the presence of God, to feel the incredible responsibility of being available to God, no matter what the conditions—to go and serve him anywhere.

What a powerful thing it is to review the moments, when that church stood and said, "Greenland needs ...," and there were those who said, "We'll go!"

Before the eighteenth-century was over, the Moravians had more missionaries on the field than all others combined. How can you explain that moment with the Moravians? You can't, unless you turn to the Scriptures. God is saying, "I plead with you, don't receive the grace of God in vain." In a divine moment of his approval, God says, "I see your heart, and I know my plan and purpose. Now is the moment."

Do you remember when some young men met under a haystack? It wasn't just a rainy day under a haystack, it was a divine moment. Something happened at that prayer meeting that you can't explain in human terms. It wasn't their devotion, it was a moment of God's favor. Through the history of missions you can see those moments when God says, "This is the moment of my favor."

The rest of that Scripture says, "In an acceptable time, in a time of my favor, I heard you." Many of you have been crying out to God for revival in America. So have I. Most of my life has been given to seeking revival in Canada and America. But there comes a time when He says, "Now is the day of my favor, and I have heard you." Would you recognize one of those moments if God did that.

The Scripture goes on to say, "And in the day of salvation, I have helped you." When God chooses a moment for a great and powerful movement to bring people to salvation, He is going to help us!

Many who look at the record would say, "I cannot remember a time in history when so many people are being swept into the Kingdom in such large numbers over the entire globe." If this is the day of his salvation, how should we then live? How should we guide what we have as a steward? Is it business as usual? When it is a moment of God's favor, and a moment of his salvation, it can never be "business as usual." because everything changes.

The apostle Paul goes on to say, "Behold now is the accepted time, the time of God's favor. Now is the day of salvation." He then talks about how we should live. He says, "We are workers together with God." One great unexplainable moment, which has been in motion for the last 10 to 15 years, is that we began to cooperate together. I've heard many an individual say, "You know, there came a moment in our history when something happened and we began to cooperate together."

Suddenly parachurch groups who wouldn't talk to each other, began to work together. Denominations began to work together. Walls and resistance came down. Can you explain what God did in our generation to bring that about? I know it has happened, because I have been involved across denominations and parachurch groups where I hear leaders say, "This is an unprecedented time."

The only one I know who could have orchestrated this is God. You can't give any man or book or meeting credit. It just happened. God chose a moment to bring his people together with one heart and one mind, to follow Him to all the peoples on the face of the earth. This is God's moment of favor.

And when God does something, we had better take notice. We had better make some adjustments in our lives. It doesn't matter how big or small we are, God is doing a mighty work to bring his people to a point where they can work together with one heart, saying "Whatever we have, you can have. Whatever ways we can cooperate, we are going to do it." It wasn't that way 20 years ago, but it is today. Never have I seen the people of God so anxious to have one heart and one mind. So, when God says, "This is my hour of favor," you had better listen. And all you do, including your planning meetings, need to take a whole new direction.

Now I am going to tell you some things that I believe. Based on the Scriptures we just looked at, we must ask, "What good is this Scripture if I can't apply it? If I can't see what God is doing, what good is it?" It is wonderful to read, "In a time of God's favor.... I will help you. I will hear you." This has incredible implications. God tells us, "I'll hear you when you cry to me. I'll hear you when you pray. I'll hear when you cry out for finances and for personnel. I'll hear you, and every time you pray in my name, I'll do it. And greater things than you have seen me do, you shall do."

Following are some areas in which I am involved, and in which I have seen enormous shift and change.

College Students

God is doing something in the hearts of college students. He is literally thrusting them around the world. For this generation, the more difficult, the more demanding and sacrificial the task, the better.

It is a different generation of college students who are responding. I don't know when I have seen more university and college students sensing that the one life they have, they want to give it to God. It is as if God is saying, "The world has had my best too long. I'm going to call my best back to myself and they will have a heart for the Kingdom of God." And the college students are responding. Has your organization made any adjustments to that? Have you made your way to the college campus? Have you looked at your own college students?

I remember when I sensed God moving to touch the world. I prayed, "God, touch my children." And I looked to see if God was going to do that. I made some changes in my life, and in my own heart, activities, and choices. Sure enough, God called all five of them. Someone asked, "You didn't expect God to call all five, did you?" I said, "Yes, I did!" I sought to live before them in an atmosphere where they would want to serve the God they saw their Dad and Mom serve.

So, I say to you, this is a generation where college students are turning to the Lord. We have a summer missions program for college students. Participation has jumped 20 times what we used to know. From just a couple of hundred, there are now 10,000 to 50,000 setting their hearts on God, and going anywhere and everywhere each summer in mission.

Teenagers

God is touching teenagers. There is hardly a place I go, if there are teenagers present, where there will not be some who come up to me with tears in their eyes. These juniors and seniors in high schools say with a great deal of earnestness, "Dr. Blackaby, we sense that the generations before us have betrayed us, and our nation is in a mess. But God is calling us to meet at 7 o'clock every morning of the week to pray that He would begin revival in America through us teenagers." This is happening all over America.

Everywhere I go teenagers are responding to missions. When you go to speak in a church, do you say, "God, I know you are moving among teenagers. Give me a message that will touch the heart of the teens. Let me be a worker together with you. This is the day of your favor for this generation of teens."

Never have I seen such an incredible movement of God among teenagers. We are anticipating that in the near future, just from our group of churches alone, we will see 100,000 teenagers on the mission fields every summer. And we are discovering that the largest percentage of those who get on the mission field feel called to missions. Why do you suppose God is touching teenagers? Because He wants a whole generation to release their life to the far-flung corners of the earth.

Global Awakening

I believe that America stands on the edge of judgment. If we don't turn back to God, and God's people don't turn back to him, the nation will not avoid his judgment. And when it comes on America, I believe it will be as severe as for any nation that God has ever judged. I have heard some people say, "Henry, God won't do it to America; we are sending missionaries all over the world." My response is, "Let me tell you a frightening and wonderful thing. Already the Two-thirds World countries are sending out more missionaries than we are!" God will not be without a witness to take the gospel to unreached people groups. If He is getting ready to judge America, and shut down many who would come from here, He is not going to be without a witness to the unreached people groups. He is raising up a force from these other countries. Their assignment, as they accept it from their heart, is to go to the hard places—the places nobody else will go. Many are going into the Islamic world.

Who is doing this? Who is putting this on the hearts of people in the Two-thirds World? Who is stirring their hearts to send hundreds and thousands of missionaries out to the ends of the earth? Only God can do that.

The greatest single need in missions today is to strengthen the home base. If we don't do that, we are lost. But what about God's activity in the rest of the world? Every country we go into, one of the first things they want to tell me is that they are sending missionaries. "We didn't do that before. But we are sending missionaries now." In one country they said, "We believe that the assignment God gave us is to the Islamic world, and Cuba, so that is where we are sending all our missionaries."

I don't know how to explain it, but I believe God has made a covenant with the Filipino people. I believe He said to them, "I see such a love for me in your heart that I could send you anywhere in the world, and you'd go even if it cost you your life." If you hear of arrests and imprisonment around the world, more often than not it will be a Filipino believer. I have wept with them, and told them, "As I see what is happening in your hearts, I know only God could do that. When He puts you in the tough places you share your witness even if it costs you your life."

I also said to them, "I don't know when I have wept more over a people, except perhaps Native Americans, than I have for the Filipino people. I think God made a covenant with you, and you said 'Yes, Lord.' God is thrusting you out by the thousands into the most difficult parts of the earth, and you are bearing witness and starting churches." This is an incredible movement of God.

The Business World

God is also touching the business world for missions in a way I have never known before. Every month I have a conference call with about 30 CEO's of Fortune 500 companies. They are Christian men who are saying, "God put us where we are. Would you help us? How do we each live out our life as a CEO of a Fortune 500 company?" These men are setting their hearts to adjust everything in their lives and in their businesses.

One of them I talked with is responsible for 30,000 employees. With tears in his voice he said, "God told me I am to touch every one of these employees and their families." Two months later, I asked him how he was doing. He said, "God is enabling me, just like He said." In a time of God's favor, and in the time of His salvation, He will hear you and He will help you. He then asked, "Henry, what do you think this means? They made me vice-president, and I deal with foreign countries." "I can tell you what it means," I said, "God is going to put you next to Pharaoh."

I don't know when I have heard of so many CEO's in the business world touching presidents and other top people of the world. I heard of one who shared from the Scripture with the Premier of China. As a result of the conversation with this highly respected layman, the Premier immediately ordered several million Bibles to be published. I hear stories from all over where it is the businessman, not the missionary, who has access to the presidents and kings of the world. And those business people have a heart stirred by God so that He would put them in a place to touch the world for Him.

One man, in charge of training all of the diplomats from his country, had his life changed by *Experiencing God*. Because he is in charge, he now has every diplomat from that nation go through *Experiencing God*, so that they can be a faithful witnesses to the ideals of their country. Who is doing that? God is. The hand of God is on the CEO's of these major companies of the world in a very significant way. And they can go where no missionary can. They can get missionaries out of or into countries because of their position, and the influence they have with leaders of nations.

God is moving in the hearts of Christian businessmen. He is saying to them, "I put you here for such a time as this. Not for the company, but for the Kingdom of God." Never have I heard so many of them ask, "Henry, can you help us know how to live our lives?" They control enormous finances and are saying, "When our company goes into a Two-Thirds World country, we do humanitarian things. We build stadiums, and spend millions of dollars." One said to me, "If you will tell me about the countries where I am going, we can direct those humanitarian funds from our country into a Christian setting. Would that be helpful?" When I add these up, my heart leaps, and I wonder if the CEO's of mission-sending agencies understand what God is doing.

Athletics

God is taking athletics into the Islamic world. Many say to the leaders of Islamic nations, "Would you like me to help you have a world-class basketball team?" The head of that Islamic country, out of his own sense of national pride says, "Would you come and help us have a contender in the Olympics?" The same thing is happening with soccer, tennis, and other sports.

God has taken some of the most qualified, wonderful athletes, and touched their hearts. He has given them a heart to say, "I want to link with the people of God. I want to know how I can use my athletic fame as an instrument in the hand of the King of kings, and do it right now in the middle of the most needy countries of the world.

Military

I have felt for a long time that God has put our military in some very interesting places to achieve his purposes. I have discovered to my delight that an enormous number of churches on the foreign mission field are started through military personnel. The Spirit of God is touching the hearts of military personnel and saying, "Let me tell you why I put you here. I want you to start a church."

Have you linked into this? Have you set your heart to find out where the military is, and asked God to show you his people who want to bring in his Kingdom where God has put them? These military personnel who do church planting on the mission field are often called to be a pastor or a missionary when they get home, and leave the military. I have talked to hundreds who have said, "I was on the mission field and God let me be a part with several other men of starting a whole new church. We started the church and many were saved. Then we moved, and God brought other leaders in. That experience did something in my heart, and I believe God wants me to go back to that country and do church planting as a missionary." Are you watching to see what God is doing through the military? It is amazing how many military personnel in other countries of the world have become Christians, and are using their influence in the Kingdom. This is a wonderful, wonderful day.

Exchange Students and Teachers

Exchange students are also being used mightily by God. But they are not going just to get an education. They have a sense of missions, and are being exchange students in some of the most interesting and difficult countries of the world in order to serve as ambassadors for Jesus Christ. Teachers are also going into some of the most difficult places in the world.

The Internet

Someone had a burden to put *Experiencing God* on the Internet. After the first round of teaching it on-line, this individual received e-mails from about 23 countries. He saw hundreds come to faith in Christ. Are you watching to see what God may have put in place to touch people through the Internet? Remember, Jesus said, "My Kingdom is like leaven." He didn't say, "My Kingdom is like an explosion or an event," but "My Kingdom is like leaven." If you go on the Internet and lead one person to Christ in a remote little village in Iran, what will be the impact for his Kingdom? You didn't just reach one person, you set in motion the principles of the Kingdom of God. They will no more be able to keep quiet than you or I could dam up Niagara Falls. And what you started, God will use to touch others around them. And if you were to go back a year later, in some parts of the world, that person who was led to Christ on the Internet, will have a whole village listening. Then they will have the village across the valley listening. It's true. I've heard the testimonies.

One person in Africa who was saved through the internet was so excited that he began to tell everyone in the village. He then drove several hundred miles to the missionaries to say, "We have 57 people ready to be baptized." They asked, "What missionary has been out there?" He answered, "None, just me. You remember, you led me to Christ and I have been talking with my neighbors, and my family, and everybody else." The Kingdom is like leaven. And God has given us an incredible opportunity to touch a world just by that means alone. You are not just touching individuals, you are touching whole villages and whole areas of the world. Because the Kingdom is like leaven, if one person is saved, it can't stay just one unless they kill him. And sometimes they do. But, oh, what an incredible story could be written about those who have used that simple means alone.

Experiencing God is now in Arabic. We worked with TransWorld Radio to put it in 65 sessions, and they broadcast it all over the Middle East. They broadcast it all over China. And they have touched other parts of the world. When God announces this is the day of his favor, and when He says this is the day of salvation, you can count on it. Whatever you did yesterday, or five years ago, even if it didn't work then, try it again, because in the day of God's favor, everything works! In the day of His salvation, everything works! And He helps us, and He hears.

I have never seen such a movement of God. He is moving so many of his people with a depth that I have never seen before. I have watched individuals sell their homes and businesses, and go to the mission field. Never have we seen so many volunteering for missions as we do today. It is overwhelming. Our International Mission Board cannot keep up with the number of people who are applying to go. We may come close to 1,000 new career appointees in missions this year. Is this the time of God's favor? We have never seen this before. And I can tell you, it has nothing to do with the International Mission Board. It has nothing to do with our promotion. It has everything to do with God touching the hearts of his people.

After the great Moody awakening, 20,000 young adults ended up on the mission field in the following 25 year period. This happened also in the great revival and awakening in Wales in 1904 and 1905. You can tell when there is a movement of God, and it is a manifestation of His favor—you see God touching the hearts of so many.

Volunteers

Another area where God is touching hearts is among volunteers. In the last year, combining our home and foreign missions areas, we had about 500,000 who volunteered to do some form of mission work. That is unprecedented. When I see this, I don't see it as marketing or institutional advancement. I see it as the time of God's favor, and the time of his salvation.

Government

Have you followed what God is doing in Nigeria? Did you know that the new president is a Baptist? Now that doesn't mean anything unless he is also a genuinely committed Christian. He will not begin government without prayer and Scripture every time Parliament meets. He is determined to be a servant of God, and to see the Kingdom of God come in his country. I'm seeing that more and more around the world. God is touching key leaders.

Do you look at this and say, "That is not on our agenda"? My wife and I recently had the privilege of being in Hungary and Romania, and we are soon to be in Cuba. When you go to a country, understand that God has been there before you got there. You don't bring God with you! I tell missionaries that the first full year of their mission term ought to be given to understanding what God has been doing in this country before they got there.

When I was in Hungary, a shy little lady came up to me and waited and waited. She then said, "I don't want to offend you. I don't want to hurt you, but would you be interested in taking a tour of the Parliament buildings?" I told here I'd be thrilled to do that.

She told me she was the secretary to the President. "Do you think the President would receive a signed copy of *Experiencing God?*," I asked her. "Oh," she said, "He'd be thrilled to receive it." And then I realized God had sent her.

How could I have possibly had entrance to the President of Hungary unless God did it? I came away with a deep sense of humility. "Lord," I prayed, "Thank you that I didn't cut off the group who wanted to talk to me." She had been third down the line, and I had my own agenda. I said, "Lord, I thank you that you put in my heart to stay until the last person who wanted to talk had come by." And she was just about the last person.

I also had opportunity to talk with believers in Hungary. I told them to "Pray, pray, pray." This president is the most beloved person in Hungary. His son has become a Christian. Maybe this will be the means God will use to bring the president to faith in Christ. And if he does, what a difference it would make in that great country.

The week before this man had sat down and talked with President Clinton, the Prime Minister of England, and other world shakers. What could happen if he came to know the Lord? Remember, this is the time of God's favor. God says, "I'll hear when you cry. And this is the day of salvation, and I will help you."

World leaders

One of the politicians that I came to know is Steve Largent. He is one of the best wide receivers the Seattle Sea Hawks ever had. He was reading *Experiencing God* as he was trying to decide whether or not to run for Congress. During the study, he concluded that God did want him to run for Congress. Do you know why Steve Largent is in Congress? By the divine will of God. He knows it, and others know it. I could name 10 or 15 others who are also there by divine assignment.

Disasters

Every time there has been a global disaster more churches have been started while trying to help people than during all the rest of our mission time put together. I turned to our mission personnel on one occasion and asked, "Do you think that disaster is one of God's greatest means for spreading the gospel?" They said, "Without a question of a doubt." "Then you ought to have a department of El Niño," I responded, "and you ought to track where the forecasters say there is going to be a disaster." In a recent disaster in the Caribbean, hundreds of churches were started. Could you do the same? Yes. But you say, "That was a disaster, we had better go somewhere else." No, whenever there is a disaster, put your life there. Put your ministry there. You can do more in a country during a time of disaster than almost any other time.

Partnerships

I've never seen so many partnerships. The local church is partnering. Associations of churches are partnering. Everyone seems to be partnering. This is a time when God is laying on the heart of his people an incredible commitment and desire to partner with the nations of the world. I don't know when I have ever seen God marshal so many of his people so thoroughly, as I see him doing it now. I come back to the Scripture, and plead: "Do not receive the grace of God in vain." Don't let God move with such mighty power while you set it all aside as though it means nothing. Don't set aside the grace of God.

Conclusion

Are you just perpetuating the same things you did last year? Or are you moving and adjusting your life as Jesus did? Jesus said, "I don't take the initiative. But whenever I see my Father at work, I join him." I have been telling you some areas where the Father is at work. There is no other explanation for it than that.

Have you been responding to partnerships? Have you been responding to college students, young people, and teenagers? Have you been responding to military personnel and businessmen? Have you been responding to the thousands who are volunteering to go on missions at their own expense? What are you doing to adjust to where God has you, and to what He is doing?

Jesus made a simple statement: "If you are not going with me, you are going against me." Let me say it again, If you are not going with Him, he said, you are going against Him. So, if you can see all the activity of God, and say that it is not what your organization is here for—you can count on it, you are going against Him. And it is an awful thing to be chosen of God, but be out of step with the Savior. You may be maintaining an organization, or practicing religion faithfully according to the traditions of our founding fathers. But if you are nowhere near where He is at work, you are not only not going with Him, you are going against Him.

I had an interesting moment in Toronto. I was asked to speak to about a hundred and twenty Christian CEO's and businessmen from the city. I spoke about God's assignment for them to be on a mission in the marketplace to bring revival. I cited the last great revival in America from 1857-59—that great movement in Manhattan which was led by lay businessmen. I began to describe what happened within the business community. I said, "God has assigned you to the business community, not to make money for the world, but to bring revival for the Kingdom." Many of these men started to weep. Nobody had ever told them that. When I went back to Toronto, I asked if I could speak to the pastors of the largest churches in the city. I spoke to about 37 of these wonderful pastors.

Sitting in front of me was a dear servant of God. He was the rector of the largest Anglican church in downtown Toronto. As I spoke, I told the pastors, "Your assignment is not to bring the people out of the business community to help you have a successful church. When those men come to you, your assignment is to bring them into such a relationship with God that, when they go back into the workplace, revival breaks out. You're there to equip those men and women to go back into the marketplace. As I shared that, this rector began to weep. He was the first person up afterwards and he said, "Are you telling me that the church is to receive the ones God is bringing out of the community and so equip them that they go back on fire to change it?" "Yes, sir, that's what I am saying," I told him. He then said, "I want you to know, the whole of our church is going to change in its focus."

God is touching His people. If I could describe it, I'd simply say this is the day of God's favor. This is the day of his salvation. He is hearing his people in ways we have never seen. He is helping his people in ways that are incredible. This is a time of God's favor.

What I have been describing to you is God pouring out his heart of love. His Spirit is moving mightily. He is expressing his grace to us. Countries are open. Places to go are open. Doors are open. People are waiting. God is marshaling every segment of our community and sending them together. He is putting them together in new kinds of teams. He is showering us with his grace. Is this one of the moments of his favor? I believe it is. We are on the front end of it. Wouldn't it be wonderful if the next generations could look back and say, "It was a time just like the Reformation, just like Wesley, just like the Haystack prayer meeting, just like when Jesus gave the Great Commission.

God came to a group of men and women and said, "This is the day of my favor. Let me show you my favor. Let me show you my grace. I am pouring out on you the spirit of grace and supplication." Wouldn't it be wonderful if they looked back and said, "And that generation knew it and responded. With one heart they released everything there was in them to follow the direction God had given them. And they did it together with the rest of his people. With one heart, the Lord brought redemption to every people group on the face of the earth."

You, spiritual leader, do you recognize God's time of favor? If it is God's time of salvation, would you recognize it? Would you release everything there is in you for God to rearrange it, so that it is in tune with Him? Because if you are not going with Him, you are going to be going against Him. And I wouldn't want any of us to be in that position. Take a moment to pray. I sense God is standing on the edge of his mightiest move, and I don't know a group of men and women whose "Yes" to God could mean so much as in this very room. It is God who is on a mission. He invites us to go with him.

Context of the New Millennium

Chapter 2

Setting the Scene for 2020: Shifting Missions into the Future Tense

Tom Sine

Introduction

Mission executives in the United States and beyond our borders tell us they have never felt so hammered by change. They are looking for help. In many parts of the world, missionaries are much more at risk than they were ten years ago. Recent refugee crises like Kosovo are raising a host of new challenges for Christian mission organizations. The Asian meltdown has seriously impacted the church in Korea and their efforts to dramatically expand their activities in global mission. Numbers of leaders in Western mission organizations tell us that raising money to support their mission initiatives has never been tougher. Many leaders report that approaches to both missions abroad and fundraising at home that worked brilliantly for years don't work any more.

One of the major reasons this is such a tough time for those in leadership is that we are living in a world changing at blinding speed. Our assignment as we enter the new millennium is to help those in leadership make sense of the change that is likely to confront the church and mission organizations in its first two decades.

We will explain why it is essential that those of us in leadership take the future seriously. Then we will take you on trips back to the future to sketch some of the possible changing landscape of tomorrow's world economically, politically, technologically, and societally. We will specifically try to identify new challenges and opportunities likely to face mission organizations, missiologists, and local churches all over the world. Then we will ask how ably the church is likely to respond to these challenges given the significant changes taking place in the church with regard to attendance and giving patterns. Finally, we will suggest some creative ways to fundamentally reinvent how we do mission, as well as how we work with supporters to address the new challenges of a new millennium.

In light of the unprecedented change we are likely to face in both the larger world and the church, it is important that we try to think outside of the box a bit on how we might respond effectively. I am persuaded that new challenges will require some radical new responses in our lives, churches, and mission organizations. I don't expect everyone to totally agree with either my assessment or recommendations but I do hope to spark an energetic discussion about how we can together advance the mission purposes of God in a rapidly changing world.

Looking Back on Missions 1990–2000

It seems like it was only yesterday that many of us were gathered together in Manila in 1989 to help set the direction for missions for the nineties. As you know, that was a definitive conference in focusing the mission of the evangelical church in the nineties on reaching unreached people groups. Looking back on the past decade there is much good news for which those working under the umbrella of EFMA/IFMA can thank God.

Dudley Woodberry, former Dean of the School of World Mission at Fuller, states that "through the efforts of the Lausanne Committee for World Evangelization, AD 2000 and Beyond, and the World Evangelical Fellowship, coordinated efforts are being made in church planting, especially in the 10–40 window...with considerable church growth."

Patrick Johnstone in his new book, *The Church is Bigger Than You Think*,[1] documents the remarkable growth of the church in much of Africa, Latin America, and parts of Asia. Through DAWN and the AD2000 movement new churches have been planted in regions with little gospel witness. Johnstone further states that while the Bible was translated into only 537 languages at the turn of the twentieth century, at the beginning of the twenty-first century it has been translated into 2800 languages.[2]

One of the most encouraging signs for the future is the advancing of the Two-Thirds World church. Increasingly churches in Brazil, Kenya, and Korea have become major missions sending churches. Ten years ago Korea was sending 200 missionaries. Today that figure has reached 6,000 and is growing. Interdev predicts that 95,000 missionaries will be sent out from non-Western churches before the end of the year 2000.[3] One of the major changes of the past decade that many haven't recognized is that North America is no longer the center of global missions. We are entering an era in which the whole church is reaching out to the whole world.

There is also much good news to report from evangelical agencies working with the global poor during the past decade. Child mortality has been steadily decreasing since 1960. As a result life expectancy is rising in almost every country on earth. Immunization is on the threshold of eliminating diseases like measles and polio. Per capita global income is also beginning to rise in most countries and global population growth is beginning to slow.

There are thousands of examples of the great things God has been doing in the last decade. Let me share just a few. IFES is doing evangelism on the West Bank using mixed groups of Palestinian and Jewish Christians to bear witness to the reconciling gospel of Jesus Christ in a community filled with bitter ethnic and religious animosities. Clive Calver of World Relief reports that the Albanian government is stunned by what 160 evangelical churches, planted in this decade, have been able to do to address the staggering needs of Kosovo refugees. Young missionaries from Brazil have gone to Portuguese speaking communities on islands off the West Coast of Africa. They went as church planters, but the community also invited them to develop a health care program and schools to address the urgent needs of the community. Remarkably, these young Brazilian missionaries chose to live at the subsistence level of everyone in their community as a part of their witness to Christ.

Everyone here could share dozens of stories of how the good news of the Gospel has made a difference in the lives of families, churches, and communities. In the 90s you and your staff were a part of this remarkable extension of the gospel of Jesus Christ all over the world. Christine and I have seen firsthand many of the ways in which God has used your ministries to touch our world. And as my Australian wife would say, "Good on you for your part in the inbreaking of God's kingdom in this decade!" Now we need to get ready for a hurricane of new challenges that are likely to face those in leadership in Christian missions in the new millennium.

Looking Forward to 2000-2020: The Importance of Taking the Future Seriously

Speaking to 60 Christian businessmen in Christchurch, New Zealand, I asked, "How many of you forecast before you plan in your business?" Every hand in the room went up. "Now," I asked "how many of you as leaders in your churches forecast before you plan?" Not a single hand went up.

While corporations routinely make an effort to make sense of how the future is likely to change before they plan, churches and Christian organizations rarely do. Too many Christian leaders, including mission executives, do long-range planning as though they are frozen in a time warp, as though the future is simply going to be an extension of the present. Anyone who has lived through the past three decades knows better. As a consequence, the church as a whole and mission organizations in particular have missed many opportunities to be pro-active instead of reactive.

Let me be clear, we cannot predict all of the change likely to fill our common future. Only God can do that. But we can predict some areas of change. For example, we can predict with a high degree of accuracy demographic trends 5 to 10 years into the future. Yet I find few executives who make any effort to research how the demographics in the nations in which they work are likely to change, and identify the challenges those changes will present. Nor do they often look at how the demographics of their donor base is changing.

We can also identify some of the new technologies that are likely to be available in the coming decade. Many missions organizations were 4 to 5 years late adopting the new internet technologies which have revolutionized missions communications in the nineties. And I find little effort to anticipate the coming of a host of new technologies and how they can be used for mission.

It is also possible to identify larger themes that are likely to change the contours of our global future. I find that some missiologists are discussing missiological issues as though we are still operating in the same global context as the seventies and the eighties. However, as we will show, we have moved virtually overnight into a new globalized society that is rapidly changing the context in which we do missions, discuss missiological issues, and nurture the church. Therefore, to lead the church into the twenty-first century we will need leaders who lead with foresight.

How to Lead with Foresight

Let me outline some of the methods that might be of use to those who are looking for ways to make sense of some of the new challenges that are likely to face us in a new millennium. I will present several examples of how both churches and mission organizations forecast before they plan. I will particularly attempt to show that if we can anticipate even a few areas of change, then we have lead time to create imaginative new strategic responses that advance the kingdom of God.

Demographic forecasting in a Baptist church in Vancouver. In preparation for doing a Millennium III Creativity workshop with a Baptist Church in Vancouver BC, Christine and I asked the pastor to provide us with a demographic profile of their congregation. The profile revealed that over a third of the church was over 65 and there were virtually no 40 and 50 year olds. The rest of the congregation was comprised of a very transitional group of young people who had been attending the University of British Columbia and Regent College. In our research we discovered why so many of the young move away... housing prices in the community started at $500,000 and go up from there. You don't have to be a futurist to realize that this congregation doesn't have a very promising future if present trends continue.

I asked the pastor to research how much apartments cost. To his surprise 8-unit apartment houses were selling for only $800,000, or $100,000 a unit. So during our creativity workshop leaders came up with the creative idea of purchasing three or four apartment blocks and transforming them into condos and selling units to younger members so that the church will have someone to lead the church into a new millennium.

Contextual forecasting at Tear Fund England. Corporations routinely do contextual forecasting before they plan. In contextual forecasting you try to present a picture of how the larger context is likely to change economically, politically, technologically, societally, and culturally in order to identify possible new needs, challenges, and opportunities. Doug Balfour, who came from a corporate background to become the CEO of Tear Fund England initiated a process called the Jordan Project. One aspect of the project was to do a contextual forecasting process in which they asked two questions:

1. How is the context in which we work with the poor in Africa, Asia, and Latin America likely to change in the next ten years?

2. How is the church in the United Kingdom and their donor support base likely to change in the next ten years?

In answering the second question they found what is an issue for many Christian agencies—their donor base was rapidly aging. In response, Tear Fund added a brand-new program to find creative ways to reach those under 30 and start creating a new constituency. They report that their new strategy has already dramatically increased the ranks of their younger supporters.

Doing scenario forecasting at Open Doors. Open Doors invited my wife and I to meet with them in their international offices in Holland to help them do some scenario forecasting. In scenario forecasting you can use information collected in contextual forecasting to draft 2 to 4 stories about the future. This provides your staff with an opportunity to play through each scenario without betting the farm on any one forecast. It is a very valuable tool to help them learn to plan contingently.

In our scenario forecasting at Open Doors we focused on their work with the underground church in China. We invited their leadership team to play through two very different scenarios for China's economic future. In the first scenario, using some material from a World Bank book entitled *China 2020,* we presented an optimistic scenario that China's economy will return to 8 percent to 9 percent growth for the next ten years. We asked Open Doors leaders to identify the possible impact of a high growth economy for those in the underground church. On the positive side they stated that greater economic growth would likely encourage a greater openness to the outside world. But growing prosperity could be as corrupting, they pointed out, for vital Christianity in China as it had been in Eastern Europe after the wall came down. Therefore, Open Doors' leaders responded by proposing the design of training materials to prepare members of the underground church to deal with growing materialism.

The second scenario focused on a future in which the Chinese economy goes into a meltdown. Here the leaders predicted Chinese society would become much more repressive toward the church, and Christians would be the first ones fired. They also predicted that the church would experience more severe hunger and deprivation.

Their response was to explore how to create micro-enterprise projects to enable the hidden church to support themselves.

In other words, because we are moving into a new millennium in which our world is changing at blinding speed we can no longer do missions planning, discuss missiological issues, or raise funds as though the future is simply going to be an extension of the present. Since most organizations have limited resources for research, I propose that they create an ad hoc Futures Watch Group using volunteers on-line to do research to identify new needs, challenges, and opportunities that are likely to confront their organization in the future. This group would have the sole task of doing research on futures trends—to enable their organization to: (1) anticipate some of the new opportunities and challenges that are likely to be a part of the changing context in which they do mission in the next ten years and; (2) anticipate how the church and the donor base that supports their organization is likely to change during that same period.

To the extent that those in leadership can anticipate the new challenges of a new millennium they have lead time to create new responses. We have the opportunity to be pro-active instead of reactive.

Back to the Future . . . Shifting Global Mission into the Future Tense

I will take you on trips back to the future to outline some of the challenges that I believe are likely to confront mission executives, practitioners, and missiologists in the first two decades of the twenty-first century. These forecasts come out of research for my new book *Mustard Seed vs McWorld: Reinventing Life and Faith for the Future,* which is intentionally written for those in leadership. First we will look at how the context in which you do mission is likely to change and then we will look at how the American church that supports your mission is likely to change. Again, if we can anticipate even a few of the changes we have lead time to create new strategic responses. It might be helpful to keep a list of the needs, challenges, and opportunities that could impact your organization in a new millennium. I am sure you could add to my list. Remember not only to anticipate new opportunities, but start imagining creative ways you might respond to those opportunities.

Globalization: A driving force for change. Futurists not only develop forecasts of ways in which the context in which we live and operate is likely to change, but also attempt to identify primary driving forces for that change. There is consensus among many that two of the most potent driving forces for change at present are fragmentation and globalization. The resurgence of nationalism, ethnic hatreds, and ethnic cleansing in places like Kosovo are a driving force for change that is likely to raise a number of new challenges for mission projects all over our troubled world. One of the reasons behind the resurgence of nationalism and concern for ethnic identity is a direct response to our rapid movement into a new homogenized globalized society. Many of these people fear they could lose their sense of identity in such a context.

Some American evangelicals live in fear of a one-world government takeover. Frankly, I don't feel that is a serious possibility anytime in the foreseeable future because we are witnessing an unprecedented movement toward political devolution and fragmentation. But we have already become a part of a one-world technological and economic order. Overnight we have all become a part of a new globalized society that is radically changing the context in which we live and do mission. In other words, the world in which we raise our young, plant our churches, and work with those in need is changing right beneath our feet. My concern is that I hear virtually no discussion in mission and missiological forums of the challenges this rapid globalization is likely to raise for the church and mission organizations

One world ready or not. Two major events have directly contributed to this process of rapid globalization. First, in the nineties we began hardwiring our planet into a single global electronic nervous system of satellites, fax machines, and internet communications capable of incredible speed. Borders are melting. Distance is dying. One and a half trillion dollars circulates through this global electronic nervous system every day. All of this is directly contributing to the rapid creation of a one-world economic order.

Secondly, with the sudden end of the cold war the model of centrally planned economies was thrown into the trash bin, and for the first time in history practically all the nations of the world joined in the capitalist race to the top. This global economic race is turning out to be brutally competitive, and is decisively changing the world in which we raise families, organize congregations, and seek to obey the Great Commission and the Great Commandment.

Not only has capitalism triumphed, but so has McDonalds. It has just passed up Coca Cola as the most widely recognized logo in the world. As a consequence, we will join others in using McWorld as a way to characterize the process of globalization. "Economic globalization involves arguably the most fundamental redesign of the planet's political and economic arrangements since at least the industrial revolution" states Jerry Mander, a senior fellow at the Public Media Center.[4]

Most of us are benefiting in a myriad of ways from being a part of this new one-world economic and technological order. Mission executives can instantly communicate with staff half a world away by e-mail. We can purchase a huge selection of fruits and vegetables from all over the world that we wouldn't have seen in American supermarkets 15 years ago. And this economy is providing more jobs, not only for the middle class, but for those at the margins in the U.S. and even in many parts of the Two-Thirds World. But the rapid globalization of the planet also raises a host of new questions for families, congregations north and south, and for mission organizations. Not the least of which is the kind of a future to which this new globalized society is likely to transport us.

Preparing for the long boom scenario. The two scenarios I hear discussed most commonly about where our new global economy could take us are the scenarios of the "long boom" and the "slow meltdown." The advocates of this one world economic order assure us that if we trust our future to the twin rockets of global free enterprise and global free trade it will raise all boats. Many of us in America, they say, will soon be living palatially, just like Microsoft millionaires.

To those who raise money for world missions this sounds like very good news. But the reality is that while the income of many American evangelicals has indeed gone up during the economic boom of the last ten years, that fact is scarcely reflected in their giving patterns. In fact, some areas of missions giving has actually declined during this boom time.

Anyone who talks to the pastors who minister in "Microsoft land" will learn that what is happening to many families who suddenly find themselves living extravagant lifestyles isn't all good news either. These pastors will tell you that many of these folks, who are living in huge mini-mansions with 3 or 4 hot tubs and gigantic yachts, were not there to see their kids grow up. They have become so caught up in the glamour and status of their upscale lifestyles that they have lost interest in the church and their Christian life, and have dropped out.

How can our leaders prepare American Christians for the possibility of the long boom scenario? There are very few resources being use in the American church today to enable believers to deal with the growing seductions and addictions of a long boom future of economic upscaling. And, as we will show, there is a direct relationship between the consumer seductions of modern culture and the declining attendance and giving patterns. Leaders must find ways to educate believers to limit their consumption to what they need, instead of what they can afford during boom times. This will be essential if we are to have a community of vital Christians who are willing to invest the kind of resources necessary to advance God's mission purposes, and to address the mounting challenges of a new millennium.

Increasingly there will also be a need for the churches of the developing world to develop a curriculum on biblical stewardship for those in poorer countries who are being seduced by our rapidly expanding Western consumerism. And it will become even more important for expat missionaries to realize that their lifestyles are often more of an advertisement for McWorld consumerism, than are their teachings regarding the gospel of Christ.

Preparing for the slow meltdown scenario. Even some of its loudest advocates express two major concerns about the reliability of this new global economic structure:

1. They are concerned that all of our national economies will be more vulnerable to rupture, recession, and meltdown as a direct result of being hard-wired together rapidly into a single global economy. The rapid spread of the Asian meltdown, for instance, reaching as far as Russia is an example of why many are concerned. The more tightly knit we are together, it would seem, the more likely that a breakdown anywhere in the network could engulf all of us.

2. The advocates are also concerned because this new global economy is being fashioned with very little substantial structure or

ground rules. This makes it more volatile and all of us are more vulnerable.

How can Christian leaders prepare those in the church for the slow meltdown scenario? Leaders need to encourage Christians in North America to reduce their vulnerability by getting out of debt as quickly as possible and seriously reducing their lifestyle costs. That way, if hard times come these Christians will not be so preoccupied by their own survival, but can be more able to minister to those in critical need in their own communities and abroad. Believers in the Two-Thirds World will also need to reduce their debt (where possible); as well as to plant churches that not only address spiritual needs, but include the creation of economic and agricultural cooperatives to help one another in good times and hard times as a witness to the gospel.

Welcome to the great world McWorld auction. Whether we enter a future of the slow meltdown or the long boom we are going to see continued rapid globalization of every aspect of God's world and our lives. We are racing into a McWorld future in which everything from jobs, to small businesses, to our own bodies are up for auction. Economists assure us it is just good common business sense to assign everything a price.

British author Charles Handy explores where this business of assigning a price to everything might take us. "...If people want to sell their kidneys, or their bodies for sex, why shouldn't they, as long as there are willing buyers? In this rhetoric the value of anything is solely in its price. It gets tempting, this commodification of everything. It reduces everything to a convenient common denominator. One can even, technically, demonstrate that the marginal productivity of some members of society is too low to allow them to purchase the cost of living. Should they then perish?" Handy concludes "A society which was a grand auction block would not be a society worth having. It might even be far less economically successful than its proponents imagine. We should not be overimpressed by the early energies released by deregulation. Everything cannot be for sale."[5]

But we are moving into a future in which everything in God's good creation is up for auction, including human DNA. There is a growing feeling articulated by Pat Buchanan on the right and Richard Gephart on the left that tilts towards protectionism because of their concerns about auctioning off "American Jobs." Wendell Berry, a Christian ecologist, expresses serious concerns about the destruction of local communities which support families when small neighborhood businesses and farms are being auctioned off to be replaced by macro-malls and huge corporate farms. If the long boom scenario continues it will also dramatically escalate the rate at which we auction off our planetary resources and pollute our environment. Therefore, in the future it will be essential that all mission projects include a creation care and a community building component.

Future of the North American middle. Everywhere my wife and I work—in Great Britain, Australia, New Zealand, Canada, and the United States—people tell us they are having to work harder and longer just to stay even in this increasingly competitive global economy. In 1977 less than half of families relied on dual incomes. Today it has dramatically increased to two-thirds, and it is still climbing. Some women are working simply to help pay the bills and keep their heads above water. Some are working to be able to buy extras.[6]

The Harris Poll reports that the average American spent 41 hours at work in 1973. In 1997 that had increased 10 hours to 51 hours a week.[7] As we gallop into a new century, McWorld will insist that we spend even more of our waking hours at work. That means we will have less time for family and friends, less time to pray and study Scripture, and less time to volunteer to be involved in missions at home or abroad.[8]

The under-35 have hit the economy at a particularly tough time. While some land high paying jobs in business and computers, many will never achieve the lifestyle levels of their parents and grandparents' generation because the relationship of what they earn to what they can buy has changed dramatically since I was a young man. When I graduated from a Christian college in 1958 it cost $700 a year for everything. I worked at a summer job for $4 an hour and had no trouble paying the whole cost in advance. School debt was unheard of. Today young people are graduating with debt loads of $20,000 to $60,000 because the annual cost of a Christian college has increased over 20 times since I was in school. And there is no way students can pay that bill off by working during the summer. Obviously grads who have high debt loads put off the possibility of missions service until their debts are paid, and many never follow through on their sense of calling.

We are running into more and more young people for whom over half their income goes into rent or mortgage. Such a percentage was unheard of when I was their age. We paid closer to 20 percent. The first house I bought in Portland, Oregon, in 1963 was a large 4 bedroom house with a full basement that had been totally restored for $14,500 and a $100-a-month payment. Working at a Christian college on a welfare level salary of $4,800 a year I had no difficulty making that payment. Today many young couples with good incomes would have difficulty qualifying for this house which is now priced at over $400,000.

The decline in generational income is documented in an eye-opening way in *The State of Working America 1996-1997*: "The average income of families headed by someone under 25 declined at an annual rate of 2.4 percent from 1979 to 1989 and 1.8 percent from 1989 to 1995. These young families in 1994 had $6,148 less income to spend in real dollars than their 1967 counterparts had when they were starting out."[9] In fact there is growing concern because many of these young people have so little left over for savings that they will have very meager resources on which to retire. This means that many of the under-35 are likely to have significantly less time and money left over to contribute to the work of the kingdom than older generations.

McWorld: Branding the young. McWorld not only wants more of our time, but also more of our money. Essential to the continued high growth of the long boom economy is persuading people to ratchet up their appetites for more. As a consequence, there will be mounting pressure on all of us to buy the message that yesterday's luxuries have become today's necessities. There is already escalating pressure on our young to consume at levels never conceived of even a few years ago. "You must get kids branded by age 5 if you want to have them as faithful consumers of your product," admonished a marketing executive in a corporate training session on the PBS documentary called "Affluenza."[10]

Christian leaders need to realize that we are in a contest for the hearts and minds of a new generation. Remember that the average child in the U.S. spends over 20 hours a week in front of the tube and is exposed to thousands of ads. Add to that the additional hours spent listening to CDs, video games, and MTV. Isn't it clear that there is no way an hour a week in Sunday School can begin to equip the Christian young to contend with these other inputs? Christian educators will need to work with churches and families to design curriculum that helps them to successfully contend with the growing influence of McWorld. And we also need to begin preparing for the rapid graying of the middle class.

McWorld: Graying of the middle class. Seventy-seven million baby boomers will begin retiring in 2010, which will make problems in Social Security and Medicare acute. By the time the last boomer retires in 2030 it could be calamitous if the politicians don't take responsible action to fix the system. The boomer generation, and those of us in the silent booster generation, are the primary supporters of the American church today. As soon as the boomers begin to retire in 2010 it will start to impact their giving. The larger church and Christian mission organizations in particular need to anticipate the extent that this demographic shift is likely to seriously depress giving.

Much has been written about the hope that the church will somehow get a generous chunk of the 13 billion dollar wealth transfer from the boomers to their offspring. But I will be very surprised if that happens. Fund raisers need to begin designing a strategy now to try and offset the serious decline in giving that can be expected between 2010 and 2030.

Future of the global poor. How will this new one-world economic order impact the global poor? Let me be clear. The architects of McWorld are eager to have all the world's people become a part of a global labor pool, as well as eager consumers in the global macro-mall. And many more people have already found jobs and are able to increase their consumer buying. But the reality to this point is that this new McWorld economy works much better for those with resources than for those without.

The United Nations Development Program states that 30 years ago the poorest 20 percent of the world's population earned 2.3 percent of the world's income. Now they earn only 1.4 percent and that figure is still declining. At the same time, the richest 20 percent increased their share of global income from 70 percent to 80 percent.[11] The point is that the race to the top seems to be dramatically expanding the wealth of the richest 20 percent, while at the same time it seems to be shrinking the resource base of the poorest 20 percent. Much more, therefore, will need to be done in education and small business development to help our poorest neighbors join this economic liftoff. The Mennonite Development Association has a very successful loan program in Haiti and a number of other countries to help the poor start small businesses to become economically self-reliant. More efforts like theirs will be needed.

Even though global population growth is slowing, it will still grow from 6 billion today to between 8 to 10 billion by 2050. Of course most of that growth will be among our poorest neighbors in the most densely congested urban areas. This means that there is likely to be much more for those who work with the global poor to do as we race into a new millennium. Today almost half of the global poor are under 15. Some estimates suggest this emerging population will need between 1.2 to 2 billion new jobs by the year 2020. This means that not only Christian relief and development agencies, but even church planting agencies, will need to be engaged in new ways—enabling new church plants to provide vocational education for both boys and girls, starting credit unions, and doing micro-enterprise development so that the youngest members have the opportunity to participate in this new global economy and support their families.

One of the new challenges that many churches in the Two-Thirds World will be facing by 2020 is the rapid graying of their national populations. Frankly, I haven't found any agencies planning ahead for this important new demographic challenge. Church planting agencies, as well as Christian relief and development agencies, need to help these churches begin to prepare now for the aging tomorrow of their communities and congregations. It is important to remember that most of our poorest neighbors have not had the resources to prepare for their own retirement, and there are virtually no government programs in these countries to assist the aging poor. Planting churches is not enough. We need to help create communities of mutual care to provide for the growing needs of aging populations in Africa, Asia, and Latin America.

The future of the global poor and global free trade. One of the major doctrines of this new global economy is the belief that if we allow everyone to fish in each other's ponds, and own one another's banks and phone systems, that somehow a tide will rise that will lift all boats. Mission organizations need to anticipate and prepare for what the long-term consequences of this doctrine are likely to be for those living in poorer countries.

After the 1986 takeover of Uganda by the forces of Yoweri Museveni, the new leader developed some very close relationships with European investors. A number of these investors live in areas of Northern Europe in which, over the past four decades, fish supplies have been seriously depleted by over-fishing. When these investors learned of the bountiful resources in Lake Victoria, they entered into an agreement with the Ugandan government to build fish factories on the edge of the lake. Reportedly they are buying, processing, and flying 200 tons of fish a week from Lake Victoria to dinner tables in Europe.

Christian families living on the edge of the lake used to be able to buy fish 2 days a week. But since the European fish factory has come to Uganda, fish prices have soared four-fold and the people along the lake can no longer afford the price. As a consequence, the only way they can get any protein in their diet is to go to the fish factory and buy the fish bones to stew with their vegetables.[12]

This new free trade doctrine is radically changing the way the global economy works, and again, it seems to work far better for those with assets than for those without. For example, American preference for white chicken meat has produced a glut of chicken legs U.S. producers can't sell domestically. So, they are dumping them at very low prices in Haiti and other countries. This practice is threatening to destroy local poultry industries in places like Haiti because they can't compete with the very low give-away prices. There is a serious need for some international Christian forums to discuss the new opportunities and challenges this new global economy, and particularly this doctrine of global free trade, are presenting to those living in the poorest parts of the world.

Debt and the future of the global poor. The global debt crisis makes it virtually impossible for many of the poorer countries to ever get ahead because such a high percentage of their income has to go to pay for the interest on their loans. For example, Nicaragua and Algeria are using over 50 percent of their export income to service interest on their debts. Recently the Anglicans gathered as a worldwide communion, and one of their major issues for discussion was debt among the poorer countries: "The Lambeth Conference

48   *Context of the New Millennium*

has demanded action on international debt and economic justice, not only from governments and banks, but also from churches. The resolution asks bishops to take money from their own budgets to help pay for international development and to cooperate with other faiths in advocacy programs."[13] Those of us who work in world mission can't ignore the forces at work that keep whole communities locked in hopeless poverty. Those of us in missions leadership need to speak out in international forums regarding the growing impact of the debt crisis on those with whom we work, and we need to work for structural change as well as for change in individual lives.

McWorld: Reducing the drag equals cutting assistance to the global poor. We are rapidly moving globally into a future in which the new one-world economic order is working brilliantly for the top 20 percent, but the bottom 20 percent are losing ground. Of course, the bottom 20 percent is also that part of our global community that is experiencing the most rapid population growth. Bottom line: all of us who work with the poor, including private and public agencies, will need to do much more in response to the mounting needs.

As the industrialized nations have joined in this brutally competitive race to the top, they are doing everything they can to reduce the drag on their economies. As a result, virtually all of the Western governments are cutting back their social programs at home and their humanitarian aid overseas.[14] David Beckmann, president of Bread For the World, has stated "The trend in cutting back foreign aid is global. But the United States is the leader of the trend, which will mean increased hardship for poor people in poor countries."[15]

In other words, since many of the world's governments are cutting back their humanitarian aid to the growing ranks of the global poor, others will have to pick up the slack. The church, voluntary organizations, and the private sector will need to do much more in the opening decades of the new millennium.

Global evangelism regress. Not only will the church need to do more to address the mounting physical needs that will fill our planet in a new millennium, but the growing spiritual needs as well. We are going to need to dramatically increase our investment in world evangelization and church planting. What isn't generally realized is that we are actually going backwards, not forwards, in world evangelization. Peter Brierley of the Christian Research Association reports that 28 percent of the world's people identify themselves as some brand of Christian: Protestant, Catholic, or Orthodox. Because population growth is outstripping our best efforts it will decline to 27 percent in 2010, and continue to decline after that.[16]

The people who are doing a brilliant job at world "evangelization" are the marketers of McWorld. They have in the past ten years become remarkably successful in creating the first borderless youth culture in the history of our planet. They have persuaded the young everywhere to change their values—they all drink the same soda, watch the same MTV videos, and wear the same jeans. The youth of this new borderless culture have more in common with one another than they do with the cultures from which they come.[17] Two Pentecostal pastors from the Dominican Republic told me at a WEF conference that they had lost their entire youth groups in two years. This was a direct result of their community suddenly being inundated with American media, MTV, and values that they weren't able to counter.

The marketers of McWorld aren't just selling products. They are actively at work persuading the young to change their values so they will buy more of their products. In other words, the Muslims aren't our only competitors. We are in a battle for the hearts and minds of a new generation, and our opponents are highly skilled in persuading them to change their values and their life priorities. Isn't it past time for us to enlist our young people to launch a major counter-offensive using the same channels McWorld uses?

McWorld and the wiring of the planet. The Internet is playing many positive roles in our increasingly globalized society. The poor in many countries are using the net to access educational opportunities not available in their own communities. Churches and mission organizations not only need to use existing Internet technologies to create new educational initiatives; they also need to design new ways to use emerging technologies for God's kingdom. For example, mission organizations should explore the possible introduction of video conferencing technology to improve communications with staff worldwide. Likewise, they should explore the possible applications of new digital and virtual reality communication capabilities for educational use. And, with the cost of photovoltaic energy technology dropping, and its efficiency increasing, mission organizations will be able to introduce solar operated electrical systems in areas without energy to start clinics, small businesses, and educational programs.

We are moving into a future changing at warp speed. The church is going to need to do more to address both the spiritual and the physical needs of those to whom God has called us to minister. The question is, to what extent is the American church going to be a part of God's response to this challenge—given changes going on in attendance and giving patterns in the U.S.?

The Future of the American Church

The church in the United States has enjoyed a period of considerable growth in the last two decades. We have witnessed the emergence of megachurches, like Willow Creek and Saddle Back. Alpha programs in evangelism imported from Britain are resulting in thousand coming to vital faith in Jesus Christ. Prayer initiatives are involving millions of American believers. Promise Keepers is not only calling men back to a vital faith, but also promoting racial reconciliation. And we are seeing significant levels of growth among Black, Hispanic, and Asian congregations in the U.S.

Unfortunately, not all the news is good. In fact, the overall trends regarding church attendance and church giving are really quite alarming as they relate to the future of missions.

In the United States, while the Catholic church is still experiencing a bit of growth, virtually all of the mainline Protestant churches are graying and declining, as they are in Europe, Australia, New Zealand, and Canada. In 1968, 11 mainline Protestant denominations represented 13 percent of the U.S. population. By 1993 that figure had plummeted to 7.8 percent, a 40 percent decrease. If the present trends were to continue uninterrupted these denominations would be totally out of business by the year 2032.[18]

Add to the problem of declining numbers that of aging congregations. For example, there are twice as many ELCA Lutherans over 75 as the general population.[19] The Presbyterians (USA), the United Church of Christ, the American Baptists, and the United Methodists are all dealing with the twin hits of declining numbers and graying congregations. The 2.5 million member Episcopal Church lost one million members from 1965 to 1989.

Wade Roof and William McKinney, in their important book

American Mainline Religion, stated that "the churches of the Protestant establishment, long in a state of relative decline, will continue to lose ground both in numbers and in social power and influence. The proportion of the population that is Protestant will continue its gradual decline in the decades to come, and within Protestantism, denominations and revitalization movements will continue their contest for power and influence."[20]

However, Gustav Niebuhr, religion editor for the *New York Times*, has recently reported that there is a bit of good news. Several mainline denominations, including the Episcopal church, the United Methodists, the ELCA Lutherans, and The Presbyterian Church (USA), saw their rate of decline begin to slow in the past three to four years. However, this doesn't alter the reality that they are slowly going out of business. It is only slowing the rate of decline.

Even the Southern Baptist Church, which has enjoyed strong growth since the end of the Second World War, is in trouble. Fraught with internal conflicts, they have seen their growth almost come to a halt at one-half of 1 percent or less from 1994 to 1997.[21] The major growth in the U.S., as elsewhere, is among conservative Protestant groupings, such as: many Black and Hispanic congregations, Assemblies of God, The Vineyard, The Evangelical Free Church, and the Covenant Church in America.

George Gallup insists, nevertheless, that in spite of the graying and declining of the oldline churches, church attendance of American Christians has remained fairly constant since the fifties, between 40 percent and 45 percent. George Barna, who has only been tracking attendance patterns since the early eighties, puts average U.S. attendance nearer 40 percent.[22]

Over the past decade other demographers have begun questioning the assumption that American church attendance patterns are remaining constant, because there seems to be anecdotal evidence contradicting this profile. Kirk Hadaway, chief statistician for the United Church of Christ, has seriously questioned the validity of these surveys because he believes Americans are over-reporting their attendance. Hadaway states "Interest in spirituality is up. But active participation in a faith community or institution is dropping." He points to the fact that mainline churches have lost one-fourth of their members in the last 30 years. Roughly 48 percent of the children in Episcopal families leave the church at age 18. Since 1965 the United Methodists have lost almost 1,000 members a week.

To check the validity of the self-reporting methods, Hadaway had his research team count cars in church parking lots in a small Ohio county over a period of several months. His findings: "Americans over-report their actual church attendance by a marked degree. Actual attendance is closer to 24 percent," Hadaway said, "and is falling slowly."[23]

If Hadaway's observational research is more accurate than the self-reporting approach, then U.S. attendance patterns would be more similar to the kind of attendance patterns we find among churches in other Western and English-speaking countries.

One trend that is identical in all these countries is that the more theologically conservative and evangelical side of the church is the lively and growing edge. And this is certainly true in the U.S. as well. Evangelicals in the United States and Canada, ". . .whether defined by denominational attachment, personal beliefs, and practices, or both, now constitute the largest and most active component of religious life in North America," states Mark Noll and Lyman Kellstedt.[24] However, this growth in the evangelical segment of the church in North America is not enough to offset the overall trend. American Christians, too, are a part of the incredible shrinking Western church. In spite of the good news about growth, the American church is graying and declining like the rest of the Western church, a fact which, if present trends continue, is likely to impact negatively the ability of the American church to sustain the present levels of mission outreach in the years 2000–2020 and beyond.

The future of the church and those under 25. There is another trend in the American church that is identical to what we have seen in the profiles of all other Western churches: those under 35 constitute a missing generation. In a recent survey of college freshmen in the U.S., 15 percent indicated no religious preference. This is the highest figure ever for college freshmen, and two-and-a-half times that of the nation as a whole.[25]

In his seminars, George Barna says the Buster generation (born between 1965 and 1983), age 18–36, is the first generation in America who aren't starting their lives with some kind of clear Christian heritage. Barna Research reports that over the past ten years, while older generation church attendance patterns range from roughly 40 percent to 60 percent, Busters come in dead last with about 34 percent attendance.[26] If the American church is to have a future it will need to strategically target the under-35. We will also need to plant new forms of churches, and institute major mentoring efforts to prepare a new generation of leaders to lead the church in the new millennium.

We need to find new ways to tell the gospel story to a postmodern generation that relies less on propositional theology, and more on story, narrative, and the arts. Our young people are key to helping us find new ways to share the story of a living Christ to their generation.

The incredible shrinking Western church and the future of mission. We can celebrate the fact that while the Western church is slowly going out of business, much of the church in Africa, Latin America, and parts of Asia is growing, thriving, and experiencing the renewal of God's Spirit. The problem is that much of the total wealth of the church is still located in Western countries. So let's look at how giving is changing in the American church. The problem with declining numbers, of course, is that it will automatically reduce the amount of time and money available to be invested in the advancement of God's Kingdom.

It is becoming increasingly evident that in a highly competitive McWorld future, many middle class people are going to have to work not only harder, but longer. So we will probably continue to see a steady erosion of the discretionary time people have available for family, relationships, prayer, Scripture study, service, and all-around church involvement. As we have seen, there will also be increasing pressure to persuade us, and particularly our young, to relinquish a growing percentage of whatever is left of our discretionary time and money at the McWorld macro-mall.

Giving American-style. Buoyed by recent economic growth, donations after inflation to all kinds of charities in the U.S. increased by 7.8 percent. However, giving to social services, like those for youth, family and employment needs actually declined by 3 percent. For those counting on the private sector to pick up the slack, this is not welcome news. If giving to social services is declining during economic times as good as these, what will the future hold if we enter a full-blown recession? Giving to religion, including the church, increased only by 2.5 percent.[27]

The Empty Tomb, which does some of the most helpful research on giving patterns in the American church, has some very alarming information on church giving over the last 28 years. First, they report that the real growth in U.S. per capita income, after taxes and inflation have been factored out, increased by 68 percent between 1968 and 1995. However, during the same period, the percentage of per capita income contributed to the church actually declined 21 percent from 3.11 percent to 2.46 percent.[28] Of even greater concern is the decline in benevolent giving to the American funds that are designed to address human needs outside of the church building. Between 1968 and 1995 income given to benevolence actually declined 38 percent.[29]

The researchers divided the American church between those mainline churches that affiliate with the National Council, and those evangelical churches that affiliate with the National Association of Evangelicals. Both groups experienced the decline. The NAE group declined from 6 percent giving in 1968 to 4 percent in 1995. The NCC group declined less sharply, from 3.3 percent in 1968 to 2.9 percent in 1995. Of particular concern was the decline in the rate of benevolent giving. Between 1985 and 1995 the giving to benevolence by NAE affiliated churches declined by 18 percent. The decline for NCC affiliated churches was 14 percent.[30]

This forecast by the Empty Tomb for the future of benevolent giving in the United States is truly alarming: "...If the giving patterns of the past 28 years continue in an uninterrupted fashion, then per member giving as a portion of income to the category of Benevolence will reach 0 percent of income...in 2045." While this linear forecast seems very improbable, the downward trend of giving should profoundly concern all those in Christian leadership.

As we have seen, those under 35 have hit the economy at a much tougher time than those over 45. As we have shown, the relationship of what the young earn to what they can afford to buy has changed. They will have both less time and less money to consider investing in the work of the church than older generations have had.[32] And if the young succumb to the growing pressures of McWorld to work longer and consume more, they could have even less left over to invest in the cause. Therefore, given these trends I believe those under 35 will not even be able to sustain the present giving levels to the church and its mission, let alone increase them.

At the very center of this emerging crisis is the dawning recognition that my generation sold their generation the wrong dream. For all the talk about the Lordship of Jesus, my generation sold them the American dream with a little Jesus overlay. The real message that has gone to the Christian young is the message that drives McWorld. Agenda one is getting ahead in your job, getting ahead in the suburbs, and getting your upscale lifestyle started. With whatever you have left over, you follow Jesus. As we have seen, if this generation puts the American dream first, they will have very little time or money left over to invest in the advancement of God's kingdom.

While the challenges of the twenty-first century are escalating, the capacity of the American church to be a part of God's compassionate response is declining at a disturbing rate. If the dual trends of declining attendance and declining giving continue uninterrupted, the American church and her mission initiatives could see a serious decline in support by the year 2020.

I sincerely pray that this assessment will sound an alarm among leaders in the American church. I urge Christian leaders in local churches, denominational offices, and missions organizations to convene forums with missiologists and demographers to develop innovative new responses—strategies to dramatically increase growth and funding of the mission of the church into the new century.

Creating New Responses to the New Challenges of a New Millennium

Clearly, business as usual won't begin to respond to the mounting challenges of tomorrow's world. All of us committed to the completion of the Great Commission and the Great Commandment will need to radically reinvent much that we are doing—in missions abroad, and in stirring up missions support at home to address the new challenges of a new millennium. Let me begin by proposing some alternative missions responses to the challenges just outlined.

Beyond planning as usual: Taking the future seriously. I am convinced that for all of us, the first step forward must be to take the future seriously. Mission organizations can only respond creatively to tomorrow's challenges to the extent that they first anticipate them. I urge all those in leadership to reinvent strategic planning, to do forecasting before they do long-range planning. For example, we are working with World Relief to help them anticipate the next ten years—the changing context in which they will work with churches abroad, with refugees in the U.S., and supporting churches everywhere. Once that is understood, then they will work to create new strategic responses to those challenges.

Beyond the American dream and Jesus too. One of the strongest messages from the advocates of McWorld is that the ultimate human aspiration is economic growth. This aspiration for economic progress is rooted in the Enlightenment and is at the root of our modern consumer driven society. The American dream of individual economic upscaling is rapidly becoming the dream of people all over the planet, so that whole societies are rapidly being homogenized into a single global culture of consumption. The message from the marketers of McWorld is a simple one—that we will find our fullest sense of meaning by increasing our appetite for more.

As I have shown, the young all over the planet are being targeted by the marketers of McWorld to change their values and increase their levels of consumption, thus increasing the growth of the long boom global economy. One of my greatest concerns is the extent to which Christians all over the world, but particularly in America, are allowing McWorld to define what is important. Increasingly, value is being defined in terms of economic upscaling, consumerism, and materialism. And too often, following Jesus is trivialized to little more than a private spiritualized faith that is worked in around the edges of all that modern culture and McWorld demand of us. I believe this growing seduction of our sense of what is important and of value is directly responsible for the erosion of attendance and giving patterns in the American church. And, therefore, those of us who care about the future of mission need to address this growing challenge head on.

We need to reawaken our biblical imagination and discover in Scripture an alternative dream to the American dream, one that doesn't define the ultimate in terms of economic growth and personal upscaling. We need this new biblical dream not just for our spiritual life, but for all of life. And we need a new vision of the redemptive purposes of God that helps us bring together the word and deed mission of the church.

In the writings of the prophets we are shown the vision of a new heaven and a new earth—the coming home of God's people as a huge multicultural family to a new mountain and a new city. At this great homecoming we will join in a festive banquet. Justice will come to the poor, reconciliation to the nations, and the blind will see, the deaf will hear, and the disabled will dance. At the center of this vision is the reign of our Creator God, and the redemption of all those who have been made alive by God through the death and the resurrection of Jesus Christ.

Jesus comes proclaiming good news that the future of God has broken in amongst us. In his servant life, his kingdom teachings, his brutal death, and his triumphant resurrection we are given a preview of all that God purposes for his people and the world. It is a much larger vision than we tend to celebrate in many of our churches. And it offers a very different vision for the human future than the one offered us by McWorld.

Beyond addressing the spiritual and physical needs of individuals: Working for the transformation of communities. The biblical vision is not just about saving individual souls and meeting individual needs; it is also about the transformation of communities. The mounting challenges that are likely to face us, and the growing pressures of McWorld itself, make it clear that simply addressing the needs of individuals will not be enough. Those working for evangelization and church planting, therefore, and those working to address the physical needs of individuals, must find ways to partner together to transform with the vision of God's new order, not only individuals, but also communities.

One example of what this might look like is the innovative community creation ministry of Agros, based in Seattle. They raise money in the U.S. to buy large tracts of agricultural land in Central America. For instance they bought 200 acres in Nicaragua, and moved 50 landless families from the cities to this land. They have helped them create a new agricultural community from scratch, where they can sustain themselves, plant a church, and create a new way of community life that honors God. People living in such a rooted cooperative Christian community will be much better able to deal with the challenges of the possible long boom, or the slow meltdown scenarios.

Beyond North American control of missions: New partnerships for the twenty-first century. With mounting pressures and declining resources, there will need to be much more emphasis on new forms of partnership to increase impact and to use limited resources more strategically. Interdev, among others, is spearheading a number of new forms of partnership.

Increasingly, the leadership in missions is shifting from the Northern to the Southern Hemisphere. This means that Americans will also increasingly need to participate in partnerships where they aren't in control. Several years ago, for example, the Eastern Mennonite Missions Board seconded two of their missionaries to work under the auspices of the indigenous Chinese Mennonite Mission Board in Indonesia. Examples of this sort are becoming more and more common.

Beyond mission stewardship as usual: doing more with less. Because there is going to be growing pressure on mission budgets, there will also be a growing need to streamline mission bureaucracy so that more of the total resource is sent to the field. For example, to reduce their facilities costs, Puget Sound Community Church in Tacoma, Washington, did something quite clever. They constructed a two-story warehouse with 35,000 feet on each floor, and they make enough income off the bottom floor, which they rent out to small businesses, that it pays the monthly mortgage cost for the entire building.

When over ten years ago Simon Pellew started Pecan, a job training ministry for the urban poor in London, he introduced an innovative approach to compensation. He paid each of his job counselors exactly the same modest salary he paid himself. He told me that he thought it was a good idea at the beginning, but even a better idea today, because he can afford a much larger staff.

With the graying of America there will be a growing number of able volunteers who can use the second half of their lives for the kingdom, while largely living off the fruits of the first half. Given all that is likely to lie ahead, we are all going to need to learn to become Christian scroungers, doing more with less.

Beyond the declining, graying of the church: strategically reaching a new generation with the gospel of Jesus Christ. If the Western church as a whole, and the American church in particular, wants to sustain and grow its mission initiatives in a new millennium, then we must find ways to reach, church, and mentor a new generation. We must strategically target those under 35, and call them to a more biblically radical form of discipleship than that for which older generations have often settled.

One the most encouraging developments today is that nearly a thousand young leaders in their twenties are planting churches all over America. The Leadership Network has come alongside this emerging and rapidly growing part of the American church to support their efforts without controlling them. They are rapidly evangelizing many members of a postmodern generation who have no Christian background at all. The churches that are forming are more local, relational, and tribal than the boomer churches of the nineties. Much more must be done to support the efforts of a new generation to reach their peers, and those of us who are older need to take their leadership gifts seriously. Churches and mission organizations need to do much more to mentor young men and women of all races and colors into significant leadership positions. If we are to have effective leadership to take the church into the twenty-first century, there is no option.

Beyond dualistic discipleship and giving out of our leftovers: Calling believers to whole life discipleship and stewardship. One of the major reasons I believe investment of time and money is declining in the American church is that we are operating from assumptions about discipleship and stewardship that are often more cultural than biblical. For all the talk about the Lordship of Christ, the real message too often is that your first allegiance is to your job, getting your house, and getting your kids off to their activities. The things of faith tend to come in way down the list. That is why over the last 20 years there has been a steady erosion in the amount of time and money many Christians have left over for their faith. There is a major disconnect between whatever is preached Sunday morning, and the decisions that are made Monday through Saturday.

I am persuaded that the only way to contend with the growing influence of McWorld in our lives, families, and congregations is to call people to whole life discipleship and stewardship. We must help believers to place the aspirations of God's kingdom, instead of those of McWorld, at the center of life. I am proposing we design a curriculum for use in our churches that assists Christians to develop personal and family mission statements that reflect the vision of God's kingdom. The remainder of the course would help participants use this sense of God's purposes to enable them to make decisions about where to spend their time and money, and what activities to sign their kids up for.

If churches would use this kind of curriculum to help their people put first things first, I am confident that it would result in a significant increase of resources invested in Christian mission. Those of us in leadership, of course, need to model lifestyles that reflects the simpler values of the kingdom instead of the upscale values of modern culture.

Beyond planting churches as a place to go: Reinventing the church as whole life communities committed to mission. Less than 20 percent of the resources of the churches we work with in the U.S. are invested in mission at home or abroad. In contrast, Spreydon Baptist Church in Christchurch, New Zealand, invests over 60 percent of their total income in mission. While many American churches don't have a single ministry outside the building, Spreydon Baptist has 25 thriving urban ministries including a trust fund to help the poor start their own small businesses.

David Bosch tells us that only after the Reformation was church seen as a place you go to once a week. Prior to that, church was seen as a community you were a part of seven days a week, where you also happened to worship. Frankly, I don't believe the average Christian family can stand up to the mounting pressures of McWorld, or deal with the possible scenarios of a long boom or slow meltdown future. We will need to live near to those with whom we are in community. I am convinced that in the twenty-first century we will need to reinvent the church as new missional communities, where we live and share mutual care as an essential part of our witness for the gospel of Christ.

Rockridge Methodist Church in Oakland, California, is a great new model of a missional community of mutual care. Not only has this church reinvented itself to place mission at the center of community life, but they have just completed construction of a cooperative Christian community in an inner city neighborhood. Part of the congregation has relocated there to work in tutoring and helping those in need in the community.

By living in this cooperative community it reduces their lifestyle costs so that they have more time and money left over to invest in mission. And like that first gospel community, they are much more involved in one another's life on a daily basis. The creator God has a much more festive way of life for the people of God than anything McWorld can offer, but we are only likely to find it in community with sisters and brothers. We are called together to be a living foretaste of the great homecoming of God.

Beyond cultural addictions: Learning to celebrate the Kingdom. One of the most important ingredients in enabling Christians in both the northern and southern hemispheres to overcome the addictions of the McWorld culture is to teach them to celebrate the inbreaking of the great homecoming of God. Instead of allowing the culture to call the tune, we need to teach people, as integral parts of their faith, to celebrate the inbreaking of the kingdom of God any time they are given an opportunity. As we reach each new milestone in mission we need to join with those we work with in celebrating the advance of God's new order. And instead of allowing McMedia to entertain us we need to teach believers to celebrate God's kingdom in every aspect of daily life.

"Working Together to Shape a New Millennium," is more than a theme for the final EFMA/IFMA Conference of the twentieth-century. It is an opportunity for all of us who are committed to the mission of Jesus Christ in a rapidly changing world to lead the church with foresight, vision, and a Spirit-inspired imagination, as together we race into a new millennium.

Endnotes

1. Patrick Johnstone, *The Church is Bigger Than You Think: Structures and Strategies for the Church in the 21st Century* (London: Christian Focus Publications/WEC 1998).

2. Ibid., p. 231.

3. "The Power of Partnership," *Interdev*, Seattle, 1998, p. 21.

4. Jerry Mander, Edward Goldsmith, editors. *The Case against the Global Economy: and for a Turn toward the Local* (San Francisco: Sierra Club Book, 1996), 3.

5. Charles Handy, "The Invisible Fist," *The Economist*, February 15, 1997, p. 3-4.

6. Tamar Lewin, "Men Assuming Bigger Share at Home, New Survey Shows," *The New York Times*, April 15, 1998, p. A16.

7. The Harris Poll #31, Table 2, "Work Hours Per Week," July 7, 1997, p. 3.

8. Shelley Donald Coolidge, "Work and Spend Cycle Makes Company Slaves," *The Christian Science Monitor*, April 4, 1995, p. 9.

9. Lawrence Mishel, Jared Bernstein, and John Schmidt, *The State of Working America 1996-1997* (New York: M.E. Sharpe, 1997), p. 47.

10. "Affluenza, Warning: Materialism May Be Hazardous to Your Health," *UTNE Reader*, September-October 1997, p. 19.

11. "A Global Poverty Trap," *The Economist*, July 2, 1996, p. 34.

12. "World Population Growth," *Global Child Health News & Review*, No. 1, 1995, p. 19.

13. Nan Cobbey, *Episcopal Life*. August 18, 1998.

14. "United States Falls to Fourth in Global Giving," *Bread for the World Newsletter*, Aug.–Sept., 1996, vol. 8, p. 9.

15. Ibid.

16. Peter Brierley, *Future Church: A Global Analysis of the Christian Community to the Year 2010* (London: Monarch Books, 1998), 33.

17. Katharine Q. Seelye, "Future U.S.: Grayer and More Hispanic," *The New York Times*, March 27, 1997, p. A18.

18. John and Sylvia Ronsvalle, "The End of Benevolence? Alarming Trends in Church Giving," *The Christian Century*, October 23, 1996, p. 1012.

19. "Trends Affecting the Evangelical Lutheran Church in America," ELCA department of Research and Evaluation, December, 27, 1966, p. 1.

20. Wade Clark Roof and William McKinney, *American Mainline Religion: Its Changing Shape and Future* (New Brunswick: Rutgers University Press, 1987), 233.

21. Gustav Niebuhr, "Makeup of American Religion Is Looking More Like Mosaic, Data Say," *The New York Times*, April 12, 1998, p. 12.

22. "Church Attendance by Generation," Barna Research Group Limited, 1998.

23. Robert Marquand, "Preaching to Empty Pews," *Chicago Sun Times*, February 22, 1998, p. 45.

24. Mark Noll and Lyman Kellstadt, "The Changing Face of Evangelicalism," *Pro Ecclesia*, Vol. IV, No. 2, p. 147.

25. "Godlessness 101," *The New York Times Magazine*, December 7, 1997, p. 61.

26. "Church Attendance by Generation," Barna Research Group Limited, July 8, 1998.

27. Karen W. Arenson, "Donations to Charities Rose 11% Last Year, Report Says," *The New York Times*, May 15, 1996, p. A9.

28. John L. Ronsvalle and Sylvia Ronsvalle, *The State of Church Giving through 1995* (Champaign, Illinois: Empty Tomb, Inc., 1997), 11-12.

29. Ibid. p. 15.

30. Ibid. p. 25-27.

31. Ibid. p. 42-45.

32. Lawrence Mishel, Jared Bernstein, John Schmitt, *The State of Working America 1996-1997* (New York: M.E. Sharpe, 1997), 47.

Chapter 3

Global Theological Challenges

T. V. Thomas

Introduction

I am sure you have heard this adage: "Coming together is a beginning. Keeping together is progress. And working together is success." Throughout this conference, I have sensed a spirit of unity, cooperation, synergism, and partnership. I believe your heart will resonate with the point Chuck Colson makes about believers, "Not only what we have in common is much more than what is different between us, but what we have in common is of greater eternal significance than what separates us."

I presently live in the prairie province of Saskatchewan, Canada, and I know what I am talking about when I say that when the harvest is ripe, the fences disappear. I believe the global harvest is ripening fast and the fences between us are quickly disappearing. Praise God!

For the preparation of this address, I owe a great deal of gratitude to the 57 friends and colleagues in the enterprise of mission—from the different continents, and of diverse theological streams and ecclesiastical traditions—who responded to my survey on Global Theological Challenges. To each one I express my sincere thanks.

Now, it is difficult to overstate the importance of careful theological reflection, though the urgency of the remaining task of world evangelization may easily press or tempt us to strategize apart from theology. Hopefully, we are all well aware that we must avoid the impatience of theologically sterile activism every bit as much as we must avoid an erudite theology which remains in the cloistered ivory tower. I believe our mission strategy must be rooted in theology, and that theology must be rooted in Scripture.

Over the decades there has been a proliferation of theologies from within the sphere of missions. Many of these were born in the crucible of struggles in cross-cultural ministry. Some of the better known include: Water Buffalo Theology of Southeast Asia, Coconut Theology of the Pacific Islands, and Liberation Theology of Latin America. In recent decades we have also come across Praxis Theology, Black Theology, Feminist Theology, Diaspora Theology, Urban Theology, Openness Theology, and Dalit Theology. Some of us are wrestling with issues in the Theology of Reconciliation, Theology of Ethnicity, Theology of Dialogue, Theology of Contextualization, Theology of Laity, Theology of the Land, Theology of State, and others.

Recognizing that I am addressing a primarily North-American based audience, I would like to first focus on two major theological challenges facing the Western Church in global mission. Then, I want to zero in on the most pressing theological challenge before us.

Theology of Supernatural Power

Have you visited a bookstore lately? If you have, I am sure you have observed the torrent of books on the occult, witchcraft, astrology, spirituality, etc. Sales of such books have never been higher.

Are you surprised by the number of psychic hotlines advertised on your television channels? It has been a banner season for such intuitive counsellors. The North American psychic industry, from storefront fortune tellers to high-end soothsayers, is booming. Psychic telephone hotlines alone generated $450 million "earthly" dollars last year. There is no doubt that there is an acceleration of interest and involvement in the supernatural, the mystical, and the esoteric. A Toronto-area clairvoyant recently reported that her client-list has quadrupled twice in the past two years. She now earns $30,000 a year reading tea leaves, up from $1,500 in 1996. This is the summary analysis she gave for her success: "People just want to get high. Religion has let us down but people still want to get in touch with a spiritual energy."[1]

Such trends can easily be explained philosophically. In the last four decades, the restrictive straitjacket that was placed on Western Christianity by the rationalism of the Enlightenment has vanished. This scientific-rationalistic worldview that flourished since the birth of the Enlightenment in the mid-eighteen century dominated the lives of most people. This worldview which dismissed as a psychological crutch belief in any sort of mystical, supernatural, or spiritual dimension to life, Christian or otherwise, has crumbled.

Postmodernism has emerged in the West as a direct result of the collapse in the belief of the omnicompetence of human reason and modernism.[2] As we transitioned from modernism to postmodernism, there was both a shift from naturalism to supernaturalism, and a shift from reason to mystery. In place of scientific rationalism, neo-paganism has become the major contender with Christianity for the heart of Western civilization. The main characteristics of this neo-paganism in the West include: (1) denial of the personal attributes of God; (2) claiming the legitimacy to worship the created order; (3) laying claim to a dogmatic tolerance; (4) seeking to intensify the life of a person rather than transform it; (5) seeking to re-establish the place of Eros in its celebration of life; (6) offering no definite, well-grounded hope; and (7) militant opposition to Christianity.[3]

In all honesty, we must admit that the church in the West was largely trapped by the scientific-rationalistic worldview of modernism. Therefore, such a Church believed and practiced a limited view of the supernatural. Through the missionary enterprise of the Western Church such a limited view of the supernatural has been exported globally. Unfortunately, it was a partial view of the supernatural power of God. What resulted was a limited and anemic demonstration of God's power in the mission field from the beginning of the twentieth century—the Pentecostal missionaries were the notable exceptions.

Simultaneous to the unchurched seeking assurance and reality in the paranormal and supernatural, Christians in the West have also delved into the realm of the supernatural—exploring its positive and negative influences in life. In the wake of this fervor, a new glossary of terms is becoming popular in the church—spiritual power, signs and wonders, spiritual battle, spiritual warfare, spiritual darkness, power encounter, demonization, prayer walks, territorial spirits, spiritual mapping, exorcism, strategic-level praying, etc. Movements, conferences, and materials focusing on healing, deliverance, spiritual-mapping, prophecy, and strategic-level praying have exploded. The miraculous is much more visible and frequent in Christendom today. Case studies are beginning to trickle in about great advancement of the Gospel and unbelievable community transformations in several locations. Such supernatural influences are not an embarrassment to the Christian worldview. They are testimony to the compassion of God for human beings trapped in sin and its structures.

It is my firm conviction that the continued neglect of God's supernatural power in missions would only further contribute to our personal loss and ministry frustrations. The need for dependency on the supernatural in missions is indispensable. Praying and releasing God's supernatural power in ministry can be a guaranteed arsenal to remove the barriers to faith in a postmodern world. I have experienced this in my ministry both here and overseas. Both Generation X (Busters) and Generation Y (Bridgers) will respond readily and favorably to the supernatural with their postmodern worldview.

Theology of Suffering for Faith

Who among us does not know that persecution of Christians today is worldwide, massive, and escalating? Reports continue to pour in of Christians experiencing threats, riots, discrimination, violence, loss of property and possessions, kidnapping, imprisonment, physical and mental torture, and even death. We hear of some misfortune weekly, and sometimes daily. These atrocities are predicted to increase sharply.

We can be consoled by the fact that the New Testament does not ignore the subject of suffering. Missionary theologian, Roger Hedlund[4] claims that Jesus himself explained that his mission and ours in this world would entail shame, insult, and suffering (Isaiah 50:4-9; Luke 9:22; 17:25; 24:46). Did not Jesus prophesy in John 15:20, "A slave is not greater than his master. If they persecuted me, they will persecute you; if they kept my word, they will keep yours also"? Jesus empathetically declared that persecution is to be expected as well as accepted. Again, in Luke 6:22-23, Jesus echoes that same theme.

Wilbert Shenk offers a terse summary about the role of the Holy Spirit in the early Church as recorded in the Book of Acts: "The activity of the Spirit in Acts appears to be concentrated in three areas of the Church's life and evangelizing mission: the fundamentally communitarian character of the Church, the universality of the evangelizing mission and the role of suffering in its evangelization."[5]

The apostles of Christ also give us a theology of suffering in their writings. Suffering is one of the apostle Paul's dominant themes

(2 Cor 11:23-27; Phil 1:12-13; Col 1:24; 2 Thess 1:4-5; 2 Tim 2:3, 10-11; Philemon 9). In fact, St. Paul is told in no uncertain terms that he must suffer much for the sake of the Lord Jesus as he fulfils his ministry (Acts 9:16). Peter's theology of suffering comes clearly through in 1 Peter (1:6-7; 4:1,3,4; 5:9-10). And in his epistle, James calls for our steadfastness in the face of suffering (1:2f; 5:10-11).

Let me pose some searching questions to the Western Church:

—Why is it then, that the Western Church has shied away from the subject of suffering in the cause of the Great Commission?

—Why is it that in our recruiting and sending of missionaries, we tend to focus primarily on risk-free environments for ministry? (There are exceptions to this, of course).

—Why do policies of most missionary handbooks dictate immediate evacuation of missionaries in times of danger or disaster? Even with the persistent protest of some missionaries who desired to stay and serve, mission policies ruled and they were forced to depart. In my travels, I have personally met numerous Western missionaries who have confessed to me that their personal consciences were violated by their mission agency's stringent order to depart. They felt such action abandoned the national Christians to suffer alone and resulted in loss of loyalty and credibility with them. Many of the missionaries were emotionally scarred and some of them have left ministry altogether.

It is clear from Scripture that to be involved in missions we must be discerning risk-takers for God. Obviously, a Christian ought not to seek or court persecution through provocation. Nor should we seek opportunities to be persecuted to attain a premature martyrdom and its accompanying glory. But we should expect and accept suffering and persecution in fulfilling the mission of the Church.

We must, therefore, determine to develop a wholesome biblical theology of suffering in our service for Christ. "A holistic theology," says evangelical missionary anthropologist Paul Hiebert, "must include a theology of divine guidance, provision, and healing, a theology of ancestors, spirits and invisible powers of this world; and a theology of suffering, misfortune and death."[6]

Such a holistic theology of suffering is important for all Christians, whether one is a mobilizer in missions, a sender in missions, an intercessor for missions, a goer as a missionary, or a welcomer in the host country. Then, when anyone in the Body of Christ suffers, we all will suffer together. A well-defined solidarity within the Body of Christ is often forged by the fires of persecution. We will then strive to "bear one another's burdens" (Gal. 6:2), and share in the fellowship of suffering (physical, mental, and emotional) as St. Paul expects us to in 1 Cor. 1:9-10 and Phil. 3:10, because we are all part of the family of the living God (1 Thess. 4:6; James 2:15-16).

Only as we express our solidarity in Christ in intercession for the persecuted can we experience the vastness of the grace of God. Such solidarity breeds confidence and strength in suffering Christians. Because of the lack of regular and adequate information regarding the Suffering Church, until very recently, Christians in the West have been robbed. They have not been able to experience the grace of God and the attending Christian growth made possible through identification, support, and intercession for Christian brothers and sisters who suffer so greatly for their faithfulness to Christ.

Human history is replete with many forms of persecution and suffering of Christians and the Church. No matter how many trials, perils, defamations, and deaths the Church has gone through, however, its suffering has almost always brought more believers into the Church. The phrase coined by the church father Tertullian, "The blood of the martyrs is the seed of the Church" has proved remarkably true over the centuries. So, why are we in the West so hesitant? We must learn to embrace the fact that obedience to Christ may include suffering, misfortune, and even martyrdom. We must challenge new generations with this emphasis as we seek to recruit them for spiritual warfare.

The good news is that such suffering never leaves us without hope. In the Scriptures, hope is a prevailing theme for God's people living under oppressive regimes, persecution, and conflict in the world.[7] Revelation 11:15 is one such verse of encouragement, promise, and hope: "And the seventh angel sounded; and there arose loud voices in heaven, saying, 'The kingdom of the world has become the kingdom of our Lord, and of his Christ; and He will reign forever and ever.'" Until then, we desperately need a theology of suffering for our faith and martyrdom.

Theology of Salvation

The most critical and pressing theological challenge is in the realm of soteriology. I sense this is the doctrine that is creating the most ferment in the evangelical world. And this is quite understandable. Dr. Roger Olson in the introduction of his newly published book, *The Story of Christian Theology*, concludes that the one common thread running throughout the history of Christian theology has to do with salvation, i.e., "God's redemptive activity in forgiving and transforming sinful humans."[8]

To fully address a Theology of Salvation one must include issues like: (1) the centrality and uniqueness of Christ; (2) the relation of the Gospel to world religions; (3) religious pluralism and relativism; (4) destiny of the unevangelized; (5) God's judgement and the existence of hell; and (6) ultimate annihilation or eternal conscious torment in hell. Polarizations on these issues within evangelical circles have been unfortunate, but inevitable.

One way or many ways of salvation? All are aware that there are different schools of thought regarding the long-established evangelical position that Jesus is the only way to God.

From the outset I must state that the uniqueness and exclusivity of Christ and Christianity is still firmly held by most evangelicals, although it is now very seriously questioned by some. Others have rejected it totally. They say that Christ and Christianity is unique, but not exclusive. What they really mean is that non-Christians can be saved by other means as well. There are five major groups with their respective approaches. The following is a summary of their claims.[9]

The Exclusivists/Particularists. The exclusivists or the particularists believe that Christ is the only path to salvation. Therefore, salvation cannot be found in other religions but only in Jesus Christ. This is the historic orthodox evangelical position.

The Universalists. The universalists believe every one will eventually be saved. Classical universalism affirms the need of salvation in Jesus Christ, but at the same time maintains that all human beings will be reconciled to God in the end. None will be eternally damned.

The problem is that the universalists lean on an extreme view of the love of God to save everyone. They envision a situation in which God imposes salvation upon everyone.[10] Unfortunately, the universalists do not take what Jesus taught in Matthew 7:13-14 with sufficient seriousness. Jesus said: "Enter by the narrow gate; for the gate is wide, and the way is broad that leads to destruction, and many are those who enter by it. For the gate is small, and the way is narrow that leads to life, and few are those who find it." Intrinsically, universalism tends to deny to humankind the right to say "no" to God.

The Inclusivists. The inclusivists believe that Jesus Christ is the only way to God and thus the *only* Savior. But the inclusivists deny that knowledge of Christ and His atoning work on the cross is necessary for salvation. Therefore, while they believe that Christ is the final and definitive revelation of God, they claim that Christ's presence and saving activity are also found in non-Christian religions. This implies, therefore, that the salvation offered by Christ can be mediated in and through faiths other than Christianity.

Thus, if people from other faiths diligently practice and follow the religion of their choice with complete devotion, they can be saved. This makes Christianity the ultimate fulfilment of the other paths, and explains why the inclusivist theologian, Karl Rahner, claimed that there were "anonymous Christians" in other religions.

Those who buy into the inclusivists' approach criticize those evangelical Christians who are seeking to convert peoples of other religious faiths to Christ. They ask, "Why do you want to convert other people?" Some of the inclusivists even suggest that instead of converting people to Christ, we should help them be better Buddhists, better Hindus, better Muslims, or better Sikhs, as the case may be. Their sincerely reasoned argument is this: "If they are true devotees of their own faith, then God will save them anyway." Yet, how do the inclusivists reconcile the words of Jesus in Luke 19:10? Jesus said: "For the Son of Man has come to seek and to save that which was lost."

The Pluralists. Pluralists believe that all religions provide different ways of salvation, and each is equally valid. Pluralism is opposed to both exclusivism and inclusivism.[11] Therefore, Jesus and Christianity cannot claim to be either the only path to God (exclusivism) or the fulfilment of other paths (inclusivism). For pluralists, each path is as equally valid as the other. In a sense, then, pluralism can be viewed as democratized universalism.

The Integrationalists. The integrationalists seek to combine the best values of each religion in an effort to create a single world faith, which they trust will be the basis for harmony and unity for all humanity (e.g. The Baha'i Faith and New Age Religion). By doing this they have only added one more religion to the many already on the world's stage.

Those of us who still hold tenaciously to the conviction that Jesus is unique, and that He is the only way to God, are often accused of possessing a colonialist mentality which still wants to conquer and dominate others. Regardless of our feelings or desires otherwise, however, we still have clear and incisive teaching from God's Word. Since we believe that the Bible is absolutely conclusive, therefore, we must also believe what Jesus said in John 14:6. In the first half of the verse, Jesus stated in the affirmative, "I am the way, the truth and the life ...." In the second half of the verse, Jesus removes any exceptions "... no one comes to the Father except through me." If we believe that statement of Jesus' in John 14:6, then, we must also obey the Great Commission that Jesus gave us (Matt. 28:18-20).

What about Popular Religious Pluralism?

We are increasingly ministering in culturally pluralistic environments, especially in the major cities of the world. Now, against this background of cultural pluralism, there seems to be tremendous pressure for everyone to adopt a religiously pluralistic outlook, as well (i.e. the acceptance of the diversity of beliefs and values held by our neighbors). On the surface, that may sound innocent enough. But the popular religious pluralism we are called upon to accept has some underlying fallacies. Let me highlight just three of the major ones.

First fallacy: None of the religions are absolute. The argument for this fallacy goes something like this. God's truth is reflected in all religions to a varying degree. Therefore, we should all accept that the differences between the religions are not a matter of truth and falsehood, but simply different perspectives on the one truth. Hence, the logical conclusion is this: all religions manifest unique reflections of the one Absolute God or Ultimate Reality, just like the different colors in the rainbow. Together they form a whole spectrum. The great danger of this fallacy is its assumption that no single religion can claim absolute religious truth.

Second fallacy: All religions lead to God. Just as all the spokes of a wheel lead to the hub of the wheel, all religions lead to God. It makes absolutely no difference which spoke you choose, because all will ultimately arrive at the center anyway. Or as one often hears it put: "We're all climbing the same mountain; we shall all meet at the top." This means any path will get you there. Therefore, all we need to do is become better people within the boundaries of our own pathways of religious traditions and frameworks.

Here's my question: When the goals of each religion are so different, how can anyone harmonize the pathways to reach those goals? The goal of Christianity is to enjoy endless personal fellowship with God. In contrast, the goal of Eastern religions like Hinduism and Buddhism is Nirvana, which involves the final extinction of individual personality. Attempting to harmonize all religions and ideologies is both impossible and ridiculous on the surface of it.

Third fallacy: All religious beliefs are relative. This fallacy is widely held in Western society, where belief is so often seen as simply a private matter. Each person is to be left to his or her own private opinion, and to find his or her own way to God. The implication of this fallacy, therefore, is that no one should seek to intentionally influence the followers of other faiths, and no religion should insist on converting others to its way of thinking. Evangelism and missions, according to this fallacy, are about the most intolerant things a person could be involved in.

In reality, that is not what is actually happening in society. Ideologies and worldviews are passionately presented, books and articles are published on them, and people are being persuaded. With fallacies like these—none of the religions are absolute, all religions lead to God, all religious beliefs are relative—popular religious pluralism in fact spirals down to become religious relativism. What religious relativism essentially says is—no belief is absolutely true for everyone. It can only ever be relatively true, or subjectively true. Herein lies the primary argument against relativism: it cannot state its case without self-contradiction.[12]

Religious relativism even goes on to say that what might be absolutely true for you, is not necessarily true for the rest of humankind. This sort of thinking slides smoothly into the core of postmodernism, which elevates emotions and feelings to be equal to rational thought or even superior to it. What results from such thinking is this: absolute truth is sacrificed, universal truth is suppressed, objectivity is surrendered, and certainty is squashed.

What about People Who Believe That All Religions Are the Same or Equal?

Two common observations need to be made here:

1. When someone says, "All Chinese look alike," we know two things about that person. First, he/she is not himself Chinese. Second, he/she lacks interest in the Chinese people, as indicated by the failure to look hard enough.

Similarly, when someone says, "All religions are the same," we know two things about that person. First, he/she knows very little about religion, and cares very little about it. Second, he/she is not committed to any one religion in particular.

2. No true Jew, Muslim, or Buddhist would ever agree that one religion is the same, or as good, as another.

The following seven questions need to be posed to people who believe that all religions are the same or equal.

1. *If all religions are the same, why do they have vastly different views of God?* Christians believe in the Trinity—but Jews and Muslims do not. Tribal religions are often polytheistic, and New Agers stress we ourselves are gods. Hindus believe in many gods and goddesses, but most Buddhists believe in none. Though some forms of folk Buddhism worship gods and goddesses, the founder of Buddhism, Gautama Buddha, claimed that there is no creator.

2. *If all religions are the same, why do they have such different views of salvation?* Jews are saved by obeying 613 Old Testament commandments, and their as-yet-unknown Messiah. Muslims (who deny original sin) find salvation through obedience to the Qur'an. Buddhists gain Nirvana through self-denial. Hindus follow cycles of reincarnation until they merge with the Ultimate. Unificationists are saved by the grace of the founder, Sun Yung Moon. Witches achieve deliverance by engaging in rituals that sometimes include sexual acts.

3. *If all religions are the same, why do they differ so much in ritual and worship practices?* Hindus use idols for worship. Zen Buddhist monks are hit with a bamboo pole during meditation in order to increase their focus. The cult leader, Moses David, taught "sacred" prostitution as a means of worship. Some fringe religious groups in the USA handle deadly snakes as part of worship.

4. *If all religions are the same, why do they differ so much on moral issues?* In India, the followers of Jainism oppose violence to any living creature. They even wear masks over their mouths lest they accidentally swallow a fly. Followers of other religions do not think twice about swatting a fly. Orthodox Jews have no taboo

against drinking alcoholic beverages, but they abstain from lobster. Christians deplore polygamy, whereas Muslim men can be married to as many as four women at any one time.

5. *If all religions are the same, why do they have different views of Jesus?* Most Buddhists have little interest in Jesus. Muslims believe Jesus is a prophet, but do not believe Jesus is the Son of God or that He died on the cross. Hindus believe Jesus was another "avatar" (revelation), but do not believe He is the Son of God.

6. *If all religions are the same, why would Jesus be crucified by other religious people?* If Jesus shared the same faith as the Jewish leadership who plotted his death, why would they have killed Him?

7. *If all religions are essentially the same, why do people have such different faiths and values?* Do white supremacists have the same faith as black preachers? Do theologians who blessed Hitler share the same gospel as those who resisted Hitler? Did Catholic inquisitors share the same faith as the people they burned at the stake as witches and heretics?

Does the militant wing of fundamentalist Islam, Hamas, serve the same God as the Jews who were slaughtered by Hamas suicide bombers? Can anyone believe that? By the same token, most Muslims believe the Hamas martyrs will go to Paradise. Would this be the view of Jewish rabbis? Would Jews expect to greet Hamas martyrs in that same Paradise after death? Observation and common sense make it patently obvious that religions are neither the same, nor equal. In fact, no two of them are the same or equal.

We are living in days when we badly need to recover and restate with the same conviction as the apostle Peter his testimony of Acts 4:12. Responding under the Holy Spirit's powerful influence to a question asked by the Jewish Sandhedrin, the apostle Peter categorically replied: "And there is salvation in no one else; for there is no other name under heaven that has been given among men, by which we must be saved" (Acts 4:12). This leaves no room for qualification, and makes clear that no one else shares the unique status of Jesus.

Here is where we can unite. We can unite around the person of Jesus Christ, the work of Jesus on the cross, and the words of Jesus Christ. The uniqueness and exclusivity of Jesus Christ is the basis of the uniqueness of our Christian faith, and the message of our missionary enterprise. The correlation between the uniqueness and exclusivity of Jesus Christ and the salvation of humankind is crucial. To reject one is to also reject the other, willfully or otherwise.[13]

What is Unique about Jesus Christ?

Uniqueness of the coming of Jesus. The Old Testament paved the way for the coming of Jesus. It is full of prophecies which fit the life of Jesus, and Jesus fulfilled all 48 of the major Old Testament prophecies. Is this due to a coincidence? The probability that all 48 prophecies occurred in one person by coincidence is 1 in 10 to the power of 157 (i.e. the number 10 followed by 157 zeros). One can't imagine a number that big, or a probability that small!

Uniqueness of the character of Jesus. Though Jesus lived in human society, He was without sin. He was not a person in search of acclaim or power over others. At one point, people wanted to make Jesus their King. His reaction was to go away and hide (John 6:15). Jesus very often charged those He healed not to broadcast what He had done for them (Mark 1:44).

Just before his death, Palm Sunday, was the first time Jesus let his disciples make public who He really was. Even then He rode into Jerusalem not with pomp and majesty, but lowly, and astride a donkey. The teachings of Muhammad, Buddha, or Confucius do not stand or fall on the character and integrity of their founders. With Christianity, however, the character and integrity of Jesus is all important.

Uniqueness of the claims of Jesus. Jesus made many stupendous claims. No one has ever made anything comparable.

—"Ultimate Judge of the world" (John 5:22-23)
—"I am the Bread of Life" (John 6:48)
—"I am the Light of the World" (John 8:12)
—"Truly, truly I say to you, before Abraham was born I AM" (John 8:58)
—"I am the Good Shepherd" (John 10:11)
—"I am the Resurrection and the life" (John 11:25)
—"I am the way, the truth and the life" (John 14:6)
—"I am the True Vine" (John 15:1)
—"Son of Man" (Matt. 8:20; 19:28; Luke 5:14; John 1:51)
—"Son of God" (Matt. 11:27; 16:17-18, Mark 12:6; 13:32; 14:61-62; Luke 10:22; 22:70; John 10:30; 14:9; Heb. 1:2)

Uniqueness of the credentials of Jesus. The credentials of

Jesus are threefold:

1. *His authority over the physical realm.* Repeatedly in his ministry, Jesus exercised authority over nature. In his first miracle, He turned water into wine at the wedding at Cana (John 2:1-9), and later on fed 5,000 people with five loaves and two fish (Luke 9:12-17). When Jesus calmed the Sea of Galilee, his disciples then understood He was the Son of God (Matt. 8:23-27).

1. *His authority over the moral realm.* Christ's words to the paralytic, "My son, your sins are forgiven," proved his deity, because only God can forgive sins (Mark 2:8-11). Jesus had authority to heal spiritual blindness (John 9:39-41).

3. *His authority over the eternal realm.* Christ raised Lazarus from the dead as dramatic proof that even death itself could not limit his authority, "I am the resurrection and the life, he who believes in me shall live even if he dies, and everyone who lives and believes in me shall never die" (John 11:25-26).

Uniqueness of the cross of Jesus. With the help of the Roman authorities, the Jews finally put Jesus to death by crucifixion. His disciples, who were devastated, frightened, alarmed, and confused hid themselves. Jesus, the Sinless One, died in the place of all the sinners. When Jesus was crucified we witnessed the most profound self-revelation of God.

On the cross, Jesus Christ did all that was necessary to secure forgiveness and new life for lost humankind. Jesus cried out on the cross, "It is finished." Jesus died once, but never again. What God accomplished on the cross can never be undone. And it will never need to be done again. The cross was sufficient and final.

Uniqueness of the resurrection of Jesus. Three days after his crucifixion and burial, God raised Jesus from the dead. The historical evidence for the resurrection of Jesus still stands firm and secure after nearly 2,000 years of scrutiny. Christianity stands or falls with the truth of the resurrection, and the resurrection of Jesus establishes Christianity as the truth. The resurrection promises new life and an eternal relationship with the living God for those who trust in Christ's salvation.

Uniqueness of the message of Jesus. Christ's message is a message of love. His death was a demonstration of the love of God for humankind. God's love seems to meet completely the deepest needs of the human heart, giving purpose to life. Furthermore,

God's personal love for us is unconditional, taking away our sins and giving us eternal life. We cannot earn it. But our part is to trust what Christ accomplished on the cross on our behalf. God's love in us enables us to love God and love other people—both our friends and our enemies.

Now, the multi-faceted uniqueness of Jesus is precisely why the apostle Peter was convinced that there was no salvation in anyone but Jesus Christ. This crucial note that Peter declared rang uncompromisingly through all the preaching of the early apostles. Why? They were absolutely convinced that there is no other name by which to be saved.

This is an issue that we must settle on individually, and corporately as churches, denominations, and mission agencies: We must unapologetically declare that there is no other name than Jesus by which people can be saved. This vital truth needs to be echoed and re-echoed in theological institutions and in local congregations all across the world.

I believe this triumphant affirmation needs to be echoed and re-echoed in the pathways of service in which God places us. It needs to be echoed and re-echoed in all the contexts of the missionary enterprise as we fulfill the Great Commission—in the board rooms of mission agencies as well as on the frontiers of our mission fields.

Conclusion

Our message is that Jesus is not only unique, but He is the only Savior and Lord. He alone claims to save humankind from sin and its wages of eternal death. Only two reactions are logically possible with that claim:

1. If it is believed, Jesus cannot be reduced to just one among many human moral teachers.

2. If it is NOT believed, Jesus cannot be raised to the level of Buddha, or Muhammad, the Dalai Lama, or Guru Nanak, for He claims much more than they do. Christ's claims are exclusive. They cannot be amended, watered down, relativized, negotiated away, or nuanced into acceptability.

This is best illustrated by the following historical anecdote: The ancient Romans built a pantheon for all the gods of the world. They invited the Christians to put a statue of Jesus in with the other gods. The Christians were told, "Be open minded. Join the fellowship of world religions." The Christians responded, "No thanks." They knew if they did that, they would be aligning themselves with those seeking to rob Jesus of the uniqueness of his divinity and saving work.

Jesus alone is Lord, and the world's only real Savior. As we march into the new millennium, let us continue presenting to the lost, with sincere humility and bold conviction, the Lord Jesus Christ as He really is. Amen.

Endnotes

1. Leah McLaren, "Seeing Things," *The Globe and Mail*, September 4, 1999, p. C5.

2. The very achievements of the scientific worldview which heralded much promise have turned sour. The two world wars, industrial pollution, the environmental debate, nuclear armaments, etc., have caused the general collapse of confidence in the Enlightenment.

3. Visser t'Hooft, "Evangelism Among Europe's Neo-Pagans," *International Review of Missions*, October 1977, pp.349f.

4. Roger E. Hedlund, *The Mission of the Church in the World: A Biblical Theology* (Grand Rapids, MI: Baker Book House, 1991), 115.

5. Wilbert Shenk, ed., *The Transfiguration of Mission: Biblical Theological and Historical Foundations* (Scottdale, PA: Herald Press, 1993), 213.

6. Paul G. Hiebert, *Anthropological Reflections on Missiological Issues* (Grand Rapids, MI: Baker Books, 1994), 35.

7. Ibid, p. 130.

8. Roger E. Olson, *The Story of Christian Theology: Twenty Centuries of Tradition & Reform* (Downers Grove, IL: InterVarsity Press, 1999), 13.

9. A broader understanding of the issues can be gained from the works by Bernard T. Adeney, Daniel B. Clendenin, Alister McGrath, Millard J. Erickson, Dennis L. Okholm and Timothy R. Phillips, Gordon C. Olson, and Charles Van Engen.

10. Alister McGrath. *A Passion for Truth: The Intellectual Coherence of Evangelicalism.* Downers Grove, IL: InterVarsity Press, 1996, p. 238.

11. Daniel B. Clendenin, *Many Gods, Many Lords: Christianity Encounters World Religions* (Grand Rapids, MI: Baker Books, 1995), 84.

12. Peter Hicks, *Evangelicals & Truth: A Creative Proposal For a Postmodern Age* (Leicester, UK: Apollos, 1998), 136.

13. Valson Thampu, *Rediscovering Mission: Towards a Non-western Missiological Paradigm* (New Delhi, India: TRACI, 1995), 22.

Selected Bibliography

Arnold, Clinton E. *Three Crucial Questions about Spiritual Warfare.* Grand Rapids, MI: Baker Books, 1997.

Adeney, Bernard T. *Strange Virtues: Ethics in a Multicultural World.* Downers Grove, IL: InterVarsity Press, 1995.

Billington, Anthony; Lane, Tony and Turner, Max, editors. *Mission and Meaning:*

Essays presented to Peter Cotterell. Carlisle, UK: Paternoster Press, 1995.

Dyrness, William A. *Emerging Voices in Global Christian Theology.* Grand Rapids, MI: Zondervan Publishing House, 1994.

Erickson, Millard J. *How Shall They Be Saved? The Destiny of Those Who Do Not Hear of Jesus.* Grand Rapids, MI: Baker Books, 1996.

Gaede, S.D. *When Tolerance is no Virtue: Political Correctness, Multiculturalism & the Future of Truth & Justice.* Downers Grove, IL: InterVarsity Press, 1993.

Geivett, R. Douglas and Habermas, Gary R. *In Defense of Miracles: A Comprehensive Case for God's Action in History.* Downers Grove, IL: InterVarsity Press, 1997.

Green, Michael and McGrath, Alister. *How Shall We Reach Them? The Christian Faith to Nonbelievers.* Nashville, TN: Thomas Nelson, Inc., 1995.

Middleton, J. Richard and Walsh, Brian J. *Truth Is Stranger Than It Used to Be: Biblical Faith in a Postmodern Age.* Downers Grove, IL: InterVarsity Press, 1995.

Okholm, Dennis L. and Phillips, Timothy R. *Four Views on Salvation in a Pluralistic World.* Grand Rapids, MI: Zondervan Publishing House, 1996.

Olson, C. Gordon. *What in the World is God Doing? The Essentials of Global Missions: An Introductory Guide.* Cedar Knolls, NJ: Global Gospel Publishers, 1998.

Phillips, James M. and Coote, Robert T., editors. *Toward the 21st Century in Christian Mission.* Grand Rapids, MI: Eerdman's Publishing Company, 1995.

Ramachandra, Vinoth. *The Recovery of Mission: Beyond the Pluralist Paradigm.* Grand Rapids, MI: Eerdman's Publishing Company, 1996.

Saayman, Willem and Kritzinger, Klippies, editors. *Mission in Bold Humility: David Bosch's Work Considered.* Maryknoll, NY: Orbis Books, 1996.

Sampson, Philip; Samuel, Vinay and Sugden, Chris. *Faith and Modernity.* Carlisle, UK: Regnum Books International, 1994.

Van Engen, Charles. *Mission on the Way: Issues in Mission Theology.* Grand Rapids, MI: Baker Books, 1996.

Working Together Theologically in the New Millennium

Chapter 4

Opportunities and Limitations

Charles Van Engen

In the summer of 1998, my house in California needed to be painted on the outside. So I contracted my son, Andrew, then 16, to work for me. Together we began scraping, priming, and working our way around that two-story house. I remember that a couple of weeks into the project I was starting to climb a ladder to prime some eaves that my son had just scraped when he came running to the foot of the ladder.

"Dad, Dad," he exclaimed. "I just thought of something I had never seen before!"

"What's that?" I asked, trying not to fall off the ladder in the wake of his unexpected enthusiasm.

"Dad, when two people work well together, they can accomplish more than twice what they could working alone!"

That discovery on the part of my son was worth the whole summer! And that fact is the heart of the issue facing us in missionary cooperation.

Introduction

Why should we work together in the new millennium? Is it not much easier to work separately than to work together? North American mission-sending during the 1980s and 1990s has seen the proliferation of what I call "mom-and-pop mission shops," small, independent, often family-owned, entrepreneurial Christian agencies, mission initiatives and NGO's. We have lived through a time of decentralization, separation, and celebration of competition and difference. All over the world we have seen the phenomenon that when persons do not like the kind of church they are attending, they simply start another one more to their liking. If they disagree with the policies of their mission agency, they start another mission.

A person, couple, family, or small group senses the call of God to initiate a mission thrust. They gather support wherever it may be found and off they go to do their "mission." Not much time is wasted on psychological testing. Little effort is spent on organizational indoctrination. There is no need to convince a large mission organization or denomination concerning their vision. They are called and they go: clean, quick, efficient, focused.

Those of us associated with large mission agencies or denominational mission organizations may also ask, "Why should we work together?" We all have our turf to care for, as well as our own fundraising needs to look after to pay our bills and expenses. We have our own working principles and procedures that differ from those of other organizations. We have our own corporate identity to define, our own specialization in mission that provides the basis on which we present ourselves to our supporters. We work hard to create our own structures, to define our own purpose and mission, to protect our own interests, and to direct our unique vision. Each of us is trained to emphasize our own special contribution to world mission. Each of us sees our mission endeavor, the Church, and the world through the colored glasses of our own agendas.

Moreover, we seem to find it easier to trust the people in our group than those who belong to other organizations. When I was young, my mother used to repeat an old Dutch proverb that reflected her own pioneering roots in Northwest Iowa. Might it also be applicable to mission partnerships?

"The whole world is crazy except you and me,
and sometimes I wonder about you!"

We all have our own special geographic, continental, confessional, cultural, national, linguistic, historical, and relational biases that affect the way we cooperate with others. The history of the Church and its mission is replete with examples of theological and non-theological factors of immense influence in mission partnership and cooperation. Well-meaning people deeply committed to world evangelization have found it hard to work together. Ever since Paul and Barnabas could not agree on their assessment of John Mark, dedicated disciples of Jesus have often found it necessary each to go their own way in world evangelization.

Conversely, creating partnerships takes time and energy, is initially expensive, tends to slow the participants down, and does not always yield the focused mission activity first envisioned by the partners. It runs the risk of diffusing and redirecting everyone's energies, and sometimes yields less creative mission initiatives than the partners might have demonstrated by doing mission independently.

In the words of the 1996 Evangelical Manifesto of the NAE, "We confess that although we value unity and united evangelical action, we too often do more to build our own ministries than to cooperate at making it difficult for someone in our own neighborhoods to be lost for eternity."[1]

The question is even sharper when we consider that the center of gravity of world Christianity has now shifted to the East and the South. Two-thirds of world Christianity is now to be found in the majority world. Christianity is no longer a Western religion—it was not originally Western—and is no longer. It is African, Asian, Latin American, Middle Eastern, Indonesian, South Pacific Polynesian, and so on. Today more full-time cross-cultural missionaries are being sent and supported by churches in Asia, Africa, and Latin America than the total sent from Europe and North America. So partnership/cooperation becomes even more complex as it begins to involve multiple cultures and global relationships. The shades of paternalism, control, bitter experiences, and power struggles raise their ugly heads when we begin to search for new forms of cooperation between those who once were the senders (and may now be the receivers) and those who once were the receivers (and may now be the senders). Former senders and receivers alike must now work as equal partners in mission endeavors with other churches and missions. Partnership in mission in the twenty-first century will involve combinations of the following:

- Church-with-church cooperation
- Mission-with-mission partnering
- Sending mission with receiving church
- Sending church and receiving mission
- Formerly receiving church, now a mission, partnering to serve a new receiving church or mission
- Multi-cultural teams that draw support from, and are accountable to, persons, churches or mission agencies all over the globe

- Local congregations who send their own missionaries, cooperating with older or newer receiving churches or mission agencies
- Global, multilateral cooperative mission endeavors.

It will not be easy to work together in the twenty-first century. So why should we?

In this paper I would like to suggest four reasons why we need to partner together in world evangelization.

Why work together?

Because...

... **Together** we belong to Jesus Christ ("together").

... **Together** we belong to each other as members of the global body of Jesus Christ ("working").

... **Together** we exercise our spirit-given gifts in ministry as we participate in Christ's mission ("diversity").

... We grow **together,** as **together** we grow into the fullness of the stature of Jesus Christ ("theological").

Why work together? So that the world may believe that Jesus is the Christ (John 17: 21). Together we can evangelize the world in our generation.[2] I was given a working title for this paper: "Theological Diversity: Working Together." In keeping with that title, I have organized this paper in reverse order as a way to get at a very complex subject: **together, working, diversity, theology**. I want to draw our reflection from a rereading of Ephesians 4:1-5:2. In each section I will review a theme from Ephesians 4, then reflect on lessons learned during the twentieth century that could help us in the next millennium.

My thesis is this:

> Because our oneness is grounded in Jesus Christ (and not found in corporate, organizational, administrative, financial, structural, or historical unity),[3] we are called to partner together for world evangelization, serving one another in love and humility as we participate in Christ's mission, offering to one another the unique gifts given by the Holy Spirit to our various organizations and churches (regionally and globally), until we all together grow up into the measure of the stature of the fullness of Christ (Eph. 4:1-5:2).

We work together as we follow (and co-labor with) Jesus Christ in mission in God's world in the power of the Holy Spirit. In the words of the Manila Manifesto: "Christ calls the whole church to take the whole Gospel to the whole world."[4]

Together We Belong to Jesus Christ

Together: *The motivation for missional partnerships—"Worthy of the calling" (Eph. 4:1).*

Why should we partner together? Because together we belong to Jesus Christ. This is our most fundamental motivation for mission partnerships.

The biblical text. A profound source for a biblical theology of the Church's mission is found in Paul's letter to the Ephesians. A careful study of Ephesians offers an overview of the missionary nature of the Church. Paul saw the Church as an organism that should continually grow in the missional expression of its essential nature. And, although I do not have space here to develop all the relevant missional themes found in Ephesians, I do want to bring out four of those found in Ephesians chapter 4. Although Paul uses at least fifteen different word pictures or images to portray the Church in Ephesians, the theme that grounds all others is the fact that when Paul speaks of the Church he uses only the singular—there is only ONE CHURCH—no more!

The apostle Paul says, "There is one body and one Spirit, as there is also one hope held out in God's call to you; one Lord, one faith, one baptism; one God and Father of all, who is over all and through all and in all" (Eph. 4:4-6). We do not confess "holy catholic churches," or "families of God" or "peoples of God" or "bodies of Christ" or "New Israels." In the biblical view of the church the plural only refers to the geographic location of local congregations, not the essential being of the Church. In its essence there is only one Church. In Ephesians *ekklesia* appears only in the singular....[5]

So we must begin where Paul starts, recognizing that we are all "prisoners for the Lord" who beg, beseech, urge churches and missions alike to "live a life worthy of the calling (we) have received."[6] Christ's calling, then, entails a life of a "new self, created to be like God," (Eph. 4:24). This new missionary way of life includes understanding that we belong *together* in one Body under one Head, Jesus Christ. This entails the cultivation of specific attitudes with which we perceive ourselves and others (working); includes the exercise of our gifts in mission and ministry (diversity), and seeks to grow as one Body into the stature of its Head, Jesus Christ (theology).

This calling is not one we predetermine or decide upon by ourselves. Rather, it is a calling extended to us by our Head, Jesus

Christ. Our oneness in Jesus Christ (Eph. 4:5, 6, 13) is not predicated on our being able to work easily together. Nor that we like each other—although, hopefully, we do! Nor does it depend upon our agreeing with one another in all perspectives, in all propositions, dotting every "i" and crossing every "t" in the same way.

Our oneness is drawn from the singleness of our one Saviour and Lord. It is Christ's calling. There is no substitute for this foundational motivation for working together. We work together because we are servants of the same Lord who want to live a life worthy of the calling our Lord has extended to us all. There is an indispensable and irreplaceable link between our mission and our discipleship in Jesus Christ. This was the original concept expressed by Cyprian in the well-known phrase, *extra ecclesiam nulla salus.* As Carl Braaten has said:

> The entire theme of ministry in the New Testament is bound to the person of Jesus Christ as the decisive eschatological event of God's reconciling Work. Christ alone is the unity in, with, and under the pluriformity of ministries that arose in primitive Christianity. Ministry is Christocentric in all the New Testament writings....If there is any authority in the church, that authority can be none other than Jesus Christ, as the authority is mediated through those whom he commissioned to be his ambassadors.[7]

"The work of Jesus the Messiah," writes Wilbert Shenk, "embodies the *missio Dei*. This is normative for all mission and must determine the character, strategy, and stance of mission in our contemporary world. This allows for neither triumphalism nor defeatism. It calls for missionary witness that embraces the fullness of the gospel in response to the times in which we live."[8]

So Paul begins by reminding us that the calling is the Lord's, in whose service and for whose sake he is willing even to be a prisoner. In the next breath Paul echoes the christologies of John 1 and Colossians 1, and draws from the cosmic christology in Ephesians 1, whereby Christ is said to "fill everything in every way" (1:19-23). Paul affirms a trinitarian perspective of oneness: "There is one body and one Spirit—just as you were called to one hope when you were called—one Lord, one faith, one baptism; one God and Father of all, who is over all and through all and in all."[9]

We are *together* because we are together in Jesus Christ. The biblical reality is that it is:
- Christ's world, not ours (context of mission)

- Christ's church, not ours (structures of mission)
- Christ's mission, not ours (motivation)
- Christ's yoke and action, not ours (means of mission by the Holy Spirit)
- Christ's leading and direction, not ours (goals of mission)
- Christ calls and selects, we do so only secondarily (agents of mission)

We are not passive agents in all this—but neither do we determine, control, or circumscribe Christ's mission. We all know this, don't we? Why then do we so often act in our churches and mission agencies as if this were not so?

Missiological concerns. Affirming the oneness of church and mission in Jesus Christ creates as many questions as answers. In the second part of each of the four sections of my presentation, I want to draw briefly from an example in mission history during the twentieth century of what that point does *not* imply, then suggest what it *could* mean for mission partnerships in the next millennium.

1. *What our oneness does not mean.* This oneness does not necessarily mean structural or organizational unity. Mission history demonstrates that affirming our oneness in Christ does not in itself necessarily signify that such unity must take structural or organizational form. A prime example of making this leap was the movement in 1961 at the New Delhi Assembly of the World Council of Churches (WCC), when the International Missionary Council (IMC) was integrated into the WCC. This was a very controversial development, with strong passion on both sides of the issue. What Max Warren has called a "preoccupation with structures" ruled the day, and the IMC was integrated into the WCC because there were those who felt that they needed to demonstrate the unity of mission and church in a structural and organizational way. Warren observes,

> Structural changes may well be necessary because change is necessary, and some structures inhibit change. But there is no axiomatic increase in spiritual vitality simply because necessary changes have been defined by new structures. Some elementary awareness of this fact might serve to curb the contemporary passion for structural change which too easily becomes an escape from obedience to more urgent demands: as, for instance, actual obedience to the Missionary Commission.[10]

One of the results of the integration of the IMC into the WCC was that a significant number of Evangelicals left the WCC and became active in the Evangelical movement later represented by such major gatherings as Wheaton, 1966; Berlin, 1966; Lausanne, 1974; Pattaya, 1980; Manila, 1989; and GCOWE in Seoul, 1994.

A second result of "integration" took thirty years to become evident. The integration of the IMC into the WCC eventually led to the loss of a commitment to biblical mission on the part of the WCC and the near disappearance of the emphases formerly associated with the IMC.[11] Stephen Neill's dictum, "When everything is mission, nothing is mission," was borne out historically in the case of the integration of the IMC into the WCC.[12]

A third result of the enthusiasm regarding structural unity led to the euphoria in WCC and NCCC circles in the 1960's regarding the "Missionary Structures of the Congregation."[13] The enthusiasm over structural unity in mission, however, was never translated into missional action that brought persons to new faith in Jesus Christ and new membership in Christ's church. Unfortunately, the "Missionary Structures of the Congregation" movement ended up following J. C. Hoekendijk's mistaken pessimism about the church and unwarranted optimism concerning "The Church Inside Out," entailing a secularized ecclesial presence in the world. If the conciliar movement had followed Johannes Blauw's lead in *The Missionary Nature of the Church* (a work he published around the same time as Hoekendijk's writings), the results would have been very different. In its early years "The Gospel and Our Culture" network in the U.S. began to repeat the same mistakes inherent in "the missionary structures of the congregation," though substantial correction and redirection of this has been offered by Darrell Guder's recent contributions.[14]

These issues and others stimulated cautions like the following from W. Harold Fuller:

> A church-centric position is usually accompanied by a strong church union attitude, which can overshadow evangelism. All Christians should be concerned about sectarianism and unnecessary divisions. Some see disunity as an obstacle to witness. However, if the goal of organizational union is put ahead of witness, it may be self-defeating. Union may demand compromise that hinders witness. Lack of church union can be used as an excuse for not witnessing ... The central force of missions for (conservative evangelicals) is not ecumenism but a personal witness of Jesus Christ as Savior and Lord.[15]

We need to be committed to giving visible expression to our oneness—but that does not necessarily entail structural or organizational unity. New structures may be needed to meet new challenges, but they do not of themselves bring transformation nor stimulate new mission endeavors. As Eddie Gibbs has said, "When denominations (and mission agencies) are in desperate need of renewal, they will restructure."[16]

2. *What this oneness could mean.* Our oneness in Jesus Christ means that the Gospel is for everyone. A christological view of church and mission implies the universality of the Gospel. Because Jesus Christ is Lord of all, because Jesus Christ gave his life for all, the good news of salvation in Jesus is for the whole inhabited earth. As Lamin Sanneh has said, the Gospel is "infinitely translatable."[17] It is not the property or right of one group—it is an offer open to all. This does not suggest pluralism or inclusivism in terms of salvation. Rather, as I have shown in *Mission on the Way*, a biblical approach to mission among the religions of the world entails a perspective that is at once "faith-particularist, culturally-pluralist, and ecclesiologically inclusivist."[18] It means that the Gospel is to be offered to all those who yet do not know Jesus Christ, to persons from every tribe, tongue, family, people and nation. This is the universality of the Church that by definition makes the church God's missionary people.[19]

Thus, for Paul, it was not optional that he was called "to preach to the Gentiles the unsearchable riches of Christ, and to make plain to everyone the administration of this mystery" (Eph. 3:8-9). When Evangelical Christians and churches begin to lose their global mission commitment and involvement, they are on a path to becoming only shadows of themselves—they are no longer fully the Church that Jesus Christ intends them to be. Mission motivation derives from our discipleship in Jesus Christ. Thus the Apostle Paul said in 2 Corinthians 5:14, "Christ's love compels us"—that together we may be Christ's ambassadors of reconciliation.

The greatest harm to the Gospel occurs when we say we obey the same Lord and believe the same gospel, but compete, contradict and conflict with one another in our witness to those who are not yet disciples of Jesus Christ. This brings us to our second word: "working."

Together We Make Up the Body of Jesus Christ

Working: *The means for missional partnerships—"With all humility and gentleness...members one of another" (Eph. 4: 2, 25).*

Why should we partner together? Because together we make up the Body of Jesus Christ. And the means by which the Body works together involves a special set of attitudes toward one another as members of the Body.

The biblical text. We normally think of Ephesians 4 as one of the primary passages having to do with the gifts of the Holy Spirit, which it is. And this will be considered in the next part. However, a closer examination of the chapter shows that Paul devotes even more emphasis to the attitudes with which Christians are to treat one another. The lists here echo the "fruit of the Spirit" as found in Galatians 5. Paul offers two other similar lists of virtues in 2 Corinthians 6:6 and Colossians 3:12-15. Applied to mission partnerships, these attitudes are profoundly practical suggestions on Paul's part as to how we may work together. They are the means by which we can partner with one another in mission. We've heard them all before. But listen to them again—this time, thinking about what it might be like to experience these in the context of missional partnerships. We are all "prisoners of the Lord." Therefore, we live a life worthy of our calling when we treat each other in this way.

> Be completely humble and gentle; be patient, bearing with one another in love. Make every effort to keep the unity of the Spirit through the bond of peace....
>
> You must no longer live as the Gentiles do, in the futility of their thinking....You, however,...were taught, with regard to your former way of life, to put off your old self, which is being corrupted by its deceitful desires; to be made new in the attitude of your minds; and to put on the new self, created to be like God in true righteousness and holiness. Therefore each of you must put off falsehood and speak truthfully to his neighbor, for we are all members of one body. In your anger do not sin....
>
> Do not let any unwholesome talk come out of your mouths, but only what is helpful for building others up according to their needs, that it may benefit those who listen. And do not grieve the Holy Spirit of God, with whom you were sealed for the day of redemption. Get rid of all bitterness, rage and anger, brawling and slander, along with every form of malice. Be kind and compassionate to one another, forgiving each other, just as in Christ God forgave you.
>
> Be imitators of God, therefore, as dearly loved children and live a life of love, just as Christ loved us and gave himself up for us as a fragrant offering and sacrifice to God" (Eph. 4:1-5:2).

Three brief observations are in order.

1. *We are in fact not the ones who work in mission.* The Holy Spirit works in mission—and works through us. Therefore, if we exhibit inappropriate attitudes and destructive interpersonal relationships, we "grieve the Holy Spirit" who is the One carrying out the work of mission. This pneumatological instrumentality of mission was recognized very early by the Jerusalem church, as we see in Acts 12 and Acts 15. Because Christ's mission is wrapped in the presence and power of the Holy Spirit, our interpersonal relationships have a profound effect on our spirituality—personally and corporately—and ultimately they affect our mission.

This is consistent with Jesus' words to his disciples when he cautioned them about their interpersonal relationships as they participated in his mission. "You know that the rulers of the Gentiles lord it over them, and their high officials exercise authority over them. Not so with you. Instead, whoever wants to become great among you must be your servant, and whoever wants to be first must be your slave—just as the Son of Man did not come to be served, but to serve and to give his life as a ransom for many" (Matt. 20:25-28). In other words, we must exercise the gifts of the Holy Spirit only in an atmosphere permeated by the fruit of the Holy Spirit.

2. *Although we customarily think of this passage in terms of a local congregation and its members, it is instructive to apply it to the corporate cultures of our mission organizations.* What does this passage have to tell us when we let it become a beacon shining into the inner workings and relationships of our mission organizations and denominational mission structures? I believe Paul is signalling here that the internal life of our Christian organizations must be consistent with our missional goals. We cannot say we are a mission agency dedicated to compassion and love if internally our mission organization is not permeated by grace, love, forgiveness, and compassion through the Holy Spirit. We cannot bring Good News if we ourselves are the bad news.

3. *The Body of Christ is a global Body.* Thus, the attitudes mentioned by Paul become imperatives (and tests of authenticity) for the way in which we should treat each other globally—between East and West, between North and South, between sending agency or church and receiving agency or church. The attitudes Paul emphasizes are the aroma that folks should smell, the taste they should get,

when they become involved in our mission structures and partnerships. In our missionary cooperation we cannot afford to be only goal- and production-oriented. Our partnerships, our inter-personal and inter-organizational relationships must be consistent with the stated goals of our mission cooperation. When this is not so, our entire mission enterprise is compromised both internally and spiritually as well as externally and proclamationally.

Our missional spirituality, then, seems to be affected more deeply by what comes from our hearts than from those among whom we carry out our mission. Like a duck that does not get wet in water, like an earthworm that does not get dirty in the mud, so our spirituality is not contaminated so much by what comes to us from outside, nor so much by those with whom we associated. Rather, we are contaminated with what comes from our own hearts (the works of the flesh of Galatians 5). So Jesus could carry out his mission among sinners, yet be the sinless Son of God. This seems to be what Jesus was referring to when he said, "What goes into a man's mouth does not make him 'unclean,' but what comes out of the mouth, that is what makes him 'unclean'"(Matt. 15:11).

Similarly, at least in the context of Ephesians 4, separation, keeping our doctrine pure, does not seem to be as foundational or essential a virtue as is living "a life of love" (5:2) in humility, gentleness, and patience, "bearing with one another in love" (4:2). "Be not unequally yoked" is used by Paul in 2 Cor. 6:14-71 to refer to the relationships of Christians with those who are not Christian—the passage has little or nothing to do with our relationships between and among believers. And even this does not preclude our participation in Christ's mission among and to those who are not yet Christian. Otherwise, the proclamation of the Gospel to the Gentiles would have been impossible for the early Christians. (See also Luke 6:45; Matt. 12:34; Acts 10:14-15; James 3:6.)

Missiological concerns. What implications might we draw for working together in the new millennium? I will briefly mention what I believe it does *not* mean, and then what it *could* mean.

1. *What these attitudes do not mean.* The attitudes of working together in mission partnerships which Paul called for in Ephesians 4 do not necessarily mean we create comity agreements in mission. One of the ways the missionary community attempted to cooperate in mission in the past was through creating comity agreements.

Especially prevalent around the turn of the century, American mission agencies (most mainline denominations) sought to divide up the territories of various Two-Thirds World countries so that Western missions would not be stumbling over each other in their mission endeavors. These literally "gentlemen's agreements" (mostly created by men) were primarily motivated by a desire to display an appreciation for each other and a respect for each other's mission enterprises. Many comity agreements seem to have been well-intentioned attempts to avoid duplication and reduce the appearance of competition. However, in the long run they have had mixed results.

An interesting case-in-point in Latin America was the situation created by the "Plan of Cincinnati" in relation to U.S. mainline Protestant missionary work in Mexico. In 1914, with many still experiencing the euphoria of the great missionary conference of Edinburgh, 1910, eight denominations gathered in Cincinnati to work out a comity agreement with regard to their work in Mexico.[20] My impression from the documentation about this meeting is that there were no Mexican leaders present. The result of the meeting, the "Plan of Cincinnati," entailed moving almost all related missionary personnel from one area in Mexico to another, since one area would no longer be Presbyterian, for example, but would become Methodist, another would no longer be Congregational, but Presbyterian, and so forth. There was to be a united seminary and a united publishing house.

Playing on the Spanish words of "Cincinnati" and "Asesinato," Mexican church leaders call this the "Plan of Assassination." The results were very detrimental for the evangelization of Mexico by mainline Protestant missions, and destructive of interchurch relations particularly in Mexico. U.S.–Mexico mission–church relations, at least in the National Presbyterian Church,[21] have never been the same. The "Plan of Cincinnati" still clouded the horizon in the late 1970s when I was personally involved in negotiating a new umbrella partnership document between my denomination, the Reformed Church in America, and leaders in the National Presbyterian Church of Mexico. Based on my experience, I do not believe "oneness" should necessarily entail comity agreements as we have known them in the past.

Comity agreements tended to create divisions and fragmentation of witness in Latin America, ended up legitimating tribal hatred and strife in Africa, and atomized the church throughout Asia. In Africa, comity agreements have resulted in the churches too often using denominational loyalties and ecclesiastical polities mostly to divide various groups from each other within their own countries rather than bringing them together as positive contributors to the wholeness of their nation.

At times, comity agreements have gone a step further and propelled churches to unite structurally and organizationally. This was the case, for example, in India and Japan. However, all over the world united churches seem to spend more time trying to hold themselves together organizationally and structurally in their internal life than taking the Gospel together to those not yet Christian in their midst. History does not support the assumption that comity agreements or church unification increase impact and innovation in mission on the part of the participants. Nor does it necessarily multiply the number of those who are presented with understandable and contextually-appropriate communication of the Gospel.

And yet, we must hasten to affirm another equally important fact. The cacophony of conflicting and competing claims on the part of divided churches and mission agencies is no longer a luxury the Church of Jesus Christ can afford in the next millennium. So we need to keep looking for ways to encourage one another to exhibit the attitudes that Paul commends to us in our internal organizational life and our inter-organizational partnerships. This points us to a brief suggestion of what such "working together" might mean.

2. *What these attitudes could mean.* As we face the next millennium, Paul's challenge in Ephesians 4 calls us to consider in "humility, gentleness, and patience," that each of us as churches and organizations belong to each other as part of the universal, global, people of God. This means that we need to rethink how we participate together in the universality of the Church. What does it mean for the Church to be inherently "ecumenical?"

Although there are a number of uses of the term "ecumenical," the most basic has to do with "the whole inhabited earth," and with the Church's mission that is directed to the whole earth and the whole human race. Thus the Manila Manifesto stated, "We affirm that God is calling the whole church to take the whole gospel to the whole world" (Affirmation # 21). This was the original meaning of the term when it was used at the turn of the century. W. Richey

Hogg writes that the first time this was used in the official title of a conference was at the Ecumenical Missionary Conference held in New York in April–May, 1900. "'Ecumenical' was used...not because the conference represented every branch of the Christian church, but 'because the plan of campaign which it proposes covers the whole area of the inhabited globe.'"[22]

This use of the term "ecumenical" refers to a basic notion of the Church-in-mission in the world. It refers to something which might be called the "worldwideness" of the scope of the "ecumenical" Church-in-mission. It is the worldwide scope of the universal Church-in-mission which calls upon all churches and Christians to be in relationship and cooperation for the sake of the task which is worldwide and too large for any one church. It is the worldwideness of the One Church which mandates the need for all churches to strive for visible, tangible unity. Kenneth Grubb spoke of this worldwide sense of "ecumenical."

> But the true nature of the Church is supranatural and ecumenical. Its very existence is a rebuke to the overweening pretensions of exaggerated nationalism whether in East or in West. It should be the glory, rather than the reluctance, of a church to enter into relations of mutual aid with other churches, without reference to nationality as a finally determining factor.[23]

This use of the term "ecumenical" is related to its original meaning in Hellenistic and then in New Testament thought. Gerard Kittel tells us that, "The word is fairly common in the New Testament.... *oikoumé* derives from current Hellenistic usage....The reference is simply to the glad message which is for all nations and the whole earth (in reference to Mark 13:10).[24]

John Mackay traced the early use of the word "ecumenical" in relation to the mission of the church. Mackay pointed out that the term "originated as a geographic term, which in both Greek and Roman civilizations took on political and cultural significance. The Greek noun *oikoumene* means literally the 'inhabited earth.'" The adjective *oikoumenikos*, from which "ecumenical" is directly derived, means "that which has to do, or is coextensive, with the inhabited earth....In the religious history of (humankind), the only force that has created the *oikoumene* which has been 'ecumenical' in a dynamic sense, has been the Gospel of Christ."[25]

After comparing the term's use in the "Ecumenical Missionary

Conference" in 1900, Mackay offered a definition of the term that was adopted by the Central Committee of the WCC in 1951, after Mackay apparently objected to restricting the term to a sense of organic unity only. The definition reflects the same global perspective we mentioned above. "We would especially draw attention to the recent confusion in the use of the word 'ecumenical.' It is important to insist that the word, which comes from the Greek word for the whole inhabited earth, is properly used to describe everything that related to the whole task of the whole church to bring the Gospel to the whole world."

This global view of "ecumenical" was supported by Hans Küng in his definitive volume on the Church. Küng related the catholicity of the Church to its sense of being essentially missionary, as "referring to the whole world; it was to serve the world through its proclamation of the Gospel, 'Go into all the world and preach the Gospel to the whole of creation' (Mk. 16:15), to 'all nations' (Matt. 28:19), as 'witnesses...to the end of the earth' (Acts 1:8), 'until the end of the world' (Matt. 28:20)...."

"We can see," wrote Küng "that from its very origins and by its very nature the Church is worldwide, thinking and acting with reference to the world, to the whole inhabited earth, the *oikoumene*. This universality can therefore be expressed in the word 'ecumenical,' 'concerning the whole inhabited earth.'"[26]

The term should be recaptured and used in its original meaning —to refer to the vision of the whole Church carrying the whole Gospel to the whole inhabited earth. If the term is used to refer to "the whole inhabited earth" and to the universality of the Church and its mission, then it fits naturally as an adjective modifying the "ecumenical" nature of the global Evangelical movement, as David Bosch pointed out in 1980. Bosch spoke then about an evangelical theology and activity in mission that is "ecumenical" in the broader sense of the term, as having to do with the whole inhabited earth. He pointed to the Wheaton Declaration (1966), the Frankfurt Declaration (1970), the Berlin Declaration on True and False Ecumenicity (1974), and the International Congress on World Evangelization in Lausanne, Switzerland (1974) as illustrative of this global orientation.[27]

We could add, among a multitude of others the Urbana mission conferences of the Foreign Missions Fellowship of InterVarsity

Christian Fellowship; the Billy Graham evangelistic ministries and crusades; the Consultation on World Evangelization at Pattaya, Thailand in 1980; the Congress on Frontier Missions held in Edinburgh in 1980; the Lausanne II gathering in Manila in 1989; the Lausanne Movement itself; the AD2000 and Beyond Movement; the World Evangelical Fellowship; the sponsoring organizations of this conference itself; the United Bible Societies; Wycliffe Bible Translators; the Overseas Missionary Fellowship; Youth With a Mission; Missionary Aviation Fellowship; World Vision; and the Third World Mission Association that met in Kyoto, Japan. These and many others are examples of a global Evangelical *oikoumene*, an evangelical ecumenical movement that has changed the face of world Christianity and world mission, an evangelical ecumenism that represents the global commitment of world Christians to bring the whole Gospel to the whole world.

Once we see ourselves in this light, we can begin to understand that we are the universal Church of Jesus Christ, the global Koinonia, a missionary fellowship of the disciples of Jesus Christ, commissioned to participate in Christ's mission to the whole world.[28] This means we are fully the disciples of Jesus Christ only as we live out our faith in the midst of the world Church. There is an increasing myopia of North American Christians with reference to the rest of the world, and the rising emphasis on mission in our backyards. Commendable as that may be, when these are set overagainst global mission involvement they become counterproductive emphases that contradict the very nature of the Gospel and of the Church. All disciples of Jesus Christ must live out their faith in participation with the Church that surrounds the globe. To be "worthy of our calling" is to be totally dedicated to being world Christians. American Evangelicalism will only be true to its Lord as it participates on a global scale with the Church of Christ that surrounds the *oikoumene*, the whole inhabited earth. In this sense, to be American or Western (or Dutch, or Mexican—to pick on myself here) is to sell one's birthright. In the next millennium we must all learn to be first and foremost world Christians, disciples of the one Lord whose one Body circles the globe.[29]

One way we can do this is by having a deep awareness of and appreciation for one another's gifts for ministry, perceived globally. This brings us to our third word: diversity.

Together We Each Exercise Our Spirit-Given Gifts in Ministry as We Participate in Christ's Mission

Diversity: The agency of missional partnerships—"To each of us...according the measure of Christ's gift" (Eph. 4:7).

Why work together? Because together we each exercise our Holy Spirit-given gifts in ministry as we participate in Christ's mission. In this third section, I want to deal with the concept of diversity not so much in terms of a plurality of faiths, or a multiplicity of faith interpretations, but rather in terms of a variety of ministries, as Paul does in Ephesians 4.

The biblical text. Jesus Christ who fills the whole universe has given gifts: apostles, prophets, evangelists, pastors, and teachers. Paul's list of gifts here is only illustrative, and we know it is to be seen in conjunction with the lists at least in Rom. 12, 1 Cor. 12, and 2 Peter 4.

One of the major themes of our passage has to do with the juxtaposition of the concepts of "one," "all" and "fullness" with the repetition here of the word "some." "We all (will) reach unity in the faith," Paul says, as various ones of us exercise our gifts. The one Body of Christ is built up as each participates through the exercise of his or her gifts: "some" in one way, "some" in another way.

Although all this is familiar to us, we customarily associate the gifts of the Holy Spirit in this passage with individual persons as they live out their ministries in the context of a local congregation. However, given the global emphasis in the rest of the chapter, is it not legitimate also to apply Paul's concept of gifts here to the world Church? In that case, the passage would be telling us that in relation to the Church that surrounds the globe, some denominations and churches have certain gifts to offer, some mission boards have specific giftedness to bring, some one gift, some another.

Let's let our mind think of circling the globe. We might conceptualize one and one-half billion Christians spread over the entire globe, representing a multitude of languages, peoples, families, tribes, and nations. We could think of them as groups of congregations, denominations, mission agencies, mission initiatives, NGO's, and a multitude of ministries circling the globe. Then we begin to understand what Paul was really after. Paul's frame of reference in Ephesians 4 was not only, maybe not primarily, the local congregation in a specific location. Rather, I believe he was thinking of all

Christians everywhere who were disciples of Jesus Christ.

A global hermeneutic of this passage has transformed the way I think of the gifts of the Holy Spirit. Now we are talking about each group of believers anywhere on the globe offering their gifts to all other believers anywhere on the globe. Now we conceptualize a Body of Christ whose members are spread throughout the entire world, dedicated to participating in Christ's mission of evangelizing the other four-and-a-half billion who yet do not know Jesus Christ as their personal Saviour and Lord. Each "member" of the global Body has something unique to offer the Body's ministry in the world. And, conversely, the Body is incomplete without the contribution of each member.

Here, then, is a perspective of missionary partnership that is spiritually grounded, world-encompassing, and missionally oriented. This is the Body of Christ that wraps its arms around the whole *oikoumene* and loves all peoples and tries to reach all peoples because "God so loved the world that he gave his only Son" (John 3:16).

Missiological concerns. There are a host of missiological implications we might draw from such a global picture of the one Body's gifts, given by the Holy Spirit. I will focus attention on just a couple.

1. *What a global Body of Christ image does not mean.* It does not mean declaring an official or even an informal moratorium on mission partnerships. A very controversial initiative that sought to give concrete shape to the oneness of the church in mission was the ill-fated and misunderstood movement in Africa, Asia, and Latin America that called for a "moratorium" on mission-sending from the Western churches and missions. The "moratorium" debate of the 1970s is especially instructive for us, given recent calls on the part of some Western Evangelical mission leaders to drastically reduce or completely stop financial aid to Africa as a way to combat the dependencies they see on the part of African churches.[30]

In the early 1970s John Gatu of Africa and Emerito Nacpil of the Philippines, along with others, wanted to see their churches and missions in the Two-Thirds World become fully mature, adult, respected, and active participants in the world mission of the world Church. One might say, they were anxious to create space for the churches in the majority world to be able to exercise their gifts of ministry and mission. Their deepest desires had to do with the churches and missions of the Two-Thirds World being taken seriously, being respected, and being accepted as full partners by the missions and churches in the West. The proposal was a response on the part of Christians, particularly in Africa, to the paternalism and dependency that had developed as a result of Western personnel and finances being offered to African churches. I believe the initial motivation was a correct one. Johannes Verkuyl suggested that the original impetus behind the talk of "moratorium" was this question: "How can we by our inter-ecclesiastical relations become a better instrument for completing the work (of world evangelization) which still needs doing?"[31]

The motives behind the call for "moratorium" could be viewed as a consistent outgrowth of churches and missions having taken to heart the "three-self" formula of Henry Venn and Rufus Anderson. One might consider a moratorium on receiving mission support a necessary step for the receiving churches to become truly self-governing, self-supporting, and self-propagating—as well as self-theologizing and self-directed in mission. As Johannes Verkuyl puts it, "[The call for 'moratorium' in Africa] was also a positive indication of the deep African desire for self-expression and self-reliance."[32]

But the shape that the "moratorium" debate took—and the negative consequences it had for world evangelization—were most unfortunate. During the late 1960s and early 1970s this led to talk (and in some cases very real decisions) to reduce the mission vision and the commitment for mission-sending on the part of churches and missions in both the West and in the Two-Thirds World. Many receiving churches that had been taught that mature, indigenous churches should become "three-self" churches—simply became selfish and self-centered.

In the author's case, the National Presbyterian Church of Mexico followed the adopted "moratorium" perspectives and in 1972, in celebration of its centennial, declared a "moratorium," stating it would no longer accept any expatriate personnel or financial support from anywhere outside of Mexico. The Mexican church may have needed time to set its own house in order and determine its own destiny as a church. However, the long-term result of that "moratorium" was an increasing myopia and insularity on the part of the Mexican church because of its total noninvolvement in world Christianity. It took over a decade to clarify the situation and re-create a format whereby the Mexican church was again able to participate in mission with the world Church—both in receiving and in sending.[33]

2. *What a global Body of Christ image could mean.* The image of a global Body of Christ implies a new and renewed commitment to partnership on the part of churches and missions circling the globe. Paul's concept of the gifts of the Holy Spirit are stimulating and creative at this point. They call us to encourage an environment of mutuality, and complementarity among the members, a climate in which all members of the Body, everywhere in the world, may participate in God's mission in world evangelization, offering to the world church what the Holy Spirit has given to each of them uniquely and to all of us collectively. The concept of the gifts of the Holy Spirit, looked at globally, moves us all toward wanting to foster healthy forms of interdependence as a way of avoiding the creation of unhealthy dependencies. As David Bosch wrote:

> The solution, I believe, can only be found when the churches in the West and those in the Third World have come to the realization that each of them has at least as much to receive from the other as it has to give. This is where the crux of the matter lies.... We know that in ordinary human situations, genuine adult relationships can only develop where both sides give and receive.[34]

The Congress on World Evangelization at Lausanne in 1974 said, "The dominant role of Western missions is fast disappearing. God is raising up from the young churches a great new resource for world evangelization."[35]

Partnership is partnership in world evangelization. The focus must not be on cooperation as such, but on the task of world evangelization.[36] Cooperation must be for something. Partnership should not be an "empty basket."[37] However, even when we may agree on the missional goal of our partnership, the way we treat one another is of utmost significance. As Bill Taylor has suggested, true global partnership in mission will include the following lessons:

> 1. Listen before entering a partnership, and be willing to learn from mistakes and try again....
> 2. Partnerships work best when there is shared ownership of the project, including finances....
> 3. Be balanced. Don't get sucked in by hard sells based solely on comparisons of cost-effectiveness. Take time to check out potential partners before signing up....
> 4. Wise churches recognize what they cannot do, and partner with those

who can assist them in their long-range goals....

> Surely there is some relationship between partnership in mission and the prayer of our Lord in John 17:11, 21-23....The global body of Christ is learning about partnerships in every language and culture. Let us continue to grow, to expand, to please the heart of God without creating artificial structures. Let us now be true partners in the gospel.[38]

Phillip Butler states rightly that partnership is not optional. For nearly 200 years, the church in the West has prayed and invested in missions to see the birth of the church in Asia, Africa, and Latin America. Now, the Third World church is taking its place alongside the Western church so that, together, they can reach the final segment of the world—the nearly 2 billion who have never heard of Jesus' love. Working in partnership has been talked of for a long time, but today we have no other option![39]

A main reason why partnership is not optional is that we really, really do need each other in order to evangelize the world in our generation. Although the total percentage of Christians in relation to world population is the highest today than it has ever been, yet the actual number of those who don't yet know Jesus Christ is larger than ever before: four-and-one-half billion! We need each other in order to evangelize the world for whom Christ died. No one church, no one mission agency, no single missionary movement can evangelize the world in our generation by itself. This has become increasingly obvious to those of us, for example, who are involved in mission in the city. In the complex metroplexes of the world of the twenty-first century, the only way the Church of Jesus Christ will impact the cities—any city—is by all the disciples of Jesus partnering together to present the Gospel through word and deed in each city.

Is it not time for all of us to take seriously what was affirmed by the Lausanne Movement in Manila ten years ago?

> We affirm that we who claim to be members of the Body of Christ must transcend within our fellowship the barriers of race, gender and class.
> We affirm that the gifts of the Spirit are distributed to all God's people, women and men, and that their partnership in evangelization must be welcomed for the common good....
> We affirm the urgent need for churches, mission agencies and other Christian organizations to cooperate in evangelism and social action, repudiating competition and avoiding duplication.[40]

For churches and mission agencies to partner together in world evangelization, they must be willing to listen to each other, learn from each other, and appreciate one another in their theological understanding of the Gospel. This brings us to our final word: Theological.

We Grow Together, as Together We Grow into the Fullness of the Stature of Jesus Christ

Theological: The goal of missional partnerships—"Until all of us come...to maturity, to the measure of the full stature of Christ" (Eph. 4:13).

Why should we partner together in the next millennium? Because we grow together as together we grow into the fullness of the stature of Jesus Christ. Our proximity or distance from Jesus Christ is the heart of Paul's theological affirmation in Ephesians 4.

The biblical text. The christological center of our passage is rather obvious. Although the chapter is about the Church and its growth in diaconal ministries, it is Jesus Christ who permeates the entire chapter. Paul is a prisoner of Jesus Christ, his Lord (4:1). There is one Lord (4:5). Jesus Christ is the one who apportions the grace, who ascended on high, led captives in his train, and gave gifts to men (4:7-9). This is the Christ who fills the whole universe (4:10). He gives various gifts (4:11). The Church is the body of Christ (4:12). The Body is built up in the knowledge of Jesus Christ the Son of God, and becomes mature, attaining the whole measure of the fullness of Christ who is the Head (4:13, 15). Paul writes to the Ephesians insisting in the Lord (4:17). The Ephesians are not to live as the Gentiles do, because that is not how they had come to know Christ (4:20). The truth is to be found in Jesus (4:21). Therefore the Ephesian Christians are called to put off falsehood, speak the truth in love, not let any unwholesome talk come out of their mouths, not grieve the Holy Spirit of God, be kind and compassionate to each other, forgive one another the way in Christ God has forgiven them (4:25-32). In short, they are to live a life of love just as Christ loved them and gave himself up for them, because Jesus Christ is a fragrant offering and sacrifice to God (4:32-5:2).

If we were to take out the christological references in this passage, there would be little left. The center of Paul's missiological ecclesiology in Ephesians 4 is, in fact, Jesus Christ the Lord. Paul shows us a comprehensive approach to theologizing that includes both propositional and experiential content.

First, a comment about theological content. When we as Evangelicals think of the word "theology," we tend to associate with a set of propositions, a "statement of faith," that neatly spells out those with whom we agree and those with whom we disagree. This has been especially true since the Fundamentalist/Modernist debates of the 1920s and 1930s. In terms of mission partnerships, our tendency has been to cooperate in terms of specific missional action, as long as our theological propositions are not questioned. Our theological affirmations have been off-limits. In mission partnerships we Evangelicals have tended to show a marked unwillingness to deepen, reexamine, and reflect on the theological assumptions that undergird our missional actions. Yet, it is also true that during the twentieth century Evangelicals demonstrated a "broadening vision" that included a degree of openness to reexamining the way they did their theology.[41] This has included a willingness to examine their theological method, bringing together their propositional reasoning with their experience of being encountered by Jesus Christ.

Stanley Grenz offers a classical meaning of the term:

> Basically, systematic theology is the reflection on, and the ordered articulation of faith....The word 'theology' does not appear in the biblical documents....The word itself is formed from two other Greek terms, theos (God) and logos (word, teaching, study). Hence, etymologically 'theology' means 'the teaching concerning God' or 'the study of God'....Theology is primarily the articulation of a specific religious belief system itself (doctrine). But it also includes reflection on the nature of believing, as well as declarations concerning the integration of commitment with personal and community life.[42]

Donald Bloesch emphasizes that both the rational and the experiential, the propositional and the mystical, are integral aspects of the theological task... "The dogma of revelation," Bloesch writes, "consists in the unity of logos and praxis....Dogma is not just an external truth but an internal truth. It must take root in one's inner being. It appeals not just to the mind but to the whole person....An evangelical dogmatics is based on the supposition that God's Word is at the same time God's act. This Word is both conceptual and personal, propositional and existential."[43]

Hendrikus Berkhof speaks of doing theology in terms of a relationship of love that seeks sanctification:

> The essence of the study of the faith is best grasped if we regard it as an element in the sanctification of the church. In the faith-relationship God seizes us for himself with his love. We may respond to that by loving him with our whole being and therefore with all our mind. The study of the faith is not the only form, but certainly one of the forms of our loving God with the mind...All right thinking about God arises out of the encounter with God and is aimed at the encounter with God....The possibility of making this true and meaningful thinking depends on the relationship which from the other side is established by the Holy Spirit.[44]

This leads to a comment on theological method. Grenz, Bloesch, and Berkhof present us with an approach to theologizing as that seeks to bring us relationally closer to Jesus Christ—and in so doing deepens its understanding of the truth of the Gospel. Lesslie Newbigin emphasized this when he suggested that we need to reverse Descarte's methodology and "believe in order to know."[45] Our passage in Ephesians 4 is both experience and objectification, both faith-relationship with Jesus Christ and propositional reflection. It draws from the "Ten Blessings" of Ephesians 1:3-14, together with all the various propositional affirmations woven through Ephesians. But it also calls for radical transformation of the spirituality of the disciples, growth toward a truer and clearer reflection of their Head. This is a growth in the biblical sense of "knowing," an intimate relationship like the way the old King James English stated that "Adam knew Eve...."—and she bore a son" (Gen. 4:1). This is the sense of "knowing" that has to do with wisdom, rather than accumulating empirical facts.[46] It is the kind of thing of which the Psalmist was speaking when he said, "The fear of the Lord is the beginning of wisdom" (Ps. 111:10).

Paul Hiebert has presented this as a "centered-set" method of theologizing, as opposed to a "bounded-set" approach. In *Anthropological Reflections on Missiological Issues*,[47] Hiebert develops the "characteristics of centered sets:"

> First, a centered set is created by defining the center or reference point and the relationship of things to that center. Things related to the center belong to the set, and those not related to the center do not....
> Second, while centered sets are not created by drawing boundaries, they do have sharp boundaries that separate things inside the set from those outside it—between things related to or moving toward the center and those that are not. Centered sets are well-formed, just like bounded sets. They are formed by defining the center and any relationships to it. The boundary then

emerges automatically. Things related to the center naturally separate themselves from things that are not....

Third, there are two variables intrinsic to centered sets. The first is membership. All members of a set are full members and share fully in its functions. There are no second-class members. The second variable is distance from the center. Some things are far from the center and others near to it, but all are moving toward it.....

Fourth, centered sets have two types of change inherent in their structure. The first has to do with entry into or exit from the set. Things headed away from the center can turn and move toward it....The second type of change has to do with movement toward or away from the center. Distant members can move toward the center, and those near can slide back while still headed toward it.

Hiebert goes on to demonstrate that "Hebrew Culture" was structured as a centered set, based on relationships, especially in terms of a covenantal relationship of the people of Israel to the God of Abraham, Isaac and Jacob.

Paul Hiebert's idea of "centered-set" thinking is helpful for doing Evangelical mission theology. It provides a means by which we can be firmly and tightly anchored in truth in Jesus Christ, yet simultaneously open to differing worldviews, different cultural glasses with which we read the Scriptures, all within the same world Church comprised of the disciples of the one Center, Jesus Christ.[48]

For us to be able to work together in mission partnerships in the midst of differences in our theological perspectives, we will need to learn to theologize comprehensively, including both propositions and experience as legitimate data for our theological task. And we will need to do this through a "centered-set" approach that asks about our growing proximity or distance from Jesus Christ our Lord. We can no longer use our theologizing primarily as a defense of our own boundaries by which we decide who is in and who is out. Rather, "speaking the truth in love" (Eph. 4:15), we will need to receive from each other—on a global scale—the insights which draw all of us closer to our Lord, the Head of the Church. In this way we can learn to cooperate without compromise. We are centered in Jesus Christ, in the midst of the multiple cultures of the globe.

Missiological concerns

1. *What theological growth does not mean.* Comprehensive theological growth of the Body of Christ means we all must struggle to avoid paternalism in missional partnerships. Paternalism was a

major source of frustration on the part of receptor churches during the height of the "moratorium" debate. And we must not underestimate the destructive power of paternalism. Though it is beyond the limits of this presentation, let me illustrate what I mean by mentioning some of the "many faces" that paternalism might include:

1. The Financier Syndrome[49]
2. The Mothering/Smothering Syndrome[50]
3. The Organization Syndrome[51]
4. The Invasion Syndrome[52]
5. The Isolation Syndrome[53]
6. The Big Cheese Syndrome[54]
7. The Prince-and-the-Pauper Syndrome[55]
8. The "Professional" Complex[56]
9. The "Fix-It" Syndrome[57]
10. The "Reproducing Ourselves" or "Cloning" Syndrome[58]

We all know that paternalism is an ever-present danger in mission and ministry. It appears mostly when we hold to some position or idea in a doctrinaire fashion, or take some action regardless of the circumstances, opinions, wisdom, and feelings of the people we have been called to serve. Can we escape paternalism altogether? Probably not. But maybe we can be aware of its traps.

One of the most insidious traps of paternalism is theological. Because we are convinced of the theological propositions to which we hold, and because we are committed to the faith we have experienced, we too easily apply that to new situations. We assume our understanding of the Gospel is universally applicable in identical fashion to the way we learned and experienced it. Thus we find it easier to contextualize the wrapping of the package of our theology than to reexamine our understanding of the actual contents of the package.

For centuries Western European theologians have thought of their theology as applicable for all time and all cultures—and have imposed a theological hegemony on the world church—a theological quality control of which they have seemed to be mostly unaware. At times, this has been accompanied by an air of triumphalism and arrogance on the part of the sending agencies and churches who have supposed they already have all the theological answers necessary to respond to all the questions faced by the church everywhere. As Lesslie Newbigin and others have been pointing out with increasing force, Western theology itself represents a highly contextualized formulation of the Gospel. Unfortunately, sometimes the excellent answers the missionary enterprise has offered have involved responses to what the recipients have considered the wrong questions. Thus Dean Gilliland, for example, has suggested that in our contextual theologizing we need to begin by asking what are the operative questions of the culture?[59]

On the other hand, as seen in Ephesians 4, Paul would be adamantly opposed to speaking of plural "theologies" like in Latin American Liberation Theology, Minjung Theology, African Theology, Dalit Theology, Asian Theology, and so forth. Rather, Paul states, "there is one hope,...one faith,...one baptism, one God and Father of all" (Eph. 4:4-6). How, then, do we theologize as a world Church, as mission partners who circle the globe, as members of the one Body who represent radically different contexts of mission?

2. *What global theological growth could mean.* I would like to suggest that our global theological task must involve growth—for all of us in our closeness to Jesus Christ, through the work of the Holy Spirit. I believe Paul offers us a way to do this in Ephesians 4. It involves all of us together in each place growing into the fullness of Jesus Christ. And as we do so, we will, and must, grow closer together with each other, as disciples of the same Lord.[60] As mission partners, we grow together as together we grow into the fullness of the stature of Jesus Christ. The size of the Head does not change. The Lordship of Jesus Christ, Christ's rule, the Kingdom of God, does not change. And as the Church grows, it is the same Church. It was not less church before it grew, nor is it more Church after it has grown. But as it grows, it reflects to the world more completely, more clearly, more thoroughly the One who is the Head of the Church. It grows toward matching the "whole measure of the fullness of Christ." It grows because of Christ's work through the Holy Spirit, looking to the day when Christ will "present her to himself as a radiant church, (the bride) without stain or wrinkle or any other blemish, but holy and blameless" (Eph. 5: 26-27). This organic picture of the Church involves a perspective of theological interdependence, complementarity, and mutuality.

We need each other. The complexity of theological issues facing us in mission in the next century demands that we partner together in the theological task, seeking to understand in a new way the old,

old story of Jesus and his love—in new contexts, facing new issues.[61]

As I pointed out in "The New Covenant: Knowing God in Context," an organic view of the Church's theological growth in closeness to the Lord Jesus Christ must now become a global perspective. In the next millennium it will be the world church that together grows in its understanding of God's covenant with God's People. It is always the same covenant, always the same Gospel, yet always new, and always deepening in its impact of transforming and sanctifying Christ's church. And this is now a global phenomenon. "As the gospel continues to take root in new cultures, and God's people grow in their covenantal relationship to God in those contexts, a broader, fuller, and deeper understanding of God's revelation will be given to the world church."[62]

This theological endeavor will involve all believers in Jesus Christ from all continents, in the midst of every culture to come closer to Jesus Christ as they read the Bible for themselves, share what they see with all other Christians around the world, and grow together as together they grow into the stature of our one Head, Jesus Christ.

As we begin to learn from each other as theological mission partners we will deepen our relationship with Jesus Christ, want to learn from each other and grow closer to our Head. Then we will begin to experience what Orlando Costas called "integral (or comprehensive) growth." Costas believed that the authentic Church of Jesus Christ was meant to grow in four dimensions simultaneously. I have added a fifth—spiritual growth, numerical expansion, organic expansion, conceptual expansion, and incarnational growth.[63]

I believe it will take us all together, working together, in theological mission partnership to begin together "with all the saints, to grasp how wide and long and high and deep is the love of Christ, and to know this love that surpasses knowledge—that (we) may be filled to the measure of the fullness of God" (Eph. 3:18-19). Such is the integral growth of the disciples of Jesus Christ who circle the globe, committed to working together in the next millennium.

Conclusion

Last July my wife, Jean, and I were in our back yard, trimming the bushes. Normally, I do that by myself. But this time we were doing it together. I was cutting and chopping, she was breaking up the branches and putting them into the trash bin. And I was amazed at how quickly the job was getting done. I stopped and exclaimed to Jean, "This goes so much faster with two of us!"

I believe the evangelization of the world in our generation will go much faster if we work together. Even the writer of Ecclesiastes knew this. "Two are better than one, because they have a good return for their work" (Eccl. 4:9).

Theological Diversity, Working Together: together, working, diversity, theology. Our partnership in mission in the next millennium must be centered in Christ, focused in the local congregation, shaped by a Kingdom of God missiology, directed to a world in desperate need of Christ, recognizing that the Gospel is for everyone, committed to cooperating together in mutuality and humility, celebrating the gifts given to each member of the global Community of the King, and growing together to become mature partners, attaining together the whole measure of the fullness of Jesus Christ our Lord.

To meet the challenges we will face in world evangelization in the next millennium, we need to take to heart Billy Graham's words that appear in the Epilogue of the NAE's Evangelical Manifesto:

> It is my fervent prayer that the evangelical community will take seriously the command of the Great Commission in the manner which Jesus described in his greatly priestly prayer—cooperating without compromise, so that the world might believe!
>
> The challenge before us calls for a strategic united evangelistic effort as we've never undertaken before. The world in our time is said to have made discipleship harder. But it has also made evangelism easier. Today's world is said to be multiplying crises all around us. But we must never forget that, for the gospel, each crisis is an opportunity....
>
> We need to rededicate ourselves to the primary task of winning and making disciples of Jesus Christ in our generation. Today's world waits to see our response to questions and challenges such as these. Evangelicalism has a future to the extent that we evangelicals ourselves are drawn by the gospel, are defined by the gospel, and are declaring and demonstrating the gospel of our Lord and Savior, Jesus Christ, in word and deed....
>
> Our faithful witness may or may not result in new understanding of the name "evangelical" by the culture and media. Our faithful united witness might result in visible Christian worship of our Lord in the public celebrations of the year A.D. 2000 rather than merely a glorification of another epoch of human achievement and existence. But our faithful united witness will result in revival and reconciliation and renewal. Let us go forward in faith together—and the very gates of hell cannot prevail![64]

Endnotes

1. NAE: 1996, 3. It is no easy thing to define what we mean by "Evangelical." Some helpful sources may be found in C. Van Engen: 1990, 205, footnote 4.

2. The "Watchword" was popularized by John R. Mott and others in the Student Volunteer Movement toward the end of the nineteenth century. In 1900 John R. Mott published a book with the title, *The Evangelization of the World in This Generation*. Gerald Anderson quotes Mott's explanation of his understanding of the "watchword." "The 'watchword,' (Mott) said, 'means the giving to all men an adequate opportunity of knowing Jesus Christ as their Saviour and of becoming His real disciples.' This is what Christ implied in the Great Commission. It means preaching the gospel to those who are now living; it does not mean the conversion of the world, according to Mott" (Anderson: 1988, 382).

The "watchword" was still a strong motivational element of the missiology of Edinburgh, 1910, the springboard of much partnership and cooperation among churches and mission agencies during the twentieth century. See, e.g., Stephen Neill: 1964, 332; William Richey Hogg: 1952; and World Missionary Conference, 1910: 1910. Neill comments, "The slogan was based on an unexceptional theological principle—that each generation of Christians bears responsibility for the contemporary generation of non-Christians in the world, and that it is the business of each such generation of Christians to see to it, as far as lies within its power, that the Gospel is clearly preached to every single non-Christian in the same generation. This is a universal and permanent obligation; it applies to Christian witness both within what is commonly called Christendom and beyond it. If the principle is to be rejected, the New Testament must first be rewritten" (1964, 332).

3. There are many different meanings of "unity." The New Delhi Assembly of the World Council of Churches explored the possible meanings of unity. See *Evanston to New Delhi: 1954-1961* (Geneva: WCC, 1961); W.A. Visser 't Hooft, ed. The New Delhi Report (Geneva: WCC, 1961), 116-135. The Conciliar Movement's preoccupation with "visible" unity moved the discussion in the WCC in the wrong directions that overemphasized structural and organizational uniformity and eventually led to losing both church and mission. See C. Van Engen: "Conciliar Mission Theology: 1930's-1990's," 1996, 145-156. Also, see Appendix B.

4. "Calling the Whole Church to take the Whole Gospel to the Whole World" was one of the two themes (together with "Proclaim Christ Until He Comes") of the Lausanne Movement's meeting in July, 1989, in Manila, Philippines. Three outstanding examples of statements that have encouraged and shaped Evangelical approaches to cooperation and partnership are the 1974 Lausanne Covenant, the 1989 Manila Manifesto, and the 1996 NAE Evangelical Manifesto. See Appendix A.

5. C. Van Engen: 1991, 49. See also Karl Barth *Church Dogmatics* 4.1.

6. Or in the language of 2 Cor. 5:14, Christ's love compels us to become ambassadors of reconciliation. As persons who have been transformed in and through the mission of Jesus Christ (2 Cor. 5:11-21), we are "God's coworkers" (2 Cor. 6:1).

7. Carl Braaten 1985, 123-124.

8. Wilbert Shenk 1993, "Contents," Chapter 1. Beginning at the Willingen (1952) conference of the IMC, affirmed at the Mexico City conference of the newly-formed Commission on World Mission and Evangelism, and popularized by Georg

Vicedom's 1965 book, *The Mission of God,* the concept of *missio Dei* has represented a mixed blessing. On the one hand, it has helped missiology to stress the fact that "mission is not primarily an activity of the church, but an attribute of God. God is a missionary God" (Bosch 1991, 390). However, as Hoedemaker points out, "In the course of the years the flag *missio Dei* has been flown on ships carrying a broad range of cargoes..." (Hoedemaker 1995, 164). So James Scherer says, "In the decade of the 1960s *missio Dei* was to become the plaything of armchair theologians with little more than an academic interest in the practical mission of the church but with a considerable penchant for theological speculation and mischief making" (1993, 85). Given these cautions, however, Bosch still felt the concept could be helpful. "On the other hand, it cannot be denied that the *missio Dei* notion has helped to articulate the conviction that neither the church nor any other human agent can ever be considered the author or bearer of mission. Mission is, primarily and ultimately, the work of the Triune God, Creator, Redeemer and Sanctifier, for the sake of the world. Mission has its origin in the heart of God. God is the fountain of sending love. This is the deepest source of mission. It is impossible to penetrate deeper still; there is mission because God loves people" (1991, 392). See Georg Vicedom 1965; D. Bosch 1980, 239-244; Arthur Glasser 1983, 90-99; D. Bosch 1991, 370; 389-393; James Scherer 1993, 82-88; L.A. Hoedemaker 1995, 162-166.

9. See also Carl Braaten 1990.

10. Max Warren 1978, 199.

11. See C. Van Engen, "Conciliar Mission Theology, 1930's-1990s," in Van Engen: 1996, 145-156. The "integration" of the IMC into the WCC provides a fascinating case study of structural unification—one that is very complex, and has a number of possible interpretations. See, e.g., Paul Pierson, "The Ecumenical Movement," Forthcoming; C. Henry, 1967, 86; Max Warren, 1974, 156-158; 1978; David Bosch, 1978, 55; 1980, 187-188; O. Costas, 1982, 36; D. Bosch: 1991, 457-461; C. Van Engen, 1996, 132-133.

12. See Stephen Neill. *Creative Tension.* London: Edinburgh House, 1959, 81. Quoted in Johannes Blauw. *The Missionary Nature of the Church.* Grand Rapids: Eerdmans, 1962, 109.

13. See WCC: 1968, 16ff, 69ff; C. Van Engen: 1981, 300-323. See Darrell Guder, ed.: 1998, chapters 1, 8, 9. It is interesting to compare this with the earlier emphases in Hunsberger and Van Gelder, eds., 1996.

14. See Darrell Guder, ed., 1998, chapters 1, 8, 9. It is interesting to compare this with the earlier emphases in Hunsberger and Van Gelder, eds., 1996.

15. W. Harold Fuller: 1980, 74-75.

16. Personal conversation with the author. See Eddie Gibbs: 1994, 101-109.

17. Lamin Sanneh: 1989.

18. Charles Van Engen, 1996, 169-187.

19. Charles Van Engen, 1991.

20. The Presbyterian Church (South), the Presbyterian Church (North), the Congregational Church, the Methodist Episcopal Church (South), the Methodist Episcopal Church (North), the Disciples of Christ, the Friends Church, and the Associated and Reformed Presbyterian Church.

21. See Saúl Tijerina Gonzalez, ed. 1872-1972, Centenario: Iglesia Nacional

Presbiteriana de México. Monterrey: Comité Pro-Centenario, 1973,154-158.
22. W. Richey Hogg, 1952, 45.
23. Van Engen: 1981, 380. The quotation from Kenneth Grubb is taken from Roland Allen: 1962, vii-viii.
24. G. Kittell, ed., 1964-1976, 158-159.
25. John Mackay, 1963, 8.
26. H. Küng, 1967, 302-302.
27. See D. Bosch, 1980, 181, 193. See also C.F. Henry and W.W. Mooneyham, eds., 1967. See also F.J. Verstraelen et al, eds., 1995, 6, 157; D. Bosch, 1991, 457-467.
28. See C. Van Engen, 1991, 90-92.
29. See Orlando Costas, 1988, 162-172.
30. For informative background on the debate concerning "moratorium," see, e.g., James Scherer 1964; Federico Pagura 1973; Emilio Castro 1973; Gerald Anderson 1974; Burgess Carr 1975; David Bosch 1978, in Daniel Rickett and Dotsey Welliver, eds., 1997, 53-64; J. Verkuyl, 1978, 334-340; Robert T. Coote, 1993, 377.
31. Verkuyl, 1978, 334.
32. Verkuyl, 1978, 337. Burgess Carr wrote, "Let it be clearly understood that selfhood and self-reliance are linked in a relationship of identity to mission. In a word, the real measure of our capacity to contribute significantly to the humanization of the world is directly dependent upon a rediscovery and perhaps even a redefining of our identity as African Christians" (quoted from Anderson & Stransky, 1976, 163).
33. See David Bosch, 1978, 56-60.
34. D. Bosch, 1978, quoted in Daniel Rickett and Dotsey Welliver, 1997, 60.
35. Lausanne Covenant, article 8; see also Orlando Costas, 1982, 65.
36. See J. Verkuyl, 1978, 339.
37. Stanley H. Skreslet, 1995.
38. Bill Taylor, 1999, 749-752.
39. Phillip Butler, 1999, 753-758; See also Wilbert Shenk, 1988; Frances Hiebert, 1997; Chuck Bennett, 1998; Daniel Rickett, 1998; John Robb, "Mission Leaders Propose New Framework," 1999; Paul Hiebert, 1991; Stan Nussbaum, 1999.
40. Manila Manifesto, affirmations 13, 14 and 17.
41. In "A Broadening Vision: Forty Years of Evangelical Theology of Mission," I examined Evangelical theology of mission from the 1940s to the 1980s and offered the thesis that "as North American evangelicals experienced (1) new sociocultural strength and confidence, (2) changes in the ecumenical theology of mission, and (3) developments in evangelical partner churches in the Third World, they responded with a broadening vision of an evangelical theology of mission which became less reactionary and more wholistic without compromising the initial evangelical élan of the World Missionary Conference at Edinburgh in 1910." (Joel A. Carpenter and Wilbert R Shenk, eds., 1990, 204-205; reprinted in C. Van Engen: 1996a, 128.)
42. S. Grentz, 1994, 2-4. H. Berkhof affirms a classical definition of theology as, "Theology teaches God, is taught by God, and leads to God." (H. Berkhof, 1979, 30.)
43. Donald G. Bloesch, 1992, 19-20.
44. H. Berkhof, 1979, 29-30.

45. Lesslie Newbigin, 1991, 36.
46. See, e.g., Lesslie Newbigin, 1986 and 1989.
47. Taken from Paul Hiebert, 1994, 123-131.
48. Taken from C. Van Engen, 1996, 95, footnote 38. See also P. Hiebert, 1978, 1983, 1989.
49. Giving money only if we can control its use; or not giving money because we feel it would not be good for them; or giving money in such a way that it makes the recipient totally dependent on us.
50. Deciding what the recipients really need and fomenting change accordingly; or hearing the recipients say they need something but deciding they really do not need it.
51. The sending agency designs a program on its own and then asks the recipients to take it or leave it; or manipulates the recipients in such a way that they have no choice but to receive their services; or they do nothing until they have been asked by recipients—and then only when the request is well-planned, in advance, and done right according to their own criteria.
52. We bring in services and people, create programs, or budget money and locate all the services in a setting without any consultation with the recipients.
53. This is an insidious double-think that wishes to assert the autonomy of the recipients but from a disconnected point of view. The sending agency decides independently of the recipients the arenas they will talk about, the arenas they will not deal with, and what areas are the problem of the recipient, not of the sending agency—with little or no consultation with the recipients. The flip side of this is the co-opting syndrome that invites the recipients to join with the donors in joint committees, but the most basic and influential decisions have already been made before the recipients join the process.
54. We decide not to do something because the recipients could never carry it on or keep it up without the sending agency's help; or the sending agency thinking that its time and money is so valuable there are many day-to-day tasks which the recipients should do, and the really important ones are to be carried out only by the sending agency.
55. The sending agency's personnel live so far above the standard of living of the people they serve that they never experience life as the recipients live it; or "going native" in such an overly self-conscious way that the sending agency's personnel live in such poor conditions they spend all their time trying to survive.
56. The sending agency offer services to the recipients in an impersonal, removed fashion, avoiding "getting personal" or developing close relationships with the recipients.
57. The sending agency is interested in a quick-fix to a problem that the receptors apparently have—and has little time to listen, learn from, and partner with the recipients who may not consider the situation a problem at all—or may know better than the sender the depth, pervasiveness and difficulty the problem presents such that it is not possible to "fix it" in a short-term manner.
58. The sending agency or church is most deeply concerned in creating clones of itself in new locations; the only really authentic and acceptable mission and church structures become those that are exact replicas of the sending group's struc-

tures, "like we do it back home." The flip side of this is to think that all cultures are so unique and different that nothing in the former culture is applicable or helpful in the new setting.

59. Dean Gilliland, 1989, 52.

60. See C. Van Engen, 1981, 438-441; and Karl Barth, IV:2, 1958, 614-641.

61. In mission we are beginning to ask theological questions again— something we have not done since the mid-1960s. The 70s and 80s were primarily concerned with "how to's" of mission. The issues mentioned here are only representative, and the order is not meant to be a priority—the priority will vary according to context, with time.

—Motivation for mission: Bible and mission
—Christianity and other religions
—Theology of mission of/in the city
—The church's role in nation-building
—Theology of compassion
—World church: Many cultures—One Gospel
—Evangelism of unreached peoples
—Re-evangelization of post-Christian West and nominal Christians everywhere
—The local church as an agent of mission
—Theological issues related to the world of the unseen

62. C. Van Engen, 1989, 95; reprinted in C. Van Engen, 1996, 88-89.

63. By *spiritual growth* is meant the depth and breadth of the covenantal relationship of the People of God in intimate spiritual closeness with God, through faith in Jesus Christ by the Holy Spirit; i.e., the depth of spiritual maturity of leaders and members, their degree of immersion in Scripture, their living out of a life-style and ethics of the Kingdom of God, their involvement in prayer, their dependence of God, their search for holiness, and their vibrancy in worship (Van Engen).

"By *numerical expansion* is understood the recruitment of persons for the kingdom of God by calling them to repentance and faith in Jesus Christ as Lord and Savior of their lives and their incorporation into a local community of persons who, having made a similar decision, worship, obey, and give witness, collectively and personally, to the world of God's redemptive action in Jesus Christ and his liberating power.

"By *organic expansion* is meant the internal development of a local community of faith, i.e., the system of relationships among its members—its form of government, financial structure, leadership, types of activities in which its time and resources are invested, etc.

"By *conceptual expansion* is meant the degree of consciousness that a community of faith has with regard to its nature and mission to the world, i.e., the image that the community has formed of itself, the depth of its reflection on the meaning of its faith in Christ (understanding of Scripture, etc.), and its image of the world.

"By *incarnational growth* is meant the degree of involvement of a community of faith in the life and problems of its social environment; i.e., its participation in the affliction of its world; its prophetic, intercessory, and liberating action on behalf of the weak and destitute; the intensity of its preaching to the poor, the brokenhearted, the captives, the blind, and the oppressed. (Lk. 4:18-21)."

With the exception of the first paragraph, this material is from Orlando Costas, *The Church and its Mission: A Shattering Critique from the Third World*. (Chicago: Tyndale, 1974) 90-91. This was later published in Spanish in Orlando Costas. *El Protestantismo en America Latina Hoy: Ensayos del Camino* (1972-1974) (San Jose, Costa Rica: Indef, 1975) 68-70. See also Orlando Costas, *The Integrity of Mission: The Inner Life and Outreach of the Church* (N.Y.: Harper & Row, 1979) 37-60.

64. National Association of Evangelicals "An Evangelical Manifesto: A Strategic Plan for the Dawn of the 21st Century," NAE Web Site www.nae.net/sig_doc11.html, 1996.

Bibliography

AD 2000 and Beyond. "The PAD (Presidents and Academic Deans) Declaration," EMQ XXXV:3 (July) 321, 1999.

Allen, Roland. *The Spontaneous Expansion of the Church*. G.R.: Eerdmans, 1962.

Anderson, Gerald H. "A Moratorium on Missionaries?" *Christian Century* (January 16); reprinted in Gerald H. Anderson and Thomas F. Stransky, eds.: 1974, 133-141.

_____. "American Protestants in Pursuit of Mission: 1886-1986" *IBMR* XII:3 (July), 1988, 98-118; reprinted in F.J. Verstaelen, et al 1995, 374-420.

-Anderson, Gerald H. and Thomas F. Stransky, eds. *Mission Trends* No. 1. Grand Rapids: Eerdmans, 1974.

_____. *Mission Trends* No. 3. Grand Rapids: Eerdmans, 1976.

Barth, Karl. *Church Dogmatics*. Edinburgh: T & T Clark, 1958.

Barrett, David B. "Silver and Gold Have I None: Church of the Poor or Church of the Rich?" *IBMR* VII: 4 (Oct.), 146-1511, 1983.

Bennett, Chuck. "Is There a Spin Doctor in the House?" *EMQ* XXXIV:4 (Oct.), 420-425, 1998.

Bennett, John C. "Working Together to Shape the New Millennium: Dreams, Hopes, Concerns, Fears" (COSIM) *EMQ* XXXV:3 (July), 314-317, 1999.

Berkhof, Hendrikus. *Christian Faith: An Introduction to the Study of the Faith*. Trans. By Sierd Woudstra. Grand Rapids: Eerdmans, 1979.

_____. *Introduction to the Study of Dogmatics*. Grand Rapids: Eerdmans, 1985.

Blauw, Johannes Blauw. *The Missionary Nature of the Church*. Grand Rapids: Eerdmans, 1962.

Bloesch, Donald G. *A Theology of Word & Spirit: Authority & Method in Theology*. Downers Grove: IVP, 1992.

Bosch, David J. "Toward True Mutuality: Exchanging the Same Commodities or Supplementing Each Others' Needs?" *Missiology* VI:3 (July), 1978; reprinted in Daniel Rickett and Dotsey Welliver, eds., *Supporting Indigenous Ministries: With Selected Readings*. Wheaton: Billy Graham Center, 53-64.

Bosch, David J. *Witness to the World: Christian Mission in Theological Perspective*. London: Marshall, Morgan & Scott, 1980.

Bosch, David J. *Transforming Mission: Paradigm Shifts in Theology of Mission*. Maryknoll: Orbis, 1991.

_____. *Believing in the Future: Toward a Missiology of Western Culture*. Valley Forge, Penn.: Trinity Press, 1995.

Braaten, Carl. *The Nature and Aim of the Church's Mission and Ministry.* Minn.: Augsburg, 1985.

_____. "The Triune God; The Source and Model of Christian Unity and Mission," *Missiology* XVIII:4 (Oct.), 415-28, 1990.

Butler, Phillip. "The Power of Partnership," in Ralph Winter and Steven Hawthorne, eds. *Perspectives on the World Christian Movement: A Reader* (third edition), 753-758, 1999.

Carr, Burgess. "The Relation of Union to Mission," *Mid-Stream: An Ecumenical Journal.* XIV:4 (Oct.), 1975; reprinted in Gerald H. Anderson and Thomas Stransky, eds: 1976, 158-168.

Campbell, Evvy. "Working Together to Shape the New Millennium: Dreams, Hopes, Concerns, Fears" (AERDO) *EMQ* XXXV:3 (July), 311-314, 1999.

Carpenter, Joel A. and Wilbert R. Shenk, eds. *Earthen Vessels: American Evangelicals and Foreign Mission, 1880-1980.* Grand Rapids: Eerdmans, 1990.

Castro, Emilio. "Editorial" *International Review of Mission* LXII: 248 (Oct. 1973), 393-398. (This entire issue of the IRM was devoted to discussion of matters related to the "moratorium" debate.)

Coote, Robert T. "Gerald H. Anderson: A Career Dedicated to Mission," in James M. Phillips and Robert T. Coote, eds.: 1993, 375-379.

Costas, Orlando E. *Christ Outside the Gate: Mission Beyond Christendom.* Maryknoll: Orbis, 1982.

Dawson, David. "A Recurring Issue in Mission Administration" *Missiology* XXV:4 (Oct.), 1997, 457-465.

Dayton, Edward R. and David A. Fraser. *Planning Strategies for World Evangelization* (Revised Edition) Monrovia: MARC; Grand Rapids: Eerdmans, 1990.

Fuller, W. Harold. *Mission-Church Dynamics: How to Change Bicultural Tensions in Dynamic Missionary Outreach.* Pasadena: WCL, 1980.

Gibbs, Eddie. *In Name Only: Tackling the Problem of Nominal Christianity.* Wheaton: Victor Books, 1994. *Transforming Transitions.* Pasadena: self-published; (Downers Grove: IVP, forthcoming), 1999.

Gilliland, Dean S., ed. *The Word Among Us: Contextualizing Theology for Mission Today.* Dallas: Word, 1989.

Glasser, Arthur F. and Donald A. McGavran. *Contemporary Theologies of Mission.* Grand Rapids: Baker, 1983.

Gort, Jerald D., ed., *Zending Op Weg Naar de Toekomst.* Kampen: Kok, 1978.

Grenz, Stanley J. *Revisioning Evangelical Theology: A Fresh Agenda for the 21st Century.* Downers Grove: IVP, 1991.

_____. *Theology for the Community of God.* Nashville: Broadman & Holman, 1994.

Guder, Darrell, ed. *Missional Church: A Vision for the Sending of the Church in North America.* Grand Rapids: Eerdmans, 1998.

Henry, Carl. *Evangelicals at the Brink of Crisis.* Waco: Word, 1967.

Henry, Carl and W.S. Mooneyham, eds. *One Race, One Gospel, One Task.* Minn.: World Wide Publications, 1967.

Hesselgrave, David J. "Redefining Holism," *EMQ* (XXXV:3 (July), 1999, 278-284.

Hiebert, Frances F. "Beyond the Post-Modern Critique of Modern Mission: The

Nineteenth Century Revisited," *Missiology* XXV:3 (July), 1997, 259-277.
Hiebert, Paul G. "Conversion, Culture and Cognitive Categories," *Gospel in Context* I:4 (Oct), 1978, 24-29.
_____. "The Flaw of the Excluded Middle," *Missiology* X:1 (Jan.), 1980, 35-47.
_____. "Missions and the Renewal of the Church," in Wilbert Shenk, ed. *Exploring Church Growth*, 1983, 157-67.
_____. "Form and Meaning in the Contextualization of the Gospel," in Dean Gilliland, ed. *The World Among Us*, 1989, 101-120.
_____. "Beyond Anti-Colonialism to Globalism, *Missiology* XIX:3 (July) 1990, 263-282.
_____. *Anthropological Reflections on Missiological Issues*. Grand Rapids: Baker, 1994.
Hoedemaker, L.A. "The People of God and the Ends of the Earth," in F.J. Verstraelen, A. Camps, L.A. Hoedemaker and M.R. Spindler, eds., 1995, 157-171.
Hoekendijk, Johannes C. *The Church Inside Out*. Philadelphia: Westminster, 1996.
Hogg, William Richey. *Ecumenical Foundations: A History of the International Missionary Council and its Nineteenth-Century Background*. N.Y: Harper & Bros, 1952.
Howell, Richard. "An Overview and Plea: Christian Persecution in India," AD2000 and Beyond Movement: e-mail from Luis Bush, 7/19/99.
Hunsberger, George R. and Craid Van Gelder, eds. *Church between Gospel & Culture: The Emerging Mission in North America*. Grand Rapids: Eerdmans, 1996.
Kirk, J. Andrew. *The Mission of Theology and Theology as Mission*. Valley Forge, Penn.: Trinity Press, 1997.
Kittel, Gerhard and Gerhard Friedrich, eds. *Theological Dictionary of the New Testament*, 10 vols. Grand Rapids: Eerdmans, 1964-1976.
Küng, Hans. *The Church*. R. Ockenden, trans. N.Y.: Sheed & Ward, 1967.
Lausanne Committee for World Evangelization. "The Lausanne Covenant," 1974.
_____. "Hindrances to Cooperation: The Suspicion about Finances," Pasadena: LCWE (*Lausanne Occasional Papers* 24); reprinted in Daniel Rickett and Dotsey Welliver, eds. *Supporting Indigenous Ministries: With Selected Readings*. Wheaton: Billy Graham Center, 1983, 84-107.
_____. *The Manila Manifesto: An Elaboration of the Lausanne Covenant Fifteen Years Later*. Pasadena: LCWE, 1989.
Mackay, John. *The Latin American Church and the Ecumenical Movement*. N.Y: NCCC, 1963.
McKaughan, Paul, Dellanna O'Brien, and William O'Brien. *Choosing a Future for U.S. Mission*. Monrovia, Calif.: MARC/World Vision, 1998.
_____. "Working Together to Shape the New Millennium: Dreams, Hopes, Concerns, Fears." *EMQ* XXXV:3 (July), 306-308.
Miley, George
_____. "The Awesome Potential of Mission Found in Local Churches," in Ralph Winter and Steven Hawthorne, eds. *Perspectives on the World Christian Movement: A Reader* (third edition), 1999, 729-732.
Mulholland, Kenneth B. "Working Together to Shape the New Millennium: Dreams,

Hopes, Concerns, Fears" (EMS) *EMQ* XXXV:3 (July), 1999, 317-320.

Myers, Bryant. *The Changing Shape of World Mission.* Monrovia, Calif.: MARC/World Vision, 1993. (Updated 1998).

———. "Another Look at Holistic Mission," *EMQ* XXXV:3 (July), 285-287.

National Association of Evangelicals. "An Evangelical Manifesto: A Strategic Plan for the Dawn of the 21st Century," NAE Web Site (www.nae.net/sig_doc11.html), 1996.

Neill, Stephen. *Creative Tension.* London: Edinburgh House, 1959.

———. *A History of Christian Missions.* Middlesex, England: Penguin, 1964.

Newbigin, Lesslie. *Foolishness to the Greeks: the Gospel and Western Culture.* Grand Rapids: Eerdmans, 1986.

———. *The Gospel in a Pluralist Society.* Grand Rapids: Eerdmans, 1989.

———. *Truth to Tell: The Gospel as Public Truth.* Grand Rapids: Eerdmans, 1991.

Nicholls, Bruce J., ed. *In Word and Deed: Evangelism and Social Responsibility.* Grand Rapids: Eerdmans, 1985.

Nussbaum, Stan. "The Five Frontiers of Mission," *Global Mapping International Newsletter* (Winter/Spring), 1999, 1,5.

Orme, John. "Working Together to Shape the New Millennium: Dreams, Hopes, Concerns, Fears" *EMQ* XXXV:3 (July), 1998, 308-310.

Padilla, C. Rene. *Mission Between the Times: Essays on the Kingdom.* Grand Rapids: Eerdmans, 1985.

Pagura, Federico. "Missionary, Go Home...Or Stay," *Christian Century* (April 11, 1973); reprinted in Gerald H. Anderson and Thomas F. Stransky, eds.: 1974, 115-116.

Peters, George. "Pauline Patterns of Church-Mission Relationships," *EMQ* IX (Winter), reprinted in Daniel Rickett and Dotsey Welliver, eds., *Supporting Indigenous Ministries: With Selected Readings.* Wheaton: Billy Graham Center, 1973, 46-52.

Phillips, James M. and Robert T. Coote, eds. *Toward the 21st Century in Christian Mission.* Grand Rapids: Eerdmans, 1993.

Pierson, Paul E. Forthcoming "The Ecumenical Movement," (pre-publication draft) in Scott Moreau, Charles Van Engen and Harold Netland, eds. *Evangelical Dictionary of World Missions.* Grand Rapids: Baker.

Piper, John. *Let the Nations be Glad! The Supremacy of God in Missions.* Grand Rapids: Baker, 1993.

Rickett, Daniel and Dotsey Welliver, eds. *Supporting Indigenous Ministries: With Selected Readings.* Wheaton: Billy Graham Center, 1997.

Rickett, Daniel. "Developmental Partnering: Preventing Dependency," *EMQ* XXXIV:4 (Oct), 1998, 438-445.

Robb, John. "Mission Leaders Propose New Framework" *MARC Newsletter* 99-2 (May), 1999, 1, 6.

Roxburgh, Alan J. *The Missionary Congregation, Leadership & Liminality.* Harrisburg, PA.: Trinity Press, International, 1997.

Samuel, Vinay and Chris Sugden, eds. *A.D. 2000 and Beyond: A Mission Agenda.* Oxford: Regnum Books, 1991.

Sanneh, Lamin. *Translating the Message: The Missionary Impact on Culture.*

Maryknoll: Orbis, 1989.
Scherer, James A. *Mission, Go Home! A Reappraisal of the Christian World Mission Today—its Basis, Philosophy, Program, Problems, and Outlook for the Future.* Englewood Cliffs, N.J.: Prentice-Hall, 1964.
_____. "Church, Kingdom and Missio Dei: Lutheran and Orthodox Correctives to Recent Ecumenical Mission Theology," in C. Van Engen, Dean S. Gilliland and Paul Pierson, eds., 1993, 82-88.
Shenk, Wilbert R., ed. *Exploring Church Growth.* Grand Rapids: Eerdmans, 1980.
_____. "God's New Economy: Interdependence and Mission." (A MISSION FOCUS pamphlet), Elkhart, IN: Overseas Ministries, Mennonite Board of Missions, 1981.
_____. *The Transfiguration of Mission: Biblical, Theological & Historical Foundations.* Scottdale, PA: Herald, 1993.
_____. *Write the Vision: The Church Renewed.* Valley Forge, PA: Trinity Press, International, 1995.
_____. *Changing Frontiers of Mission.* Maryknoll: Orbis, 1996.
Silvoso, Ed. *That None Should Perish: How to Reach Entire Cities for Christ Through Prayer Evangelism.* Ventura: Regal, 1994.
Skreslet, Stanley H. "The Empty Basket of Presbyterian Mission: Limits and Possibilities of Partnership," *IBMR.* XIX:3 (July), 1995, 98-106.
Steuernagel, Valdir R. "An Evangelical Assessment of Mission: A Two-Thirds World Perspective," in Vinay Samuel and Chris Sugden, eds. *A.D. 2000 and Beyond: A Mission Agenda.* Oxford: Regnum Books, 1991, 1-13.
Stearns, Bill and Amy. "The Power of Integrated Vision," in Ralph Winter and Steven Hawthorne, eds. *Perspectives on the World Christian Movement: A Reader* (third edition), 1999, 724-728.
Taber, Charles R. "Structures and Strategies for Interdependence in World Mission," in Wilbert Shenk, ed. *Mission Focus: Current Issues.* Elkhart, IN: Overseas Ministries, Mennonite Board of Missions; reprinted in Daniel Rickett and Dotsey Welliver, eds. *Supporting Indigenous Ministries: With Selected Readings.* Wheaton: Billy Graham Center, 1980, 65-83.
Taylor, Bill. "Lessons of Partnership" in Ralph Winter and Steven Hawthorne, eds. *Perspectives on the World Christian Movement: A Reader* (third edition), 1999, 748-752.
Van Engen, Charles. *The Growth of the True Church*; reprinted in 1995 by University Microfilms, Inc, Ann Arbor, MI, 1981.
_____."A Broadening Vision: Forty Years of Evangelical Theology of Mission, 1946-1986," in Joel A. Carpenter and Wilbert Shenk, eds., 1990, 203-232; reprinted in C. Van Engen: 1996a, 1990, 127-144.
God's Missionary People: Rethinking the Purpose of the Local Church. Grand Rapids: Baker, 1989.
_____. *Mission on the Way: Issues in Mission Theology.* Grand Rapids: Baker, 1996a.
_____. "The Gospel Story: Mission of, in, and on the Way" (Installation address in the Arthur F. Glasser Chair of Biblical Theology of Mission), Pasadena: FTS; adapted and reprinted in *Theology, News and Notes* June, 1998, 3-6,22-23; to be reprinted in C. Van Engen, Nancy Thomas and Robert Gallagher, eds. *Foot-*

prints of God: Reflections on the Church in Mission in the 21st Century. Monrovia: MARC, forthcoming, 1999b.

Van Engen, Charles, Dean S. Gilliand and Paul Pierson, eds. *The Good News of the Kingdom: Mission Theology for the Third Millennium.* Maryknoll: Orbis, 1993.

Verkuyl, Johannes. *Contemporary Missiology: An Introduction.* Grand Rapids: Eerdmans, 1978.

Verstraelen, F.J., A. Camps, L.A. Hoedemaker and M.R. Spindler, eds. *Missiology: An Ecumenical Introduction—Texts and Contexts of Global Christianity.* Grand Rapids: Eerdmans, 1995.

Vicedom, Georg. *The Mission of God: An Introduction to a Theology of Mission.* St. Louis: Concordia, 1965.

W.A. Visser 't Hooft, ed. *The New Delhi Report.* Geneva: WCC, 1961.

Warren, Max *Crowded Canvas.* London: Hodder & Stoughton, 1974.

_____. "The Fusion of the I.M.C. and the W.C.C. at New Delhi: Retrospective Thoughts After a Decade and a Half," in J.D. Gort, ed., *Zending Op Weg Naar de Toekomst*, 1978, 190-202.

Winter, Ralph and Steven C. Hawthorne, eds. *Perspectives on the World Christian Movement: A Reader* (Third Edition). Pasadena: WCL, 1999.

World Council of Churches. *Evanston to New Delhi: 1954-1961.* Geneva: WCC, 1961.

_____. *The Church for Others and the Church for the World.* Geneva: WCC, 1968.

World Missionary Conference, (9 vols.) N.Y.: Revell, 1910.

Response to Van Engen Regarding Opportunities and Limitations

John H. Orme

I greatly appreciate the work of our good brother and use his text, *Mission on the Way*, regularly, in my Theology of Missions courses at Moody Graduate School. It is stimulating and energizing to be together because as Chuck says, "We all have our own special geographic, continental, confessional, cultural, national, linguistic, historic, and relational biases that affect the way we cooperate with others." This has been true since the time of Paul and Barnabas when they could not agree about John Mark.

At the same time, we also know that undue concern with total agreement can cause us to diffuse and redirect energies from the tasks of ministry. Today, finding agreement can be especially challenging with partners from Africa, Latin America and Asia working alongside Europeans and North Americans in the same organization. Chuck has helped us in the way he has addressed the nuances of these important issues.

Chuck uses four words, *Together, Working, Diversity*, and *Theological* to organize his thoughts. I will follow that same pattern to facilitate our interchange.

Together

I was glad to see the organic emphasis on the union of believers in the Triune God. The Body emphasis of Ephesians is helpful. The unity of believers is spiritual. Our unity is in Christ (John 17). We as believers are already one in our common union in Christ and, furthermore, we are one in our common mission in the world.

As a point of clarification, it would be helpful to define what is meant by "we" in our discussions of unity in mission. Care must be taken to distinguish between individual believers who are each a member of the body of Christ and their respective organizations and joint efforts in mission. Too often this teaching is put into organizational terms before the Scripture is relentlessly applied to individuals—individuals within the church, individuals within the mission, and individuals within a team. The oneness that we enjoy in Christ is positional; the partnership that we desire is a practical outworking of our individual positional oneness in Christ.

Also, "partnership" must be defined. Are we talking about individuals, mission teams, or whole organizations in joint projects? Then again, are we not "partnering" when we enjoy and recognize our oneness in the Spirit, work harmoniously in common fields, yet without any "partnering agreement"?

Furthermore, I would have enjoyed a broader perspective as could have come from the larger New Testament witness. The terms Temple, Priesthood, Flock, Bride, New Creation also speak of corporate relationships.[1] I will comment later on the need for a more complete biblical witness, but the need shows up here.

The church is One, Holy, Catholic, and Apostolic. The debate over the usage of these words is long and goes back at least to the Reformers. Are these designations verbal or substantive, or both?[2] The essence at the least, however, is that we are one and we are to be sent to the world and we are missional in nature.[3] This means, as Van Engen citing Harold Fuller says, that organizational union is never to be put ahead of witness and that the central force of mission is for personal witness of Jesus Christ as Savior and Lord. Structure is never to replace nor diminish our energies from the priorities of message and ministry.

Working

In his paper, Chuck makes "three brief observations." These are important points. First, I, too, want to emphasize that our working together must be as a result of the fruit of the Spirit. Our model is the Servant, the *ebed Yahweh*. Our model is not the entrepreneurial marketplace, where the motivation is self and pride. Secondly, it is not only local, but global. To be sure, individuals must be in the Body in order to be his disciples.[4] But with that critical qualification made, is it not thrilling to realize that our small group here is part of something much bigger? There are over 160 million who are part of the World Evangelical Fellowship alone. Then thirdly, in our organizational work, we must dedicate the time and energy to simply be together, break bread together, pray together, and sense by the Spirit our oneness as we plan and exchange ideas on the best ways to present our Lord to a disintegrating culture.

With these brief observations of my own now made, I want to turn our attention to the need for a larger New Testament witness. Chuck states, "Similarly, at least in the context of Ephesians 4, separation, keeping our doctrine pure, does not seem to be as foundational or essential a virtue as is living 'a life of love'" (4:2).

It is at this point that I suggest that a larger witness is demanded that goes beyond the Ephesian letter. Acts 20:28-31 warns the elders at Ephesus about savage wolves from among the flock who will attempt to draw away disciples by distorting the truth. The Colossian parallels refer to heresies. This is not to speak of the larger biblical witness of Israel's struggle to maintain ethical-exclusive monotheism among the pagans. Added to this would be 2 Thess. 2:15, the Pastorals, Jude 3, 4, 17; 1 John 2:19; 2 John; 3 John. In the same Ephesian region, the churches of Thyatira and Pergamus had doctrinal problems in the first century. Most severe of all are the words of our Lord in Matthew 7:21-23. Words and works without a living relationship to Christ the Head are not validated. This I believe is implied in Ephesians 1-3 and is presuppositional in Chuck's words (he as much says so in *Mission on the Way*.)[5] However, they need to be always stated clearly each time we speak of these things in our postmodern world. I would take this opportunity to draw your attention to the current editorial and focus on "The Gospel of Jesus Christ: An Evangelical Celebration," in *Christianity Today*.[6]

Having stated some issues of theological importance, it is now time to address clearly some matters of practical missiology. Just how do we work together? Since this is the EFMA/IFMA/EMS Triennial Meeting 1999, I would like to review for our encouragement some clear evidences that we do indeed work together now—and that we have worked together in the past. The following few details I have gleaned from the work of Dr. Jack Frizen entitled *75 Years of IFMA: 1917-1992*.[7]

Since the founding of the EFMA in 1945, Clyde Taylor, as EFMA's first president (1945-1975) was a catalyst in forging relationships with other evangelical organizations. Throughout the 50s and into the 60s, there were many cooperative efforts, meetings, and conferences between the EFMA and the IFMA. In 1960, at the IFMA Annual Meeting, a resolution was passed that "There should be an earnest seeking to work together with those of like precious faith." This led to the first Joint Study Conference, which we now call the Triennial, in 1963 in Winona Lake, Indiana.

Known by few today is that in 1962, the EFMA and IFMA formed the Africa Evangelical Office in Nairobi, Kenya with Ken Downing of AIM as its director. This later became the AEAM (the Association of Evangelicals in Africa and Madagascar) which was supported with substantial financial subsidy until 1991. Mr. Eric Maillefer on loan from the Evangelical Free Church served the AEAM for eighteen years. The same group was the initial force in starting BEST (The Bangui Evangelical School of Theology). There were at least four African congresses held largely through the support of the EFMA and IFMA. At the Urbana Missions Conference in 1984, Dr. Tokumbo Adeyemo expressed his appreciation for all of this and more.

During those years, the IFMA Business Administration Committee published the 1958 Mission Administration Manual. In 1962, a supplement on certain tax issues was published. This became what is known today as the Accounting and Financial Reporting Guide for Christian Ministries published by EJAC, the Evangelical Joint Accounting Committee, (1982), formed by the EFMA, the IFMA, ECFA, CMA, and CCCC. You see, even in money matters, we can and do work together!

At the 1963 Joint Study Conference (EFMA/IFMA) mentioned earlier here, some significant agreements were made that give strong evidence that we indeed do partner together. At least seven agreements out of those meetings merit our attention here.

1. All agencies should share mobilization pamphlets under their own logos at the original cost to the originating agency.

2. As mentioned above, this is when AEAM was envisioned.

3. Steps were taken to launch the EMIS (Evangelical Missions Information Service).

4. The committee that became CAMEO (Committee for Assisting Missionary Education Overseas) was named. This continued until its mission was determined to be completed in 1991.

5. The initial steps were taken that resulted in the Congress on World Mission held in Wheaton in 1965.

6. It was resolved to continue the triennial meetings of the associations.

7. Other joint committee work was begun including the ECLA (Evangelical Committee on Latin America) which functioned from 1957 to 1990.

In 1964 a significant joint effort of the EFMA and the IFMA resulted in the formation of the Evangelical Missions Information Service (EMIS). Its chief publications, the *Evangelical Missions Quarterly* and *World Pulse*, have served us all very well. A joint EFMA/IFMA committee served until 1997 when it was agreed that to serve the missions community better, another publisher was needed to advance the ministry, at which time the Billy Graham Center of Wheaton College took over admirably. The present boards are still very representative of both the EFMA and the IFMA.

One of the most active and enduring joint efforts of the EFMA and the IFMA was formalized in 1971 as the Personnel & Student Affairs Committee. In 1977, the name was shortened to the IFMA/EFMA Personnel Committee. The dynamic of partnering, however, was the energy that goes back to 1964 when representatives from the EFMA, IVCF, Moody, and the IFMA met in Chicago and later that year at Urbana. The EFMA and IFMA continued the dialogue until the formal committee was begun. This December at the IFMA/EFMA Personnel Conference '99 in Colorado Springs, we expect more than 275 registrants. It is the privilege of the IFMA to serve the missions community by acting as facilitator for these annual conferences.

Without undue further detail, brief mention should be made of other efforts in our joint ministries. Through the years, both the EFMA and the IFMA have jointly sponsored conferences on issues relating to China and Islamics. There were other joint committees on Bible translations and Asia. For thirty years, the Summer Institute of Missions was held at Wheaton College. This institute was begun in 1957 as a joint effort and only ceased when it was absorbed into Wheaton's summer program. Mission evaluation was not ignored. Through the middle 70s, a joint task force on mission evaluation had meetings and in 1978 published a fifty-page booklet of guidelines. In 1971, papers from the Green Lake consultation were published under the title, *Missions in Creative Tension*.

Lastly, it should be mentioned that the efforts of the EFMA and the IFMA were strong in the formation of the ACMC. In 1974, the executive directors of both associations served as special consultants at the initial meeting regarding ACMC in Pasadena. Not to be forgotten are the efforts with other groups such as WEF (World Evangelical Fellowship), the NAE (National Association of Evangelicals), and the Association of Evangelical Professors of Missions, now the Evangelical Missiological Society (EMS).

There is no doubt that more could be said about the partnering of the EFMA and IFMA, and partnering in general. A review of the IFMA library shows shelves and shelves of reports, compendiums, conferences, and committee publications. My regret is that in our (my) activism of today, we write and record very little. As a result, many are simply not aware of the reality of our working together.

Now very briefly, a comment about the use of the word "ecumenical." Ideally it would be nice to restore the root meaning of the inhabited earth and Mackay's missional sense. Yes, ideally, as Bosch comments, the evangelical emphasis is different and focuses on the invisible and the spiritual.[8] The understanding in the average evangelical pew and pulpit based on current usage, however, is heavily laden with World Council of Churches implications and liberal understanding. After so many years of visible and organizational usage, it is doubtful that the original sense of the word can be restored.

Diversity

Just as no part of the body can do it all, neither can we. This is easier to see in technical missions such as those working in Bible translation, radio, and aviation, and in ethnic specialty agencies. But, every time I visit a more general church planting agency, I also hear, "We are unique." And that's the way it should be! There should be singular reasons for the existence of every mission agency. One of Verkuyl's last comments is, "No single person has all the answers, and this is good. . .".[9] With all of our missiological acumen, God desires that we all be active in the vineyard where God has placed us. Missiological stratagems must never substitute for action. The diversity of the local churches is the real wonder of the Body. No association or organization should be the center. In fact, the vast majority of congregations in Africa and Latin America are not formally affiliated with organizations beyond their own borders.[10]

Theological

I would like to comment on four matters. First, I will comment in regard to theological content as it relates to mission partnerships.

I would raise a strong caution about questioning propositional issues about the way we "do" theology. While it is true that there has been a "broadening" among evangelicals, I believe the broadening is more to do with relationships and partnerships in a changing world context than to theological method itself.

In regard to content, the issues are, of course, hermeneutical and this is not the place to enter that dialogue. Nonetheless, Osborne's treatment of hermeneutics as only a singular example should be examined particularly in reference to propositional truth, speech-act, and issues of meaning (reader and text). Personally, I don't believe Stanley Grenz has sufficiently finished his exploration in theological method to be used as a model.[11]

Secondly, there is no doubt about our appreciation for the insights of Lesslie Newbigin. At the same time, it appears to me that when Newbigin discusses truth and knowledge, he is overly dependent upon Michael Polanyi and Polanyi's attempt to undo "scientific method" and positivism. We must be careful not to fall off the other side of the horse into the swamp of subjectivism or community hermeneutics which can lead to despair in truth and theological structure.

Thirdly, we must be careful about the distinction between Hebrew "knowledge" and Western ways of knowing. Linguistically speaking, we dare not ignore the significant contributions of E. D. Hirsch, Jr. and James Barr.[12] Brevard Childs referred to biblical theology as being in crisis because of the rigid distinctions.[13]

Fourthly, I have benefited greatly from Hiebert's oft-published discussions of bounded and centered sets. It is to be remembered, however, that his original purpose was to assess the question, "What does it mean to be a Christian?"—not, "What does it mean to partner?" The issue is Christian conversion and religious change. Our "theologizing" can well be along the lines of bounded sets, but our partnering and relating can be centered sets.[14]

In conclusion, I, like Chuck, am excited that we are thinking theologically in missions. The WEF consultation in Brazil and the consultation on mission language and metaphors are good examples. I would add just one more to Chuck's list. We need to address what mission formation means and implies for the new millennium. Dare I mention the overused word "paradigm?" Dare I suggest that a new paradigm is needed in mission formation?

Each of our organizations must be permeated by grace, love, forgiveness and compassion through the Holy Spirit. This will only happen as we as individuals are permeated by grace, love, forgiveness and compassion through the Holy Spirit. Organizations aren't spiritual, people are spiritual. Only as we each open our hearts to God and then to each other, as we are doing here, can we have anything more than structure in our partnering. As personal relationships join, they form that important "inter-organizational relationship" that we all desire.

John Piper relates a wonderful story about William Carey and Henry Martyn. Carey was a Particular Baptist and a dissenter from the Church of England. He even advocated closed communion. Martyn, on the other hand, was an evangelical Anglican. Nevertheless, Carey wrote, "A young clergyman, Mr. Martyn, is lately arrived, who is possessed of a truly missionary spirit. . . We take sweet counsel together, and go to the house of God as friends."[15]

Let us go and do likewise.

Endnotes

1. Compare John Driver, *Images of the Church in Mission* (Scottdale, PA: Herald Press, 1997).

2. George W. Peters, *A Biblical Theology of Missions* (Chicago: Moody Press, 1972), 214-223 and Charles Van Engen, *God's Missionary People* (Grand Rapids: Baker Book House, 1991), 59-71.

3. George R. Hunsberger, "Mission Vocation: Called and Sent to Represent the Reign of God," in Darrell L. Guder, ed., *The Missional Church* (Grand Rapids: Eerdmans Publishing Company, 1998), 77-109 and David J. Bosch, *Transforming Mission* (Maryknoll, N.Y.: Orbis Books, 1991), 368-378.

4. Robertson McQuilkin, *Good News of the Kingdom*, p. 177.

5. He as much as says so in *Mission on the Way*. Charles Van Engen, *Mission on the Way* (Grand Rapids: Baker Book House, 1996), 35-43; 169-187.

6. *Christianity Today*, June 14, 1999.

7. Edwin L. Frizen, Jr., *75 Years of IFMA: 1917-1992* (Pasadena: William Carey Library, 1992).

8. David J. Bosch, *Transforming Mission* (Maryknoll, N.Y.: Orbis Books, 1991), 460.

9. J. Verkuyl, *Contemporary Missiology* (Grand Rapids: William B. Eerdmans Publishing Company, 1978), 408.

10. Ibid., p. 239

11. See particularly D.A. Carson, *The Gagging of God* (Grand Rapids: Zondervan, 1996), 481 and J. Erickson Millard, *The Evangelical Left* (Grand Rapids: Baker Books, 1997), 45-49, 80-86.

12. James, Barr, *The Semantics of Biblical Language* (London: Oxford University, 1961) and E.D. Hirsch, *Validity in Interpretation* (New Haven: Yale University Press, 1967).

14. Osborne integrates Hirsch, Childs, and Barr in his thoughts, passim. Grant R. Osborne, *The Hermeneutical Spiral* (Downers Grove, IL: InterVarsity Press, 1991).

15. Dean Gilliland has a good summary of the concept. Dean S. Gilliland, *Pauline Theology & Mission Practice* (Grand Rapids: Baker Book House, 1983).

16. John Piper, *Let the Nations Be Glad* (Grand Rapids: Baker Book House, 1993), 72.

Chapter 5

Working Together with Conciliar Groups

Charles Van Engen

I have been asked to offer some thoughts on how Evangelical mission organizations and persons may cooperate with conciliar mission organizations and persons associated with the World Council of Churches of Christ (WCC). In the short time allotted to this complex issue, I would like to offer a question, three observations, three suggestions, and a challenge. The thoughts offered here are preliminary musings—more questions than answers. Our subject is complex, controversial and emotional for most of us here. So I simply want to raise some questions for our own reflection and self-examination. First let me introduce myself.

Introduction

I was born and raised a son of missionaries. Because my parents were members of the Reformed Church in America (RCA), I am part of a church that was a charter member of the WCC and the National Council of Churches of Christ (NCCC). Our denomination has been involved in cooperation in mission since the earliest days of mission-sending from the U.S. The RCA was part of the American Board of Commissioners for Foreign Missions from its inception in 1810. The RCA was also a member of the International Missionary Council and other cooperative ecumenical organizations. South of the Mexico-U.S. border, I grew up a member of the National Presbyterian Church of Mexico (NPCM), one of the largest and oldest Protestant denominations in Mexico. The NPCM has steadfastly refused, until recently, to be a part of any multi-denominational cooperative endeavors of any kind, standing equally aloof from both Conciliar and Evangelical movements—as well as refusing to cooperate with

Roman Catholics or Pentecostal/Charismatics.

I left home when I was fourteen to attend high school in North Carolina at Ben Lippen School, associated with Columbia International University. Some years later, I received my M. Div. from Fuller Seminary, where I now teach. This strand in my pilgrimage has placed me within the Evangelical movement in the U.S. I identify myself as solidly Evangelical in theology, hermeneutics, missiology and perspective on spirituality. Of course, just the task of defining what an Evangelical is today is no easy matter—and is beyond the scope of these reflections.

All of this is to say that my own pilgrimage has made me wonder whether the designation "ecumenical" (or "conciliar") and "evangelical" are necessarily mutually-exclusive, or whether they in fact reflect completely different theological and missiological worlds, and whether to some extent their use over-against each other may be somewhat artificial. I consider myself an ecumenical-evangelical and an evangelical-ecumenical. And there are many people like me in the Christian Church around the world—and particularly in the world of mission.

This leads me to my first point: a question.

A Question

It is interesting to me that the organizers of this gathering chose to have us examine the matter of how we can cooperate with Conciliar, Orthodox, and Roman Catholics. Why are we not also asking about cooperation with Pentecostal/charismatics and with non-Christian organizations like NGO's? It seems to me that there are many theological and biblical questions arising out of a Pentecostal/charismatic hermeneutic which a traditional Evangelical would want to ask. Might one say that these questions may be as profound and pervasive as those related to the Conciliar movement? Yet I wonder why as Evangelicals we find it easier to cooperate in mission with Pentecostal/charismatics than with conciliars? Further, in a number of cases Evangelicals have found it necessary and even desirable to cooperate with totally non-Christian agencies. And we seem to be able to do that more easily than to cooperate with conciliar agencies. I wonder why that seems to be less difficult for us? I don't have an answer to this, but I believe the question may draw us forward in our reflection on this topic.

Three Observations

I wonder if some of our deepest difficulties in cooperating with folks from the conciliar movement derive more from non-theological factors than theological ones? We know that Evangelical relationships to conciliar folks is colored in the U.S. by the history of the Fundamentalist/Modernist debates of the 1920s. In those debates, the main-line, culture-affirming Protestantism of the day was immensely optimistic regarding "the Kingdom of God in America," and the positive effects of industrialization, modernization, secularization and technology. The twentieth century was to be the height of American culture and Protestantism, and was to be the great Christian century. On the other hand, the early Fundamentalists read their reality with very different eyes. They were mostly counter/cultural folks, out of the mainstream of society, not strongly positioned in politics and economics of the day. They were pessimistic about the culture, feared the rise of evil, and rightly foresaw the coming of wars and rumors of wars. I wonder. Were the predictions made by the Fundamentalists closer to the reality of a twentieth century filled with wars and rumors of wars? The difference in cultural make-up and outlook has colored the relationship between Evangelicals and conciliar folks since that time.

Secondly, when the IMC was integrated into the WCC in 1961 at the New Delhi Assembly of the World Council of Churches, many ecumenically-inclined Evangelicals left the WCC and became a part of the Movement that would find its expression at Wheaton, 1966, Berlin, 1966, and Lausanne, 1974. This migration from the WCC into the North American Evangelical missions movement was in part fueled by theological questions about the relationship of mission and church. But maybe it was also encouraged by a cultural reaction by American Evangelicals to the very strong European influence in the WCC. That had pushed the WCC in certain socio-political directions as a result of Europe's uneasy conscience over the silence of the churches regarding the atrocities of the Third Reich. This historical and cultural difference continues to impact us to this day—seen, for example, by comparing the make-up of the Evangelical Missiological Society (EMS) with that of the International Association of Mission Studies (IAMS).

Thirdly, the post World War II European issues fueled the rise of a theology of relevance and, subsequently, humanization, and then

Liberation Theology as the foundation for conciliar mission in the 1970s and 1980s. This socio-economic and political agenda for radical change was not shared by the Evangelicals.

Instead, the Evangelicals in the U.S. were becoming more comfortable in their wealth, more culture-affirming in their view of reality, and increasingly influential (from the Carter era onward) in the economic, social and political arenas of North America. The two perspectives were like two ships passing in the night. Yet each movement has historical, cultural and theological branches that touch the other. Maybe that is what makes it so difficult for us to cooperate with conciliar folks. Do they remind us too much about that which we are trying to avoid in ourselves?

Three Suggestions

I would like to offer three suggestions as to how we might proceed in seeking new avenues of cooperation with those involved in the conciliar movement.

1. We need to stress the importance of local cooperation in mission alongside larger, macro-level, world congress-type cooperation. As I talk with pastors and missionaries all over the world, I find that new, creative, and unexpected avenues of mission cooperation arise when Christians get to know one another, to trust one another, to pray together (as, for example, in Ed Silvoso's prayer-based ministries), and to share vision and commitment with each other. I believe we need to emphasize the missional potentials of local trans-denominational and trans-tradition cooperation "so that the world may believe." I recognize the inherent difficulties that local Christians may face in relation to theological issues we all hold dear. But I find that everywhere, personal trust and shared vision seem to provide a new venue in which people seem to be able to work around such difficulties.

2. We need to remember that the Conciliar or "Ecumenical" movement is not at all monolithic. There is huge diversity among those who are members of WCC-related organizations. Among the member churches there are tremendous theological differences—and some of the member churches would be much closer theologically to an Evangelical position (and in many cases closer to an outspoken charismatic perspective) than to that of other members of the WCC. Remember also, that the WCC is a council of churches.

This at times makes it difficult for Evangelical sodality-type mission agencies to cooperate with conciliar structures. So one of the ways to be able to cooperate with conciliar structures and persons is to be familiar enough with them to be able to identify those that are closer to Evangelical perspectives. Remember, also, that the conciliar movement as we have known it since the birth of the WCC in 1948 is a movement in decline, in the midst of deep soul-searching. Now, when it is down, is probably not the time to kick it. Rather, now may be a time for offering correctives, new vision and new initiatives that draws conciliar-related organizations and persons back to a more biblical and Evangelical missiological point of view.

3. We need to strongly affirm the more Evangelical statements and views that have been expressed in the WCC and other conciliar circles. The "Mission and Evangelism" statement of 1983, the "Statement of the Stuttgart Consultation on Evangelism" of 1987, parts of "The San Antonio Report" of 1990, and some statements in the 1993 statement on "Mission and Evangelism in Unity" contain portions which Evangelicals could commend and encourage. The Salvador 1996 gathering of the former (and no longer existing) Commission on World Mission and Evangelism and the WCC Assembly in Harare in 1998 had little new to offer. Yet as Evangelicals we could be of assistance to the global Christian Church if we, using the Apostle Paul's words in I Thess 5:21, took some time to "test everything and hold on to the good" found in conciliar circles.

A Challenge

I believe Evangelical missiologists have something to offer the conciliar movement—especially at this time of crisis in world ecumenism. Although the "conciliar" segment of Christianity is rapidly shrinking in its percentage representation of world Christianity, yet many European, some North American, and many older churches in Africa, Asia and Latin America still maintain their conciliar relationships. This includes many of the older mission agencies, united churches (Japan and India and China, for example), and seminaries. I would like to challenge us to find ways to offer the conciliar movement new vision, vitality and groundedness in a truly Evangelical missiology. The IAMS, for example, needs Evangelical presence.

And a path for such input seems to me to be available when we foster conversations by asking specifically missional questions in particular locations and contexts: What should be our biblical motivation for mission—and how does that hold accountable both our own Evangelical perspective and the conciliar one?

What should be our biblical means of mission—and how does that hold accountable both our own Evangelical perspective and the conciliar one?

What should be our biblical perspective with regard to the agents of mission—and how does that hold accountable both our own Evangelical perspective and the conciliar one?

What should be our biblical perspective of the goals of mission—and how does that hold accountable both our own Evangelical perspective and the conciliar one?

As the Apostle Paul wrote, "It is fine to be zealous, provided the purpose is good" (Gal. 4:18).

Conclusion

Our mission is not our own: it is Christ's mission. We participate in the mission of Jesus Christ. The appropriateness or rightness of our mission is not determined by whether it is "Evangelical" or "Ecumenical" or "Conciliar." It is right and good if it is biblical, centered in Jesus Christ and governed by a careful reading of Scripture. We might be able to learn to relate to, and cooperate with, "conciliar" mission structures and agencies if we give ourselves the chance to examine their perspectives and our own assumptions in the light of biblical revelation. We can learn from the past, but we also need to leave much of the past in the past—and look forward to new and creative ways the Holy Spirit is leading us for the evangelization of the world in our generation. May we be open to the Spirit's leading to find new ways of "Working Together with God to Shape Mission in the New Millenium."

Chapter 6

On the Theological Possibility of Orthodox/Evangelical Cooperation in Mission

Edward Rommen

Introduction: On the Nature of the Dilemma

Unlike my fellow speakers, I am not an Evangelical speaking about Orthodoxy, I am Orthodox. I speak as a member of the Church and it is that commitment which empowers me to speak on her behalf.

My presentation, then, is not primarily professional, but intensely personal. It has the character of a confession rather than an apologetic defense of the Church. For the purposes at hand, I am not particularly interested in defending or trying to prove the superiority of one idea or the other. But I am interested in sketching the outlines of what I think it will take to move us toward the possibility of bridging our differences and cooperating in missions.

When I first became Orthodox, I was driven by an optimism based on my conviction that, at least at the level of the Gospel, Orthodoxy and evangelicalism were compatible. For example, I saw no reason for discontinuing my involvement in evangelical institutions. In fact, I considered that participation an honor and an opportunity to build bridges of understanding and cooperation. Unfortunately, things that I have experienced, heard, seen, and read since becoming Orthodox have pushed that initial optimism to a distant horizon. It is not altogether lost, but it has become very faint.

Until now, the vast majority of evangelicals with whom I have been involved seem determined to systematically eliminate or prevent every opportunity for significant exchange. Others have said and published things usually reserved for one's worst enemies rather than those with whom one supposedly wishes to cooperate. Recently I read an article in which the Orthodox Church's teaching on salvation was compared to "a bowl of manure permeated" with cream.[1] Another essay disqualified the beauty of the Church as repugnant.[2] I, personally, have been called all manner of names (a threat, a danger) and even traveled a great distance to participate in a conference only to be told, as I was about to arrive, that because I was Orthodox, my services would not be needed. For whatever reasons, there seems to be a steady stream of inaccurate, erroneous, slanderous things being propagated about the Orthodox Church.

Obviously, drawing "battle lines" does not aid the cause of cooperation. Some Orthodox, for their part, have also been very reluctant to seek and to facilitate cooperation with evangelicals. They too have published their share of unfair and unhelpful statements. Some of the most outspoken opponents of evangelicals are evangelical converts to Orthodoxy. In a recent book by a former Baptist, the author states "The ultimate concern of Protestantism is neither God nor the Scriptures nor anything that could reasonably be labeled truth, but rather the sovereignty of the individual."[3]

These then are the horns of our dilemma. How can we seriously speak of cooperation in an environment which is characterized by such polemic—an environment which is more like a battle zone than a field of common endeavor? And yet, someone must have had the courage or the foresight to put this topic, if only for 15 minutes, onto the conference schedule and my Bishop has given me his blessing to address this gathering. Let us then, take heart in these small indices of goodwill and press on.

Since I have been asked to focus on a theological framework for cooperation, allow me to suggest five aspects of theological activity to consider as you look towards the possibility of corporation with Orthodox believers around the world.

Presuppositions: Do You Really Want to Cooperate?

It seems to me that it may be somewhat premature to be talking about a framework for cooperation when, as I suspect, the question of cooperation itself has not yet been settled. You may think that the fact that you have scheduled a discussion on the subject is itself indicative of an answer to the question.

However, I imagine that there are many of you sitting here who still seriously question the possibility or the wisdom of evangelical cooperation with the Orthodox. The fact that you use your own theologians to speak for other groups such as the Roman Church does not engender confidence in your desire to cooperate. Unless you actually engage members of the other groups, the only thing you will be cooperating with are your caricatures of those groups.

To establish a framework for cooperation you are going to have to at least assume the possibility of cooperation. If you do not, the deliberation of this conference remains a fruitless exercise. It might make you feel better, but it certainly will not lead to cooperation.

Theology and Introspection: Self-Examination a Neglected Component

Let us assume for the moment that you think some form of cooperation is possible and desirable. Where do we go from here? One thing about cooperation is that it usually requires some form of self-examination. Since becoming Orthodox, my experience with evangelicals is that they are generally not willing to look at themselves. For example, as I made my journey into Orthodoxy, one of the most important questions for me was the nature and form of worship. When I raised this issue, very few seemed willing to discuss the questions I posed. As I made my way toward the Church, no one seemed willing to ask "have we in some way contributed to this move?"

My father helped establish a church, which grew within a few years to about 300 members. After some time, they hired a new pastor who introduced a radically different approach to worship. The net result was that they lost about 60 percent of their attendees. Interestingly, when my father asked whether or not that might be the result of the new worship policy, no one was willing to entertain the idea and insisted that everything was being done correctly.

I recall distinctly the exasperation I experienced when trying to discuss the things that I was discovering about Orthodoxy with evangelical colleagues. People certainly asked me questions. But after giving my answer, the usual response was "thanks for your answer," but there was almost never any real engagement of the issues.

Theology and Love: Showing the Mind of Christ

All theological activity must, of course, be guided by the authoritative truth of Holy Scriptures, but it must be done in a way that shows that the participants are in communion with Christ. That is, they should, in all that they do and say, remain cordial, sensitive, loving, and compassionate. That ought to be obvious to a group of missionaries. They are, after all, tuned into cross-cultural differences. Nevertheless, your own conference schedule shows a lack of sensitivity. You have me representing the "Orthodox Movement." The Orthodox are a Church, not a movement. It may seem a small point, yet, if this indiscretion can happen in the cultured atmosphere of this gathering, what must go on out in the "trenches?"

I don't want to belabor the point, but if the articles I mentioned earlier are any indication, some significant changes will have to be made in the way you speak about, speak to, and treat the Orthodox—at least if you really want to cooperate with them in the fulfillment of the Great Commission.

Theology and Integrity: Honestly Identifying the Real or Actual Differences Between Orthodoxy and Evangelicalism?

One of the most difficult things about this dialogue is that we are dealing with two very distinct mind sets, two cultures, conceptual frameworks which are the result of different histories, different cultural paths. Consider just a few of the resulting differences: a) the East tends to be more interested in relationships whereas the West concentrates on propositions; b) the East emphasizes person, the West focuses on nature; c) the East unites reality and symbolism while the West tends to associate symbol with that which is not real.[4]

Each of these differences gives rise to areas of apparent disagreement: a) when defining salvation the East is primarily interested in the "new life in Christ," whereas the West concentrates on our change in legal status—justification; b) when exploring the doctrine of God, the Eastern theologians emphasize the Person of God, in the West the focus is on the Nature of God; c) when venerating an icon, the Eastern believer has no difficulty relating the reality of an icon's prototype with its symbolic representation, while Western believers have considerable difficulty.

These differences are the seedbed of ineffective communication and tend to cause misunderstandings and false identification of theological issues. For example, in a *Trinity World Forum* article,

Bradley Nassif laid out a brief framework for cooperation based on his conviction that Orthodoxy and evangelicalism are compatible.[5] In a response to that article it was suggested that the two were not compatible because Orthodox teaching inserts additional mediators (priest, Eucharist, etc.). This is typical of the misidentification of issues about which I am speaking. In Orthodox theology there is only one mediator, our Lord God and Savior Jesus Christ. So the real issue is not the number of mediators, but the place of these things—things generally neglected by evangelicals. The fact that these things play a more significant role in the life the Orthodox, does not justify the evangelical assumption that these elements assume the status of mediators.[6]

I get the impression that we have a situation similar to that described in the famous book *Flatland*:[7] trying to approach the three-dimensional from a two-dimensional plane, i.e., evangelicals forcing their uni-dimensional presuppositions on multi-dimensional Orthodoxy. Of course this type of misunderstanding can be addressed and, to some degree, resolved.[8]

Theology and Growth: Learning From Others

Finally, all theological activity rests on the assumption that it is a human endeavor and therefore incomplete. As a result, it is incumbent upon all theologians to develop a humble willingness to learn from others. With respect to the question before us, I would like to point to several case studies, some informative, some challenging, and others exemplifying the attitudes and values I have elaborated on here.

1. Gospel Light Publications is helping Russian Orthodox Christians teach Sunday school. The key to this endeavor is the attitude expressed by a Gospel Light spokesperson, "We did not want to promote our own ideas or theology. Lessons use Byzantine illustrations and follow Scripture readings in the church calendar."[9]

2. Cooperation between Western Mission agencies and the Coptic Church is described and documented in *Turning Over a New Leaf: Protestant Missions and the Orthodox Churches of the Middle East*. London: Interserve, 1992.

3. Dialogue is being fostered by the Society for the Study of Eastern Orthodoxy and Evangelicalism (SSEOE). The SSEOE is a Christian "think tank" that serves both the academy and the Church.

Through its annual meetings and published papers, it seeks to identify the similarities and differences between the Eastern Orthodox and Evangelical traditions.

4. Finally, let me mention the recently published book *Proselytism and Orthodoxy in Russia*, by John Witte Jr. and Michael Bourdeaux (Maryknoll: Orbis, 1999). The book contains a wealth of information on the religious, cultural, and legal situation in Russia. In chapter 16 Lawrence Uzzell even sets out a few "Guidelines for American Missionaries in Russia."

Conclusions

Is cooperation possible? I think in some areas it may be. For that reason, I am still committed to the idea of building bridges. At this point I am not sure what those areas of compatibility are. Determining that will take considerable good will and effort on both sides.

Endnotes

1. Doug Jones, "Imperfectly Justified," *TableTalk* (June 1999), 11ff. The following two quotes illustrate the tone taken by some, who obviously do not understand even the most fundamental aspects of Orthodox doctrine. "Eastern Orthodoxy shows no concern for conforming any aspect of its worship to the requisites of the Lord. They rejoice in imitating the inferior worship of the Old Covenant temple and shallowly overturn the ancient prohibition on venerating images." "Since deification is grounded in the incarnation rather than the atonement, Christ's cross becomes, in principle, non-essential, a quaint sideshow in deification." Douglas Jones, "Eastern Heterodoxy," Credenda/Agenda, Volume 6, No. 5. Cf. www.credenda.org/issues/vol6/them6-5.htm

2. R. C. Sproul, "Repugnant Beauty," *TableTalk* (June 1999), 5ff. Not all evangelicals are engaging in this kind of "smear tactic." It seems the crudest and most ill-informed attacks against the Church come from the Calvinist's corner of evangelicalism.

3. My own experience over the last few years lends credence to his statement. Clark Carlton, *The Way* (Salisbury: Regina Press, 1997), 65.

4. Obviously this is an oversimplification. However, it does accurately indicate significant differences in conceptual frames of reference or thought paradigms. See Alexander Schmeman, *For The Life of the World* (Crestwood:SVS Press, 1963), 135–151.

5. Bradley Nassif, "Evangelical Missions in Eastern Orthodox Lands," *Trinity World Forum* (Winter 1996), p. 1-5.

6. Another example of setting up dialogue without dealing with the actual issue can be found in R. C. Sproul's article "Repugnant Beauty," *TableTalk* (June 1999), 5ff. He suggests that Orthodoxy has defended its use of icons on two grounds: their beauty, and pedagogical value. In fact, however, the Orthodox defense rests on the nature of the incarnation—Jesus the very icon of God himself. As Leonid

Ouspensky puts it "The Church declares that the icon is an outcome of the Incarnation; that it is based upon this Incarnation and therefore belongs to the very essence of Christianity, and cannot be separated from it," *Theology of the Icon*, Vol 1. (Crestwood:SVS Press, 1992), p. 36.

7. Edwin Abbott Abbott. *Flatland*. Princeton: Princeton University Press, 1991.

8. Yet, we must honestly face the fact that there are areas of disagreement which are not likely to be bridged. Some things lie outside the realm of cooperation, e.g., participation in the Eucharist.

9. See www.glint.org/projects.htm for a complete description of the project.

Chapter 7

Theological Guidelines for Working within a Roman Catholic Context

John Nyquist

In the present context of ecumenical dialogue between Protestants and Roman Catholics, it is worthwhile to consider the prospect of significant interaction between the Evangelical community and the Catholic community. In our day, the Lutheran-Catholic discussions have resulted in substantial agreement in several areas, and specifically regarding justification. This is not the place to evaluate that discussion, except to note the opportunity it creates for similar discussions among Christians of goodwill. Additionally, we note the documents produced in the wake of the original publication of "Evangelicals and Catholics Together: The Christian Mission in the Third Millennium" (ECT). A subsequent document, "The Gift of Salvation" emanated from many of the same authors of ECT, punctuated before and after by rebuttals from both the Evangelical and Catholic quarters.

Is it possible to consider that Evangelicals and Roman Catholics could extend the gospel in missionary contexts as part of the same team? At this venue in Virginia Beach, the conveners thought that such possibilities deserved a forum, alongside similar prospects between mainline Protestants and Catholics, as well as between the Eastern Orthodox and Roman Catholics. My approach will, of necessity, be unique among my colleagues here at the Triennial. Both Dr. Van Engen and Dr. Rommen can represent their respective communities with integrity: conciliar Reformed and Eastern Orthodox. My perspective must be considered from a certain distance—I am not Roman Catholic and carry no brief on their behalf.

However, it has been my privilege over the past several years to observe a kind of "ad hoc" ecumenism based on theological principle. This is not a pragmatic approach that resorts to "peace at any cost" for the sake of immediate ministry gratification. Nor is it naively uncritical of the recent ECT documents, but this is not the place for that discussion.

Additionally, I have interacted with many Roman Catholic theologians and missiologists (and many missionaries) in the process of ministry in Europe and the United States. This has led to two significant things from my perspective: invitations to speak and teach alongside and within the Catholic community, and the development of a seminary course at Trinity Evangelical Divinity School entitled "Contemporary Roman Catholicism." It is from these various perspectives that I venture some brief reflections on the possibilities of cooperation between Evangelicals and Roman Catholics in the missionary enterprise.

My friend and former colleague, Harold O. J. Brown, evaluated some years ago the various responses which have emerged in the contemporary conversation: "Enough has been written by Protestants criticizing the church of Rome. Some of it is intended to win over disillusioned Catholics, some to frighten wavering Protestants away from Rome, some to encourage Protestant smugness and self-righteousness. Some of it is even written in an admirable desire to get at the essence of Roman Catholicism and to see what it really is and where it is actually going... (I)n our ecumenical era, there are Protestants who romanticize the Roman church, putting it in a better light than most of its members would" (*The Protest of a Troubled Protestant*, Zondervan, 1969, pp. 146-7). Hopefully, our criticism is "Christian" in every respect, void of "smugness and self-righteousness." It is also the intention of this paper to avoid the "romantic" approach, attempting rather a sober and realistic reflection by integrating the insights gained from biblical theology, missiology and intercultural experience.

I recall with ironic humor an invitation to present a series of lectures at a prestigious Catholic university in Eastern Europe (prior to the fall of communism). The topic of the lectures was simply, "How Do Evangelical Protestants Understand and Practice Ecumenism?" I began the first lecture by stating that this could be the shortest lecture series in recent memory. In fact, evangelical Protestants have kept their distance from the international ecumenical movement for sound historical and theological reasons.

Our Lord's prayer on the eve of his crucifixion certainly emphasized the marks of the true church: unity and love for one another. But the application of this challenge requires theological and doctrinal integrity, demanding that the context of John 17 be interpreted without importing later ecclesiastical developments into this text. Furthermore, as theological liberalism has developed in the mainline Protestant denominations, evangelical theology and practice has attracted the attention of conservative Catholics. This, in turn, has provided the opportunity for in-depth dialogue along several lines between Roman Catholics and Evangelical Protestants. In North America, recent conversations have produced several interesting documents under the rubric of "Evangelicals and Catholics Together" (1994-). Some rather high-level dialogue continues between members of the Catholic hierarchy and evangelical theologians.

What kind of theological guidelines would assist us in making our way forward in the event that God opens doors for cooperative ministry?

The ongoing Evangelical-Catholic dialogue has focused on the gospel and its significance for considering any ministry opportunities. The gospel is referred to often in the New Testament as "the Gospel of God" and thus it is. It centers on Jesus Christ, God's unique Son and on the fulfillment of Old Testament prophecy. The several statements of the Great Commission (the gospels and Acts) point to a pattern of gospel proclamation initiated by the Good News beyond one's own cultural boundaries. Plans to collaborate in ministry demand basic agreement on the content of the biblical gospel and its trinitarian nature.

The Jerusalem Council (Acts 15) served as a watershed from the global perspective of the Great Commission. The hostility between Jews and Gentiles represented a formidable barrier to church extension plans. And yet through the courageous and bold witness of unlikely persons, the dividing wall was penetrated. Those of us who have engaged in cross-cultural ministry readily confess the difficulties which are present in such attempts. Disagreements will certainly need to be confronted with candor; they cannot be swept under the rug. But the opportunities must not be dismissed out of hand.

They require the wise and seasoned counsel of mature Christians, asking for God's discernment at every point.

An important guideline to ponder is found in Paul's defense of his own ministry in 1 Corinthians 9:19-23. Paul's freedom to engage both Jews and Gentiles with the "dynamite of God" was undergirded with a profound understanding of gospel freedom. He states with openness: "To the weak I became weak, that I might win the weak; I have become all things to all men, that I may by all means save some. And I do all things for the sake of the gospel, that I may become a fellow-partaker of it" (verses 22-23). From Acts 9 through the end of Acts, and continuing through his letters, this principle is consistently carried out. Paul ran the risk of being misunderstood and so will we. Nevertheless, the integrity of the entire enterprise is assumed to include the essence of the gospel without compromise.

Paul's communication with the Philippian church included surprising information—at least for Evangelicals. Paul was able to rejoice at the spread of the gospel, even though it was being done by his enemies. However, a careful examination of this text in Philippians 1:12-18 ff. doesn't allow for any syncretistic interpretation. Paul was always careful to distinguish between "his" gospel, i.e., the gospel that came to him via revelation, and "a gospel contrary to that which we have preached to you..." (Galatians 1:9). Twice in the space of two verses in that same chapter, Paul warns that heterodox gospel preachers would be "accursed" (verses 8-9). Therefore it wasn't just "any" gospel that was being spread by Paul's enemies. We can assume that it was the biblical gospel, even though Christ was being preached "from envy and strife..." as well as from "selfish ambition rather than by pure motives" (Philippians 1:15,17). The question here concerns the methods and techniques of evangelization, not the essence of the gospel itself.

While Evangelicals have always been characterized as zealous for truth, we have not always been willing to acknowledge acceptable diversity within the universal Body of Christ. The cultural realities of cross-cultural ministry help us to understand that God's truth can be expressed in myriad ways, with power and effectiveness. Even the disciples needed an occasional lesson from the Master in this regard. We discover two different occasions when those closest to Jesus were puzzled by those who were engaging in "unauthorized" ministry. In Luke 9:49ff. we hear one of the 12 saying, "Master, we saw someone casting out demons in your name; and we tried to hinder him because he does not follow along with us." But Jesus said to him, "Do not hinder him; for he who is not against you is for you." The interesting point about the context of this passage is that following this little sermonette, Jesus asked the disciples to go ahead of him into Samaria to get things ready for his entry into the area. In Luke's attempt to portray the disciples' attempt at applying this message, they could only resort to the "strategy" of commanding "fire to come down from heaven and consume them" (verses 52-54). If we can accept guidelines like these for possible ministry opportunities, can we also envision some concrete suggestions for Evangelical-Roman Catholic cooperation in mission?

For many years, scholars have met together in the academic arena, granting each other freedom of expression within their respective traditions. It is assumed that at least one of the reasons why such scholarly societies attract the best scholars each year is that there is much that can be learned outside the parameters of one's own experience and training. Evangelicals can continue to demonstrate sound exegetical methods, while adding to it a "hermeneutic of love"—listening and learning and growing in Christlikeness. Among missiologists, it is common knowledge that scholarly research is both appreciated and practiced across the board. *Missiology* (April 1995) published an article by Steve Bevans entitled "What Catholics Can Learn from Evangelical Mission Theology." I have been invited to join the discussion by writing a similar piece on "What Evangelicals Can Learn from Roman Catholic Mission Theology." The article is still "in process" but this kind of interchange illustrates my point.

As missiologists, we are always interested in staying on the "cutting edge" of what God is doing around the world, and in our particular disciplines. Opportunities for dialogue between Evangelicals and Roman Catholics take place at several levels. Perhaps the most fruitful level of conversation is the local one, because without the added burden of structural expectations, discussions may proceed in a profitable manner. Could we add that one is often invited to participate in such conversations by virtue of a certain type of "reputation." Simply put, if we can be trusted to engage one another with Christian charity, avoiding a strident and shrill anti-Catholicism, it is more likely that we will be invited to contribute. It is amazing how "open doors" present themselves once we have assured our Catholic friends that we will not take advantage of the situation in an unethical manner.

It has become well known that more conservative Roman Catholics often find it easier to engage in dialogue with Evangelicals than with many of their liberal counterparts because of "our" basic agreement on many fundamentals, including a high view of Scripture. We can invite Catholic colleagues into our classrooms to present "the Catholic view," and we can anticipate a reciprocal invitation in the future. To our evangelical students, this authentic approach to those with whom we differ is very attractive—an honest using of "primary sources" in a manner of speaking.

In the wake of Vatican II, as well as the more recent developments in Evangelical-Roman Catholic conversations, it must be acknowledged that the climate for ecumenical dialogue is indeed unique in our time. Even the critics of the ECT documents have recognized the value of exchanging ideas between the two communities. Much of the rhetoric of past generations has receded and discussions of substance are taking place in these final days of this century.

Lutherans and Catholics continue their engagement relative to "justification by faith," along with similar discussions between Catholics and Southern Baptists, Catholics and Pentecostals. Those engaged in these conversations are committed to their own formulations, and yet there is a certain amount of wonder as the listening and learning take place. On the local level here at Trinity Evangelical Divinity School, we have a number of colleagues participating in various discussions with Roman Catholic scholars and clergy. One of my friends and colleagues in another discipline was asked in a recent ecumenical discussion why he was taking part. His answer was straightforward: "I ask my students to be committed to learning, and as their mentor, I must do the same. I want to learn more about the Catholic church and supplement my own knowledge, as well as to be disabused of misconceptions and misunderstandings."

Finally, it must be said that in many of these gatherings, opportunities for genuine witness present themselves. Just a couple of months ago, I was invited by the Chicago Archdiocesan Office for

Ecumenical and Interreligious Affairs to give an address along with the Director of Evangelization for the Archdiocese. My topic was "Evangelism: An Evangelical Protestant Perspective." The audience was primarily Catholic and I understood the invitation as an opportunity to define, describe and declare the gospel of Christ's saving grace. As I was preparing for this event, I wondered how many of my colleagues at Trinity, to say nothing about the large number of evangelical pastors and Christian workers, would have given anything to be invited to such a wonderful opportunity. We can only thank our gracious God for providing such platforms for the gospel. Certainly, the apostle Paul would have made room in his busy schedule for that kind of address.

Listen to what he writes: "And pray for us, too, that God may open a door for our message, so that we may proclaim the mystery of Christ, for which I am in chains. Pray that I may proclaim it clearly, as I should. Be wise in the way you act toward outsiders make the most of every opportunity. Let your conversation be always full of grace, seasoned with salt, so that you may know how to answer everyone" (Col. 4:3–6).

Response to the Three Contextual Papers on Working Together Theologically

James J. Stamoolis

It is a privilege to be on the program with three fine presenters. I will limit my comments to interacting with what I see as the main thrust of each of their papers and phrase my response in the form of six questions. These questions are not only for the presenters, but for the rest of us to consider regarding the underlying issues of cooperation.

The easiest paper to respond to is Chuck Van Engen's, because of the overlap between the definitions of evangelical and the self-understanding of some in the conciliar movement. He was smart to resist the temptation to define "Evangelical." One might think that as a representative of the World Evangelical Fellowship, I would be willing to supply a ready definition. I am willing, but the point we are discussing is not a matter of definitions, but of hermeneutics, relationships, and culture. Underscoring this, one of the many good points made by Van Engen, is the theological difference between charismatic and non-charismatic evangelicals. We know of instances where there is no cooperation between these two groups because of problems from one side or the other.

Ed Rommen raises the question of whether we really want to cooperate? I am sure the question could be answered many different ways. Some would like to see a revitalization of Orthodoxy without any commitment to close ecclesiastical communion, something the Orthodox, if they really hold to their doctrine of truth, should find unacceptable. As Protestants, we should admit that some evangelicals would hold that cooperation with Orthodox, and for that matter Roman Catholics, is only a precursor to the eventual conversion of the adherents of both these confessions to the doctrines of grace as that particular evangelical group defines it. If both sides of a discussion hold exclusive truth claims, as I know both Evangelicals and Eastern Orthodox do, then the question of cooperation is a two-edged sword. Neither side can yield without giving up something of the claim to truth they possess. As we will note below, we need to ask what the essential truths are that neither side can give up. These truths form the limits of cooperation.

John Nyquist correctly points out that there is much to learn from Roman Catholicism, especially citing Donald McGavran's comment on the Vatican II document, *Ad Gentes*. But in the case of Roman Catholicism, as in the case of the Eastern Orthodox Church, we must remind ourselves that we are not dealing with monolithic structures. We need to avoid the temptation to generalize from a single example, whether it is good or bad. We should also avoid that in our evaluation of other evangelicals. Strangely, we don't seem to heed that warning because our trust level of one another's *bona fides* in evangelicalism is generally not high enough.

While we like to categorize people and movements, believing that if we have named something we understand it, this does not make for either good theology or good practice. Not every Orthodox is bad; not every Evangelical is good. There may be a greater number of bad in the tradition that we don't like for theological or personal reasons, but unless we have done a thorough statistical analysis, we can not make any verifiable claims.

In the end, does cooperation with the Eastern Orthodox and Roman Catholics simply boil down to learning from each other since joint work is impossible? Time will tell.

I would like to pose six questions to move us beyond our comfort zones and hopefully produce some reflection on the issues that cooperation raises.

1. What is Our Purpose in Being Involved in the Work of Spreading God's Kingdom?

It seems to me that there are only two alternatives: we are either planting the Church, or we are planting our church. If we are involved in planting the Church then we must trust the Holy Spirit to create the appropriate structures for each time and place. This does not mean that we accept any variant of "church" as a true church. To do so would force us into a position of recognizing cults as true expressions of the God's Kingdom. None of us are willing to do that. However, in our zeal to defend doctrinal orthodoxy we could very well be guilty of projecting our own view of what the Church is with regard to every manifestation of the work of the Holy Spirit. To do so may be limiting inappropriately what the legitimate forms of expression of faith in the Triune God should look like.

Our purpose should be the spread of the Church in all culturally and theologically appropriate forms, rather than the spread of our church. This leads to my second question.

2. What is Our Definition of a Christian?

This is the critical question because there are only three possible answers: (a) a believer in the Lord Jesus; (b) a believer in the Lord Jesus after our pattern of belief (which is a subset of one of the possible answers to our first question); or (3) a believer in the Lord Jesus after some pattern, by which we mean there is some minimal set of requirements for belief or action that determine whether a person is truly in or out.

In truth, we cannot determine who is really in or out because we cannot with certainty determine the work of the Holy Spirit in a person's life. We can only go by testimony and whether or not the person's life matches the profession they make. We are on much safer ground determining who is out on the basis of behavior and/or beliefs that are clearly unchristian. We cannot go only by lifestyle, but must insist on some articulation of faith in Jesus Christ. We want to see both identification and fruit. Otherwise we could claim all righteous people of whatever religion as anonymous Christians.

Missiologists have long recognized the distinction between the initial point of entry into the Christian faith, and the perfecting of that faith through a discipling process. We need to be careful not to apply standards of a mature disciple to situations where the person involved is only a convert. The early church had a category of catechumen for someone who believed but had not completed the instructions in the faith which lead to baptism.

Often, in our day we are often dealing with people who have been baptized, but may have only rudimentary knowledge of what it means to believe. This was my case; I considered myself a Christian since I was a baptized Greek Orthodox, but I had very little understanding of the Christian faith. It was only when I went to university and heard the gospel from those involved in InterVarsity

Christian Fellowship that I came to a real understanding of the Christian faith and consequently a true commitment to Christ. I have often told my Orthodox friends that I believe more Orthodox doctrine now as a Baptist than I ever did as an Orthodox, because I had almost no understanding of the doctrine of the Orthodox Church.

When I was involved in direct student ministry, we would often come across a student who would identify himself or herself as a Christian. However our initial conversation would reveal no evidence of a personal commitment to Christ. Rather than challenge the person's self-understanding at the outset, we would say, "Then as a Christian you will be interested in the opportunities for growth that InterVarsity provides: Bible Studies, retreats, etc." We saw many nominal Christians become real believers through this approach.

I believe this is a paradigm we can use for cooperation. Rather than be judgmental, we can encourage the other person to join us in growing as a disciple of the Lord Jesus Christ.

3. What is the Expectation of Our Constituency?

By constituency I mean everyone involved in our organization: donors, staff, mission churches. In short, anyone who identifies with our agency. The various elements of the constituency have their own thoughts about what we are doing. Cooperation will be affected very differently by whether they believe we are planting or building up churches that are worshipping in the truth revealed in the Scriptures, or more precisely, we are planting or building up churches that are worshipping in the truth revealed in the Scriptures according to a proscribed pattern. Obviously, the second option puts limits on the viability of any type of cooperation, but we must be realistic about the expectations of our constituencies. At a minimum, any attempt at cooperation will involve educating our constituency as to what we are trying to accomplish.

4. What is Our Own Capacity for Ambiguity and/or Diversity?

There are fuzzy edges around some of the externals. Even within the evangelical camp we have deep differences over church government, order and doctrine. We have all adopted a particular practice that determines how we celebrate the two clear expressions of our faith that the Lord left for us: the rite of initiation (baptism) and the rite of fellowship (communion). But when we talk about ambiguity or diversity, we need to understand that we are not speaking about our preferences. I don't see how our preferences have much to do with the sovereign work of the Holy Spirit. We are too easily hung up on the externals because it is by them that we make judgments about others.

Our Lord, in response to a question of what is the greatest commandment provides us with a pattern to consider. In Matthew 22:36-40 Jesus declares the two great commandments on which hang all the others. If we see a person whose life is marked by adherence to these two commandments, can we not cooperate with them, even if their ecclesiology is different?

5. What Do We Believe about Unity in Diversity?

Can we recognize true faith in Christ as Savior and Lord even if it is not expressed as we express it? Is it not a sign of maturity to be able to recognize a sister or a brother even if they express their devotion to our Lord in a manner different from ours? And, in practice, we often do this, acknowledging a person from another tradition as a believer.

6. What Are the Limits of Truth/Cooperation?

There are limits, but only as our Lord gave them. We are like the disciples, who wanted to limit the work to their own circle. We see the Lord's limits outlined in Mark 9:38-41 and Luke 9:49-51. He admonished His disciples not to hinder those ministering in his name. On the other hand, as we see in Matthew 12:30 and Luke 11:23, not every religious expression is on the side of our Lord. The key issue is, Are these people doing acts of the Living God in the Name of Jesus?

We cannot endorse wholeheartedly any group which claims to be Christian simply because they claim it. Nor can we agree that because some in a group or denomination are truly converted, all persons, especially all clergy in that denomination, are truly converted. We know better than that, even in our evangelical denominations. Teaching discernment, therefore, must always be part of the discipling process, so that our constituency is able to rightly discern the spirits, as John urged his hearers to do (1 John 4:1-3).

Working Together Doxologically in the New Millennium

Chapter 8

Calling an Army of Artists

Frank Fortunato

The arts are one of the mighty weapons that God uses to build the kingdom. As Ronald B. Allen said in *Discipleship Journal*:

> Some look upon the arts as merely ornamental, like the frosting on the cake or the decoration on a truly useful object....The arts may debauch or ennoble...soothe the savage breast or make one into a savage beast. A poem may describe the beauty of a flower or impel a revolution....The arts are part of God's gifts to us. He gives art for our enjoyment, for instruction, and for worship.

God is calling artists to make the greatest possible impact for the Kingdom.

The Call to Classical Artists

Patrick Kavanaugh heads the Christian Performing Artists' Fellowship, a nondenominational ministry of classically trained musicians and dancers headquartered in Fairfax, Virginia, near Washington D.C. Patrick sees his artists as missionaries who proclaim the gospel through their performances. The world of professional music is a spiritually needy place, a virtually unreached mission field. This is a huge people group, many of whom have never heard the gospel presented in a credible way. Our job is to bring them the love of the Lord. But Kavanaugh would be the first to say "you can't just preach and run."

Virtuosos like Christopher Parkening, perhaps the greatest living guitar virtuoso alive today, see their playing as a means of glorifying God. Their concerts provide many kinds of opportunities to share the Gospel. Classical artists in dance, ballet, orchestras and other institutions like HCJB radio have, likewise, effectively used their talents to serve Christ.

For many classical musicians, God is calling them beyond their own culture to places abroad where Christ is not known. As a professional violinist and orchestra conductor, Gilberto Orellana became aware of the great spiritual need in Morocco. He was able to secure an invitation from the National Conservatory of Music to teach violin and study Arab music. Being a witness in sensitive parts of the world is not for the spiritually fainthearted, however. After seeing fourteen Moroccans put their faith in Christ, Gilberto was arrested, spent time in prison, was freed, then rearrested, and finally expelled from the country. He is now praying for many professional musicians to take his place and follow his example.

The Call to Contemporary Artists

Scott Wesley Brown is a unique contemporary artist and song writer, whose concerts combine great music with strong calls to commitment, and enlistment in God's overseas army of musicians. Scott then sets the example with regular trips to Asia and Africa, to the villages and cities, concert halls and open air sites.

Many mission organizations have used contemporary music very effectively as part of evangelism efforts around the world. These include groups like YWAM with its Musicians for Missions program, Campus Crusade for Christ, Youth For Christ, OM, International Teams, Celebrant Singers, Continental Singers and a whole host of others. Many of these efforts are like mini "arts festivals" as dance, mime, and drama combine with music to attract people to Christ.

One of the most powerful attractions to Christ are contemporary musicians who use worship as a powerful tool for spiritual warfare in hostile situations. Steve Fry, a gifted songwriter and missions statesman shares about the time his musical, "We are Called," was performed in France. In attendance were some militant Muslims. Two Muslim women were deeply moved by the praise, and during the finale of the program one of them had a vision of the Lord Jesus compelling her to follow Him. She was soundly converted, and upon returning to Algeria became very active in spreading the gospel throughout the nation.

The Call to Cross-Cultural Artists

In many parts of the world artists and musicians are discovering the privilege of using their gifts as cross-cultural artists/missionaries.

The Southern Baptists have over 100 "music missionaries" as part of their huge missions force, and have built scores of recording studios around the world. International Teams also has established studios in various countries. Greater Europe Mission and other groups have deployed resident teams of artists in cross-cultural outreach and church planting for many years.

Chris Hale, son of the famous missionary doctor and author Tom Hale, grew up in Nepal and learned to speak Hindi fluently. After studies in music composition at one of the world's most prestigious music conservatories, he went back to the subcontinent and learned the sitar. Chris and his team do rock concerts with lively mime and drama in India's cities, and do sitar and tabla concerts with Indian classical devotional music in the villages. Hale recently teamed up with an OM evangelist in North India to do a concert of classical devotional music interspersed with readings from the Bible. The audience, which comprised a group of high caste Hindus, had been invited to the event by missionaries who had befriended these people over several years. Following the three-hour event, the missionaries continued to meet with their friends to further explain the truths presented in the concert. They report that this resulted in the planting of two churches, and it all began with an MK doing his "cross-cultural" concert. When not doing rock concerts or classical Hindi concerts, Chris and his team disciple students at a coffee bar near Lucknow. Recently the band won major awards at secular music competitions.

But perhaps the greatest challenge today is to see an army of daring musicians and artists willing to leave their own culture to join church planting teams in frontier missions areas. Reaching unreached people groups does not usually happen with a two-week tour to an area, so great commitment is required. It takes intense discipline to learn another language, particularly for North Americans. Understanding the deeper layers of a culture in order to grasp the mindset of a people doesn't happen with one or two summer or short-term outreaches.

On the other hand, just think how thrilling and challenging it would be to be part of a church planting team, to see congregations of believers emerge, and then to encourage the artists and musicians to develop their own gifts for the Lord. What a wonderful contribution to a people group just to get a small recording studio established so that local worship songs could be recorded and distributed throughout an area. Frontiers mission did that among the Sundanese people and saw phenomenal results.

It has been my own joy to help set up recording studios at mission bases in Tajikistan and Uzbekistan. Two more are underway in Kazakhstan and in the Gulf region of the Middle East. These studios will enable indigenous musicians who cannot go to a commercial studio to record their worship songs, and to disseminate worship tapes to scattered groups of believers in these lands.

The ethnomusicologist missionaries of SIL and several other groups are the truly cutting edge musicians of our time as they pay the price to obtain the training needed, not only to become quality musicians, but to analyze foreign music systems and develop a music notation system. Think of the treasure that these music servants are giving to the present generation of believers as they help them get their songs written and recorded. And think of the ongoing heritage they leave behind as local musicians pass on to future generations how to notate these songs and maximize the dissemination of worship materials throughout a people group.

I am mid-way through my own graduate program in ethnomusicology, and this past summer I was quite awed that our class used the latest computer tools, technology and musicology principles to analyze the music of a tribal group from the Solomon Islands. As a result of our work we were able to generate some of the first Christian songs in that cultural music system. Our teacher sent the songs to the small group of believers there for feedback. These may be part of the first worship songs available for that tribal group.

Whether classical, contemporary, or cross-cultural, let us challenge a generation of Christian musicians and artists to take up the task, and to join the army of artists and musicians laying down their lives so that "the earth may be filled with the knowledge of the glory of the Lord as the waters cover the sea."

Chapter 9

Contextualized Worship and Arts in World Evangelization

Byron Spradlin

The world these days is changing at light speed velocity—and we mission and ministry leaders stand responsible, especially given this rapid rate of change, to give special attention to the task of working together with God and with each other to shape ministry that will bear Kingdom fruit in this rapidly shifting new millennium.

In the midst of giving this special attention, I find it a special privilege to suggest two very important issues related to world evangelization. First, contrary to much thinking within the established church and missions leadership, God is affirming contextualized worship as He releases his worshiping people and communities around the world. Therefore, the evidence suggests that we need to pursue even more aggressively contextualized worship as one of the high priority goals on all our mission fields. And second, God is raising up a new breed of missionary specialists, worship and arts ministry specialists, to help intentionally accelerate contextualized worship and evangelism in his efforts to penetrate every tongue, tribe and people with his Gospel. Again, the evidence suggests as another high priority goal on our mission fields that we need to even more aggressively weave this new breed of mission and ministry specialists into the fabric of our mission strategies.

Many *Are* Noticing What God is Doing

Many readers might already be noticing how God is making more and more of us aware of the importance of contextualized worship and arts ministry specialists in world evangelization. But in my role, directing a mission board specifically for creative Kingdom servants pursing Kingdom ministry through artistic methods, I'm seeing these realities every week. Let me give you an example.

In July of 1999—while giving a challenge to over 400 Christians-in-the-arts concerning the task of world evangelization—I looked to the Lord to provoke these Christian artists towards personal involvement in world missions with the following comments:

> "Sometimes" says Dallas Willard, an evangelical believer and USC philosophy professor, "important things can be presented in literature and art that cannot be effectively presented in any other way."[1] The arts are absolutely important to God and Christian ministry! And when our time together is said and done, that is what God wants you to know, feel, and experience.

Then I told these arts ministry specialists:

> You are not strange—you are beautiful.
> You are not crazy—you are passionate.
> You are not eccentric—you are unique.
> You are not bizarre—you are imaginative.
> You are not rebellious—you are innovative.
> God has hard-wired you that way, *and* He likes it—He likes you. Look around. You are *not* alone. There's a whole room full of us.

And at that, they burst out in a resounding cheer. Why do you think they did that? And an even more basic question: why were 250 Christians in dance, 75 Christians in music, 50 Christians in theatre and drama, and 25 others in visual arts, puppets, and a few other artistic expressions—and most of them with some clear sense of God's tugging them towards ministry—why were all those folks together there to cheer at my comments in the first place?

It was because God's Spirit is already at work shaping the ministry strategies for this coming new Millennium . . . theologically, strategically, and tactically towards the Father's intentions to win new generations of post-moderns from every tongue, tribe, and nation to become his worshipers.

For this reason alone, though there are many more, I want to suggest several strategic reconceptualizations that we've already been experiencing in the task of world evangelization. Specifically I urge that all of us in Christian ministry leadership:

1. Reconceptualize the Great Commission in terms of "winning worshipers" from every tongue, tribe, and nation (since worship, in its most complete sense, is what we will engage in fully when we move into our glorified everlasting state once we're done with our

earth-bound assignments on his behalf).

2. More energetically, embrace the new breed of missionary and ministry specialists God is raising up, Kingdom servants specifically suited to reaching into the post-modern cultures of the world—those servants I have labeled worship and arts ministry specialists.

3. Embrace a more biblical working definition of artistic expression, a definition that will release us to more proactively recruit and deploy these worship and arts ministry specialists in the development of ministry plans, budgets, and projects; and do it because we realize God has specially equipped them—like He did King David—to sling his Word straight to the hearts of the myriad of diverse and unique cultures of the world.

A Good Question and a Helpful Scripture Passage

Why did those 400 Christians-in-the-arts cheer when affirmed for the way God Himself had sculpted them? We find part of the answer in Scripture. Take a look at Exodus 35:30 through 36:1 for example:

> Then Moses said to the Israelites, "See, the LORD has chosen Bezalel son of Uri, the son of Hur, of the tribe of Judah (31) and he has filled him with the Spirit of God, with skill, ability and knowledge in all kinds of crafts (32) to make artistic designs for work in gold, silver and bronze, (33) to cut and set stones, to work in wood and to engage in all kinds of artistic craftsmanship. (34) And he has given both him and Oholiab son of Ahisamach, of the tribe of Dan, the ability to teach others (35). He has filled them with skill to do all kinds of work as craftsmen, designers, embroiders in blue, purple and scarlet yarn and fine linen, and weavers all of them master craftsmen and designers (Ex 36:1). So Bezalel, Oholiab, and every skilled person to whom the LORD has given skill and ability to know how to carry out all the work of constructing the sanctuary are to do the work just as the LORD has commanded" (NIV).

When you are confronted by a passage like this, you have to ask, Why would God go to all this artistic trouble? Why didn't He just tell this people, "Listen you all: Just get it. I'm God!"

The answer is simple: many important things about God, about participation in his worship, about proclaiming his salvation, about shaping his believers as a contextualized worshiping community, are just too big for words alone. They almost always can be presented, expressed, and embraced more fully through the artistic use of metaphors, symbols, and media. In fact, God Himself went way beyond words to reveal Himself, his truth and his salvation offer to us, through the ultimate contextualized creative revealing of Himself—the Incarnate Christ.

As we face the challenge of reaching the postmodern cultures of today's world, I trust you can clearly see that contextualized worship and artistic ministry strategies are central to accomplishing the biblical mandates of world evangelization before us. I submit that we cannot present the fullness of the Lord, his love and his salvation to a culturally diverse world arena without them.

So many things related to God—his accessibility, his worship, his reality, his healing and help must be addressed artistically . . . because they cannot be presented effectively any other way.

God is stimulating contextual worship and arts ministry—and raising up artistic Christians who want to make a difference for God—all over the world.

It is interesting to see this being manifested throughout our mission community. It is readily apparent from my own schedule, shown below, over the last twelve years.

—The 1987 Lausanne-sponsored Singapore Younger Leaders gathering was dominated by international contemporary praise and worship expressions (what I like to call contextual praise and worship—worship that plucked the heart strings of the younger internationally-exposed mission leaders).

—To prepare for the Washington, D.C., Leadership 88 conference, the Lausanne Consultation asked me and a few others to design a "Baby Boomer" environment suitable for "younger leaders"—and that environment was manifested though the worship style, visual environment (especially the banners and lighting), and the music that made up so much of that event.

—At the Manila Lausanne II conference in 1989, Coreen Bakke was asked to put together a wide international array of contextualized worship expressions, which she did in marvelous fashion, and worship in a new way was itself profiled.

—At the 1995 and 1997 Global Consultations on World Evangelization there was a clear mandate that the activity of worship be a major emphasis (not simply a tag to the speaking presentations), and in the 1997 Consultation, "worship and the arts" was one of the 10 formal streams of the event.

—The entire thrust of the 1996 annual meetings of the American Society for Church Growth in Orlando, Florida, was "the Role of

Worship in Church Growth."

—At the 1997 meetings of the same association, in his presentation on urban ministries in a postmodern world, Tom Wolfe, head of the Mission Department at Golden Gate Seminary in the San Francisco Bay Area, made the pointed observation, "If we don't sing the Gospel to those in need of it in this new millennium, we will not communicate it to them at all."

—The student mobilization person for the Southern Baptist's International Mission Board, Mike Lopez, has just called my organization asking us to help recruit committed Christian musicians from the Nashville area. They are experimenting with new ways to get their North American campus workers exposed to missions through short-term mission discovery trips.

—I, along with Marty McCall of the contemporary Christian music group "First Call," was invited in August of 1999, to Beirut, Lebanon where we helped do the first ever (as far as we could tell) worship and arts outreach ministry training conference in that part of the Arabic-speaking Middle East.

And much more is happening, a lot of it right in the midst of your own ministry agencies.

Another Example: Jews for Jesus

It is easy to understand that contextual worship and arts ministry strategy really are key—by looking at how the Lord has, over these last 27 years (1972–1999), reached into the resistant Jewish community with the Gospel and borne new fruit. I've volunteered in Jewish evangelism ministries as a board member of Jews for Jesus through all this period, and was the first musical coach for their music evangelism team in 1972-73. In 1972 the Jewish community said, "You cannot be for Jesus and be Jewish." But, a bunch of Jewish kids went out on the streets of San Francisco with Jewish-looking signs, while singing, "For God so loved the world that He gave his only begotten Son . . . ." The reality that Jews could believe in Jesus became very evident. How? By God piercing the hearts of numerous Jewish people with the truth of the Gospel, largely through the contextualized artistic expression and worship of these young Jewish believers in Jesus.

The Major Points

For the sake of clarity, let me repeat my major points: I am suggesting that: (1) Contextual worship and artistic expression are absolutely important in life and Christian ministry—given the way God is shaping ministry for the new millennium; and (2) therefore we must aggressively pursue efforts to release into world evangelization the new breed of arts ministry specialists that God is currently raising up.

To support these suggestions I want to do four things:

1. Give some biblical definitions related to the area of artistic expression;

2. Provide a snapshot definition of worship;

3. Answer, at least briefly, why arts ministry specialists are so needed in world evangelization;

4. Offer a few possibilities of how to get in step with what God is doing to deploy contextual worship and arts ministry specialists for his mission of world evangelization.

Biblical Definitions Related to the Area of Artistic Expression

1. *What are the arts, really?* Biblically speaking, I submit that the arts are the imaginative arrangement of metaphors, symbols, and human signal systems. And in submitting that definition, let me define human signal systems using Dr. Don Smith's good list, to include at least the following: (1) verbal expression; (2) writing; (3) numbers; (4) pictures; (5) things [objects and artifacts]; (6) audio [sounds and silence]; (7) movement [motions, expressions, posture]; (8) optics [light, color]; (9) touch; (10) space; (11) time; and (12) smell.[2]

2. *Who are artists, from the Bible's perspective?* The terms in the Bible that best express what we today consider to be "artists" are craftsmen and artisans. In the Old Testament alone I've found nineteen artistic CRAFTS mentioned,[3] four words (really word-areas) that label specialist creative types whom we today call "artists,"[4] two words (verbs) that describe specialized artistic activity,[5] and four words (adjectives) that describe creative types as specialized.[6]

To the Hebrew mind of 1500 BC, all of these terms seem to have conveyed the basic idea that the people we call "artists" today are people especially endowed by God with wisdom in creative things;

they are the creative- and imagination-specialists.

Please note, I'm not saying what is often assumed, that there are only a few who are truly creative, and that others are not creative at all. What I am saying is that though we are all creative . . . by virtue of being made in God's image . . . there are a smaller number of us whom God has specially gifted in this area, i.e., given unusually large and specialized capacities to imagine and then skillfully rearrange our various human metaphors, symbols, and signal systems.

3. *What is the purpose of the arts?* God has endowed some people with a high degree of creative capacity to: (1) declare his glory, and reveal his truth, beauty, and, when appropriate, his reconciliation in Jesus; (2) creatively express the realities of human existence, whether depicting the base or the beautiful, religious or general (a process which I believe always brings focus back to God Himself); and (3) help us . . . beyond words . . . express in the realm of the natural the realities of God's supernatural person and Kingdom.

A Snapshot Definition of Worship

Worship is a central issue in God's agenda for world evangelization. In a nutshell, I'm convinced that worship is first, repeated real and substantial encounter with God. Think of the many pictures in the Scriptures of the supernatural God allowing real and personal "encounter" with humans (For example: Adam and Eve, Enoch, Abram, Isaac, Jacob, Moses, Joshua, each of the Judges, Samuel, David, any of the prophets, the disciples of Jesus, and the scores of people running into Jesus and the Apostle Paul. In addition, think of the scores of not-so-famous ordinary people encountering God through history) . . . all of whose lives were changed through real transactional "encounter" with the true and living God.

We see throughout Scripture that worship consists of the various lifestyle responses in obeisance and of obedience that come out of encounter with God (for example: Joshua 5:13ff; Isaiah 6:4-8; Romans 12:1; Rev. 22: 3).

With regard to our agenda in missions, if we in fact are successful in being vessels through whom the Lord works to effectively penetrate a culture or sub-culture with his Gospel, then one of the clear objectives is that the newly established Christian community will begin to grow in worshiping God and proclaiming its faith in their own heart-languages and cultural styles. These heart-languages and cultural styles are almost always facilitated by indigenous worship and artistic specialists. That is, though in every culture there are both generalists and specialists involved in human expression (all people and all human societies express themselves through their indigenous metaphors, symbols, and signal systems), it's the 'human expression specialists' (what I'm terming the arts ministry specialists) who lead the ministry team into culturally meaningful contact with the target community. It is they who facilitate the believing community in its corporate expressions of worship (whether ceremonies, liturgy, pageants, visual or movement expression, architecture, music, story telling, or other dynamics of gathered expression).

Given these considerations, the strategic link should be readily apparent between, on the one hand the development and deployment of spiritually mature arts ministry specialists, and on the other hand the winning of worshipers (cf. worshipers as understood in John 4:23, Romans 12:1, Rev. 22:3). The unifying goal then is the releasing of these worshipers into worshiping God and declaring His salvation to their own people in their own heart expressions and cultural styles.

Why Arts Ministry Specialists are Needed in the Cause of World Evangelization

Without artistic expression . . . and without those specialists God has endowed to lead us all into participating in culturally relevant expression ourselves . . . we humans could not, in our natural world and with our limited minds alone, grasp in a full enough way, the divine, the supernatural, the mysterious realities of life, both seen and unseen. How can we adequately express love without artistic expression? How can we fully express grief without it? . . . rejoicing without it? . . . worship without it? In fact, the human capacity for creativity and imagination is, for me, one of four key proofs revealing that we are made in God's image.

Along with humans being spiritual, cognitive, and moral, we are imaginative. Animals have instinct, but people have imagination in a highly developed way. And that imagination reflects in a small way our Creator Himself. No wonder, as Paul reaches the limitations of language in describing the scope of Christ's love for us—its width and length and height and depth—he leans into the poetic to more fully express to us that this love ". . . surpasses knowledge . . ." as he struggles to articulate his prayer for us to ". . . be filled to the measure of all the fullness of God" (Eph. 3:18-19, NIV).

And therefore, when it comes to the jewel of human activity, the activity of worship, more than just "propositions of fact" are required. Worship must make sense to us in the context of our culture if it is to have meaning at all, and it requires symbols and metaphors and rituals that help us connect with the invisible realities of God Himself. It moves us to press toward the edges of our human capacities to express. Whether private or public, it demands that we take the realities of God and his truths beyond the languages of the head into the languages of the heart. And that realm, for lack of better terms, is the realm of artistic expression.

Getting in Step with What God is Doing

To follow on from here then, let me offer a few possibilities of what can be done to cooperate with what God is already doing to deploy contextual worship and arts ministry specialists for his mission of world evangelization.

1. Start or strengthen your Great Commission efforts to draw worship and arts ministry specialists into your strategy and implementation staff and teams. Obviously, without drawing into our assignments mature arts ministry specialists, we will be in no better position than if we did not use their resources at all. But there are many of these creative Kingdom servants who are feeling God's tug on their life, and are ready to respond to your mentorship and guidance.[11] Identify them, involve them, deploy them.

2. Redefine artistic expression in you own mind and heart. Move away from a Western European, post-1500s secular humanistic definition of the ARTS, an elitist view that flies in the face of God's design and purposes for the marvels of the human capacity to creativity, beauty, and imagination. Move toward a more biblical view of artistic expression that affirms the marvel of how God has crowned us with glory and honor, a little less than Himself, says Psalm 8, designing us as his creative image bearers.

3. Redefine worship as encounter and engagement with God that produces responsive contextualized expression in corporate worship and in lifestyle worship.

4. Recognize the need to disciple and deploy creative Kingdom servants and arts ministry specialists into the heart of your mission

strategy, plans, budgets and teams deployed.

5. Recommit to identifying national believers who manifest God-given aptitudes in creative capacity, release them for ministry leadership, and then follow their lead with regard to what contextual expressions you employ.

6. Prayerfully look afresh at your own ministry context—this time scanning for the people and the contextualized worship and arts strategies God has already begun to implement through your own people and projects. You'll most likely discover that the Lord is already at work within your own sphere of influence.

7. Identify fruitful arts ministry specialists you know, those with solid ministry track records and solid artistic abilities. Encourage them to gain theological and biblical depth, with a view to seeing them move into your mission. And along the way, help them get the biblical and theological grounding that will give them the credibility your system needs to draw these specialists to the center of your ministry strategies and teams.

The Lord is moving. Let us prayerfully and vigilantly stay alert to what He is doing.

A Few Miscellaneous Thoughts

On the "wacky-ness" of artists. In the midst of this discussion over the inclusion of artistic types in world evangelization, I'm well aware of the liabilities that some artistic types bring. For example, since many of them have been trained in the hallowed halls of secular humanistic thought, where the creative process (art) and not the Creator (the greatest artist) is worshiped, they are sometimes a challenge. While we can never tolerate the idolatry of worshiping the creative process rather than the Creator, God is changing many of these people. And He is bringing many of them to you with the desire to be mentored and discipled by you.

On whether or not artists are special. Christians-out-of-the-arts are *not* special; but they *are* specialized, and by God I might add.

They are also feeling God's call into his Kingdom mission, and many are ready now to go. Yet, it seems, there are still too few mission agencies who take them seriously. They are *not* worldly. But they *are* quite in touch with the world systems around them—especially the ways their "market place world" expresses itself.

If we will let them, they will lead us under the guidance of his

Spirit and his Word—to express the Gospel and to worship the Lord in the heart-languages and cultural styles of the world's peoples.

They are God-enabled to play specialized roles in the contextualized declarations of God's glory, and the contextualized proclamations of salvation in Jesus. They know how to affirm that which is beautiful and unique in each people's culture, and in the work of each culture's indigenous arts specialists.

On why this is important. As I've said, it's not because these creative Kingdom servants themselves are special. It's because they are specially endowed as Kingdom agents to whom God has given the privilege and the responsibility to help lead the church in contextualized praise and declaration of God's salvation. They are also able to comment creatively on the beauties and realities of God's creation—its troubles, tragedies, and triumphs—which may, if done well, even communicate great respect for the host culture to its unchurched and unbelieving people.

Conclusion

Remember those 400 Christians-out-of-the-arts I told you about? At the end of my talk I challenged them this way: so what? If God's glory and salvation cannot be adequately expressed without artistic expression, and if He has hard-wired you as his worship and arts ministry specialists, then you need to passionately pursue Him—now! Surrender more fully to Him. Fall more deeply in love with Him. No matter what the cost. No matter what the criticism. No matter what your frailties are. He will come and save you. He will come and mold you. He will come and heal you. He will come and hear you, and help you, and guide you, and guard you . . . in Jesus. Then He'll be flinging you all over the world joining bands of his choicest servants helping lead his peoples into culturally relevant worship and proclamation of his salvation and community impact.

Then I said: "If you're serious about laying your artistic creativity on his altar . . . as an expression of that seriousness . . . stand to your feet now, telling Him by taking this stand, 'Take me, I'm yours.'"

And they all stood to their feet.

What does that mean for us as mission and ministry leaders today?

Read the signs of the times. God is doing something special again. He's moving among new types of people to reach new kinds of people, cultures, and subcultures. Pause, look around and pray. Take note of what God is doing, and who He's raising up to join with you and other mission and ministry specialists to undertake the glorious task of world evangelization. Then notice how the Lord is shaping your assignments to include this new army of specialized servants. As you do, you will see God's hand of blessing on you, even as He moves forward in his plans to win worshipers from every people, tongue, and tribe, by adding into his missionary forces a new breed of specialists, worship and arts ministry specialists all for his glory and praise now, and into the new millennium, and on into eternity. Remember the exhortation of Psalm 115: 17-18 (NIV):

It is not the dead who praise the Lord,
those who go down to silence;
it is we who extol the Lord, both now and forevermore.
(So) praise the Lord!

Endnotes

1. Dallas Willard, *Divine Conspiracy* (New York: HarperCollins, 1998), 79.

2. Donald K. Smith, *Creating Understanding: A Handbook for Christian Communication Across Cultural Landscapes* (Grand Rapids, MI: Zondervan Publishing House, 1992), 146.

3. The nineteen artistic crafts listed are: (1) brickmaking; (2) carpentering (woodworking); (3) carving (engraving); (4) ceramics; (5) dyeing and cleansing; (6) embroidering (needlework); (7) glass-making; (8) grinding; (9) mason work; (10) metalworking (mining); (11) oil-making; (12) painting; (13) paper-making; (14) perfume-making; (15) plastering; (16) spinning and weaving; (17) tanning; (18) tentmaking; and (19) wine making. James A. Patch, *International Standard Bible Encyclopedia*, Electronic Database, copyright © 1996 by Biblesoft.

4. The four words (word areas) that label specialist types—those we today label as "artists" are: (1) *shiyr* (sheer) 7891 or (the original form) *shuwr* singer, musician; (2) *machashabah* 4284, master craftsman; (3) *chashab* 2803, craftsman; and (4) *chakam* 2450, skilled person. James A. Patch, *International Standard Bible Encyclopedia*, Electronic Database, copyright © 1996 by Biblesoft.

5. The two words (verbs) that describe specialized artistic activity are: *zamiyr* 2158 or *zamir*, and *zemirah* from *zamar* 2167—to touch the strings or parts of a musical instrument, i.e., playing upon it; to make music accompanied by the voice; hence to celebrate in song and music. James A. Patch, *International Standard Bible Encyclopedia*, Electronic Database, copyright © 1996 by Biblesoft.

6. The four words (adjectives) that describe creative types as specialized: (1) *yatab* 3190, skillfully; (2) *da'ath* 1847, knowledge; (3) *tabuwn* 8394, understanding in; and (4) *chokmah* 2451, wisdom in. James A. Patch, *International Standard Bible Encyclopedia*, Electronic Database, copyright © 1996 by Biblesoft.

Chapter 10

What's in the Middle? The Implications of Doxology for Missions in the Twenty-first Century

Dave Hall

In the movie hit, "Forrest Gump," Forrest recalls how his mother always told him that, "Life is like a box of chocolates...you never know what you're gonna get." I would suggest to you that looking over the landscape of theological paradigms in evangelical missions is similar to looking at a box of chocolates. What's on the outside looks great, but with each new delicious-looking choice we are caught musing to ourselves, "What's in the middle?"

This is the question that I'd like to address, "What's in the middle of our theological discussions of why the church exists?" Much debate is taking place today over the ultimate purpose of the church. For years now, I have been involved in itinerant ministry that has taken me into hundreds of churches both inside and outside North America. Rarely have I visited a church where something like the following is not expressed publicly by the leadership: "The reason we exist as a church is to see the lost won to Christ." Often it is put this way: "The primary purpose of the church is the fulfillment of the Great Commission" or "The reason God saved us is to save the lost."

It is probably safe to say that many, if not most of us, grew up under preaching that espoused this understanding of our purpose, both as individuals and as a corporate body of believers. The aim of this paper is to revisit this paradigm in light of biblical teaching and ask ourselves afresh, "What is the ultimate purpose of the church?" or as Forrest Gump might ask, "What's in the middle?"

In the wake of what one might call a "worship awakening" in the Global Church in recent years, a growing number of leaders have been sounding a call to a new paradigm of ministry and purpose in the church and missions. John Piper has said it as succinctly and powerfully as anyone when he writes, "The primary purpose of the church is not the fulfillment of the Great Commission. Worship is. ...Missions exists because worship doesn't."[1] William Taylor, in an address given at the International Workshop for Pastoral Care and Attrition in London, England, referred to worship as, "the mother of all paradigms."

Are these assertions true? Do they carry biblical weight? Before we answer these questions, it is important, not only for the purposes of this paper, but also for our own spiritual health and well being, that we understand clearly what we mean when we use the word "worship."

Many evangelical Christians today espouse a very truncated understanding of biblical worship. When asked to define the word, they respond by saying, "It's singing," or "It's praising God." Worship, from a biblical perspective, is far more than singing or praising God in the assembly of the saints (as right and wonderful as that is).

For years now, I have been a student of the word "worship" and have begun to collect definitions of the word. One of the best I have found was penned by Dr. Bruce Leafblad. I have expanded it slightly and include it here in hopes that it will provide a framework for our understanding: "Worship is both a lifestyle and an event in which believers, by grace, center their mind's attention and their heart's affection on the Lord, humbly glorifying God in response to his greatness, his mighty acts, and his Word."

From an article written for *Missions Frontiers*, Special Issue, 1998, I have reproduced a diagram presented at an ACMC seminar entitled, "A Paradigm Shift in the Church" (See page 176).

The article states: "The idea of putting missions in the middle seems, at first, a very biblical view (especially for a room full of zealous missionaries). The Scriptures are replete with references to God's heart and passion to reach every tribe and tongue with his redeeming love. However, upon further reflection and study the temporal nature of this paradigm becomes apparent. Missions is for the here and now, worship is forever."[2]

John Piper eloquently extols the priority of worship. He writes, "Worship is ultimate, not missions, because God is ultimate, not man. When this age is over, and the millions of the redeemed fall

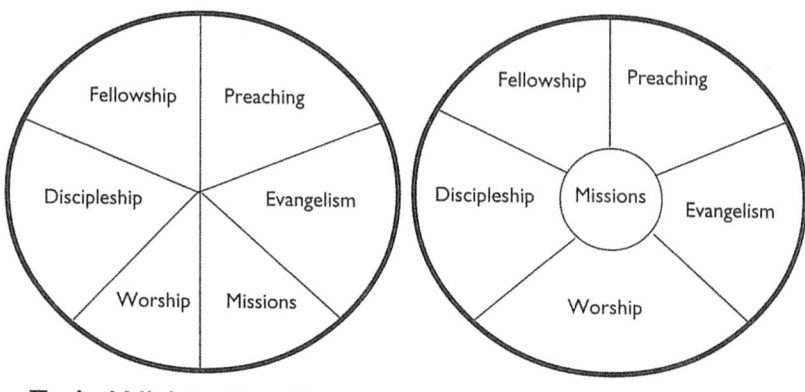

Typical Ministry Paradigm   **Biblical Ministry Paradigm**

on their faces before the throne of God, missions will be no more. It is a temporary necessity. But worship abides forever. . . . If the pursuit of God's glory is not ordered above the pursuit of man's good in the affections of the heart and the priorities of the church, man will not be well served and God will not be duly honored. I am not pleading for a diminishing of missions, but for a magnifying of God."[3]

This paradigm of the centrality of worship is expressed in Exodus, where again and again Moses goes to Pharaoh and demands, "Let my people go." However, the sentence doesn't end there. Eight times Moses tells Pharaoh why God is calling his people out of their bondage: "Let my people go, so that they may *worship* me." (emphasis mine).[4] The purpose of our redemption is worship.

Throughout the gospels there is a divine synergy between the Great Commission and the Great Commandment. However, when a religious leader came to Jesus and asked in effect, "What is God's top priority? What's 'numero uno'? What's the most important thing we can do with our lives?" Jesus did not say, "Go into all the world and preach the gospel." Rather, Jesus repeated God's command given originally through Moses, "Love the Lord your God with all your heart and with all your soul and with all your mind and with all your strength" (Mark 12:28-31).

The primary purpose for our existence is to worship God by loving Him with all our heart, soul, mind and strength! Every occurrence of the Great Commandment, whether spoken by Moses or Jesus, emphasizes loving God with the heart first (before "soul," "mind," or "strength"). The primary instrument for the expression of our love for God is the heart and the primary means of this expression is worship (cf. Ps. 95:1-8).

When our Presbyterian brethren gathered to write the Westminster Catechism they asked, "What is the chief end of man?" Their answer, grounded in the truths of scripture, was simply, "The chief end of man is to glorify God and enjoy Him forever."

Consider the following scenario. We have five children. Let's say that each morning we gathered our children just after breakfast and said something like the following: "Now Ben, Caleb, Micah, Elisabeth and Hannah, let me remind you that the reason Mommy and Daddy had you was so you can share the gospel with your friends and see them come to know Jesus. So go, have a great day and don't forget to tell everyone you know about the Lord."

It seems to me that we would be setting our children up to incur some significant psychological trauma in later years. Yet, the theology that drives such a preposterous scenario is standard fare in many evangelical pulpits. I am not saying that I believe that God loves us as his children more than he loves the lost. I am saying that I believe the primary passion in the heart of God is for his children, and as his children He calls us first of all to be, then to do. God did not make us human doings, he made us human beings. He is concerned first with our relationship (our "being"), and secondarily with our task (our "doing").

In light of the above, we might be closer to a truly biblical paradigm for ministry if we view it like the diagram below.

In my assertion that worship is central, I in no way desire to imply that missions is, therefore, peripheral. On the contrary, it is the heart filled with a passion for God that will be most attuned to God's heart for the nations.

Dr. Henry Blackaby has described the tremendous movement of God he is seeing among North America's young people.

Toward a Truly Biblical Ministry Paradigm

He sees it as a "time of God's favor among college and high school students," in which students are initiating movements to take the Gospel to the farthest corners of the earth. What he could have gone on to say is why these young people are so fired up about missions. It's because they are so fired up about God! It's their passion for God, the worship of his glory, that burns like a fire within them. This is what is thrusting them out to the nations—to see his glory proclaimed and his name exalted among every tribe and tongue.

What is this good news that we are proclaiming to the nations if it is not a growing, vital, passionate love for God expressed through worship? And the worship of which we speak is not merely a once-a-week corporate event; it is a daily lifestyle seeking to glorify God in every thought, every attitude, every response, and every action.

We are seeing a new Christian life paradigm emerging with worship at its heart. As an outgrowth of this paradigm of the centrality of worship, I would submit the following nine theses. All of these have been developed and/or influenced significantly by the executive committee of the AD2000 Worship and Arts Network.

1. We believe that worship is both a life to be lived, and an event in which to participate. It is "the submission of all our nature to God. It is the quickening of conscience by his holiness; the nourishment of mind with his truth; the purifying of imagination by his beauty; the opening of the heart to his love; the surrender of will to his purpose—and all this gathered up in adoration..." (Archbishop Wm. Temple, *Readings in St. John's Gospel*, p. 68). In and through worship, believers, by grace, center their lives (heart, soul, mind, and strength) on the Lord, humbly glorifying God in response to his attributes, his acts, and his Word.

2. We believe worship to be theologically, practically and strategically central to our lives, to evangelism, and to church planting.

3. We believe in order to more fully facilitate corporate worship in spirit and truth in the heart language of any given people, that appropriate elements of a people's rich heritage of the arts, music, dance, etc, must be tapped.

4. We believe that every church planting team should have a worship-arts leader—someone who serves the team by facilitating the use of indigenous music and the arts for the purposes of developing culturally relevant forms of evangelism and worship.

5. We believe that the time is ripe for the development of a new

discipline of theological and missiological study that explores the worship of God among other cultures. The term we suggest is "ethnodoxology," which is the theological and anthropological study of why and how the God of the Bible is worshiped through the unique lifestyles and artistic expressions of all peoples.

6. We believe that unity and cooperation in the body of Christ are necessary to complete the task of winning worshipers for God, and seeing worshiping churches established among every people. These goals will best be accomplished in partnership with the local church. It is the church's responsibility before God to equip the saints for the work of ministry, and to foster and facilitate worship both as a life lived and as an event participated in at home and around the world.

7. We believe that a "kingdom mindset" is necessary to complete the task of world evangelization. We will actively seek, therefore, to partner with churches, mission agencies, Christian organizations, and individual believers.

8. We believe that our lives and ministries should be marked by excellence; doing our best for his glory (Col. 3:23,24; Ps. 33:3).

9. We believe that we must saturate all we do and are in prayer.

If Forrest Gump gave this presentation he might enlighten us, "Theological paradigms are like a box of chocolates, they may all look good on the outside, but it's what's in the middle that matters."

I would submit to you that worship is in the middle.

Endnotes

1. John Piper, *Let The Nations Be Glad* (Grand Rapids, Baker, 1993), 11-12.
2. Dave Hall, "Taking Worship to the Nations: Three Biblical Foundations for the Task," *Mission Frontiers*, Special Issue, 1998, 7.
3. John Piper, Ibid., 11-12.
4. Exodus 4:23, 7:16, 8:1, 8:20, 9:1, 9:13,10:3,10:7.

Working Together Strategically in the New Millennium

Chapter 11

Southern Baptists: Working Cooperatively to Reach the World

Avery T. Willis, Jr.

Southern Baptists are known for doing things their own way. Because we are both the largest denomination in the United States and the largest denominational missionary sending agency, we have felt that we could take on the world ourselves. We did not denigrate what others were doing, but felt self-sufficient.

However, God has done a great work among us. He has revealed that his mission is much larger than us and that if we are to have a part in it we need to join other Christians on mission with Him.[1] Corinthians 12:12-14 clearly says:

> The body is a unit, though it is made up of many parts; and though all its parts are many, they form one body. So it is with Christ. For we were all baptized by one Spirit into one body—whether Jews or Greeks, slave or free—and we were all given the one Spirit to drink. Now the body is not made up of one part but of many.

The Body of Christ was made to:
- Worship together
- Evangelize together
- Minister together
- Make disciples together
- Go on mission together with God and each other

In light of the Scripture's teaching the International Mission Board (IMB) adopted a vision statement in 1994 that says, "We will lead Southern Baptists to be on mission with God to bring all the peoples of the world to saving faith in Jesus Christ." The "leading of Southern Baptists" was recognition of our assignment, rather than an abrogation of leading other Christians to be on mission with God. We believed that if we did our primary assignment and were open to God's leadership He may choose to use us to help other Christians and mission groups in ways we had not previously anticipated.

The part of the mission statement that showed our shortcomings was the phrase "to be on mission with God." As we evaluated how many people groups did not yet have access to the gospel, we realized that we were not keeping up with God. He had given us so many opportunities in the closing years of the twentieth century that we had to admit there was no way that we could enter all the open doors and reach all the peoples of the world by ourselves.

God humbled the Senior Executive Team of the IMB: President, Jerry Rankin; Executive Vice President, Don Kammerdiener; and myself. In a prayer retreat we offered the IMB back to God to do with us whatever pleased Him so that we could be fully on mission with Him. In effect, after 153 years we gave it all back to Him and said, "Here is a blank slate. Tell us how we need to restructure ourselves and how we need to work together with others to be on mission with You." Our trustees supported us unanimously in taking unprecedented steps to get on mission with God. Dramatic changes have led us to focus on getting to the edges of lostness, targeting all people groups, and committing ourselves to begin and nurture church planting movements among all peoples of the world.

Beyond what God led us to do internally, He led us to realize that we could not do the job alone. As we segmented the world into all the people groups and population segments we realized that with almost 5,000 missionaries and 25,000 volunteers there was no way we could reach them all.

As early as 1989, the past president of the IMB had called together other "Great Commission Groups" for a consultation in Singapore on how to work together to reach all the peoples of the world. Thomas Wang, who was at that meeting later called for an organization that would mobilize Christians to work together to reach those peoples who had the least access to the gospel. Out of that call the AD2000 and Beyond Movement was born.

At the first meeting of the AD2000 and Beyond Movement that I attended, I was drafted to lead a group of representatives of several denominations who were participating. I was then asked to lead the Denominational Leaders Track.

At the Global Conference of World Evangelism held in Seoul, Korea in 1995, I was asked to give a report on what the Southern Baptist Denomination had done in addressing the world. In the speech I said among other things:

> Our Convention voted in 1976 to launch Bold Mission Thrust. Its overarching objective was to give every person on earth an opportunity to hear, understand, and respond to the Gospel by AD2000. Since then many other denominations and organizations have adopted a similar goal. Rather than share with you what has happened, let me share with you some lessons we have learned over the past twenty years.
>
> First, be careful that the goals you set are from God and not man. We set many goals and the churches we are working with grew almost 500 percent. God is good and He glorified Himself in this unprecedented growth. However, it was clear that at this rate the vision was not going to be reached.
>
> A second lesson we learned was that we cannot do it by ourselves. We cannot do what God intended his whole Body to do. God used these sobering realities to bring us to repentance for our pride. He caused us to admit that we need to work together with other Christians to accomplish this worldwide task.
>
> Today we Southern Baptists come to this Global Conference on World Evangelization to ask forgiveness for thinking for so many years that we could do it alone. We want to affirm our commitment to work together with you so we can fulfill our slogan, "A church for every people, and the Gospel for every person." To help us do that together I am offering each denomination and mission organization our research data on 10,500 people groups by countries free.
>
> A third lesson that we learned was that business as usual will not get the job done. We repented for having stopped at the borders where only declared missionaries could go.
>
> —We made prayer our foremost strategy. No government can stop prayers from being sent in.
>
> —We began to focus on the unreached world that had no access to the gospel.
>
> —We developed innovative structures and platforms to enable us to enter the "closed doors."
>
> —We commit to partner with other Great Commission Christians to do together what we cannot do alone.
>
> A last lesson that I will mention is that God convinced us that it is not our mission. It is God's Mission. God is our Chief Operating Officer. He knows his strategy. Let's lay down our strategies and join Him in his mission to start a church for every people and get the Gospel to every person. Jesus' prophecy that the Gospel of the Kingdom must be preached to all peoples will have to happen in ONE generation. Why not this generation?

I was not prepared for the wave of appreciation and support to this confession. In country after country I meet people who were radically affected.

Since then we have made cooperative agreements with other agencies, such as Campus Crusade for Christ, Wycliffe/SIL, and so on. We have seconded our first missionaries to Wycliffe/SIL. We pay the bills and SIL supervises the missionary translators who work on a church planting team. More importantly we now work with a multitude of agencies, churches, denominations, and Christians on the field. In each case the church planting team decides the level of cooperation and then works accordingly. The diagram on page 187 and the accompanying explanation will clarify with whom we work at different levels.

Examples of IMB Relationships with Other Great Commission Groups at Each Level

IMB missionaries relate to non-IMB entities at different levels depending on their goals and needs. These relationships range from expedient to eternal in their significance. The deeper the level, the greater its significance.

Level one: Entry into people groups. These are introductory and entry level relationships. We have little screening control at this level. If the IMB missionary utilizes Southern Baptists at all it will probably be only Volunteers in Missions due to the brevity of the relationship. In order to make a suitable contact with his target population, he may ride on the coattails of a wide array of Great Commission partners. Here are a few who have worked as partners: UNHCR (United Nations High Commission on Refugees), Tunisian Ministry of Tourism, Kazakhstan Ministry of Education, Xinjiang Normal University, Altyn-Alma Foundation, Global Partners, Consortium for Global Education, Ethiopian Aid, Pacific Resources International, Management Technologies International, Asian Opportunities International, Nike Inc., the Atlanta Braves, and ELIC (English Language Institute in China). Even the Jesuits have helped introduce our IMBers to contacts among remote target peoples.

Level two: Prayer and ministry to felt needs. These are Christian relationships aimed at ministering to specific spiritual (e.g., prayer) or physical (e.g., disaster relief) needs. Some of those we've worked with at this level include: InterDev, North Africa Partnership, Amity Foundation, Global Partners, SIL (Summer Institute of Linguistics), Consortium for Global Education, Ethiopian Aid, Pacific Resources International, Management Technologies International, World Vision International, IAM (International Afghan Mission), TEAM (The Evangelical Alliance Mission), Asian Opportunities International, ELIC (English Language Institute in China), and World Vision International.

Level three: Evangelism and Scripture distribution. These are more significant relationships aimed at evangelism and thus require a shared purpose and gospel orientation. Some of those with whom we have worked at this level include: Campus Crusade for Christ, Navigators, Christar (formerly International Missions Incorporated), OM (Operation Mobilization), WEC (Worldwide Evangelization for Christ), YWAM (Youth With A Mission), EE III (Evangelism Explosion), Friends Missionary Prayer Band, Christian and Missionary Alliance, Church of the Nazarene, the United Bible Societies, SIM (formerly Sudan Interior Mission), TWR (TransWorld Radio), FEBC (Far East Broadcasting), DAWN Ministries (Disciple A Whole Nation), Arab World Ministries, Presbyterian Church in America, ACEB (Association Chretienne Espression Berbere), Frontiers, Partner International, et. al.

Level four: Planting New Testament churches. This level of relationship is very strategic. Many who would join us in doing evangelism might not have the same commitment to church planting. This is where we would seek a much more concentrated IMB input, as well as that from Baptist and other partners from all over the world who would share our understanding of New Testament church polity. Those with whom we've partnered at this level include: National Baptists around the world, NIMs (National Indian Ministries, Asian Partners (India), Frontiers (Muslim world), ACEB (Berber mission agency), and CBI (Conservative Baptists International).

Level five: Theological and ministerial training. At this level we are seeking to influence the ongoing shape of Christianity from the target population to the rest of the world. Theological integrity is of prime importance and we want to ensure that those assisting the target population be biblically sound and theologically reliable. At this level we've partnered with our own SBC seminaries, as well as some Bible training institutes in the U.S. such as Columbia International University and J. Vernon McGee's "Through the Bible."

Relationships: Levels, Goals, and Controls

IMB missionaries relate to non-IMB entities at different levels depending on their goals and needs. These relationships range from expedient to eternal in their significance. The deeper the level, the greater its significance.

Level 1: Goal: *Entry to the target population (e.g., tourism, business, education, etc.).* Basis: *Suitability to the target population.*

Level 2: Goals: *Prayer for the population, ministry to felt needs or purpose of pre-evangelism.* Basis: *Response to spiritual and physical needs*

Level 3: Goals: *Evangelism & scripture distribution.* Basis: *Commitment to biblical evangelism*

Level 4: Goal: *New testament churches (e.g., Baptist).* Basis: *Commitment to new testament church planting.*

Level 5: Goals: *Ministerial training, theological education, ordination, deploying missionaries, etc.* Basis: *Doctrinal purity.*

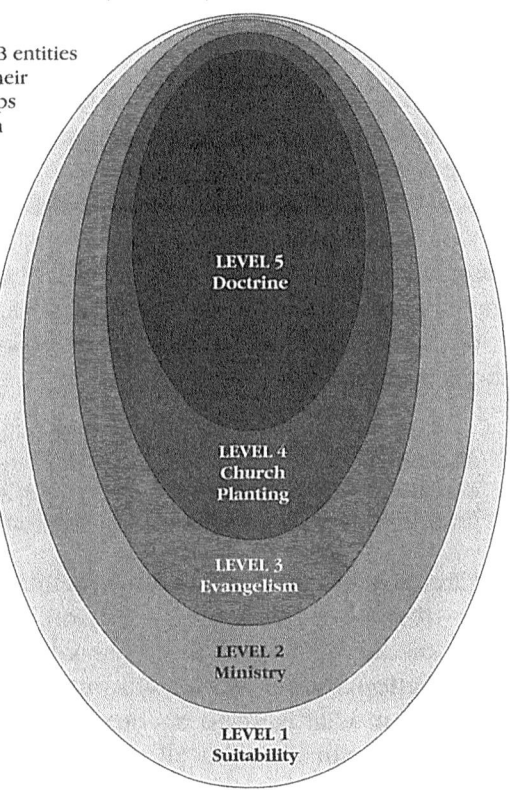

Observations

While the nature and degree of our relationship with other entities varies, the constant at each level is the career IMB missionary. We seek to ensure that they are well-trained, theologically sound, and fully aware of their strategic role as a gate-keeper and shaper of the ultimate destiny of their target people. While IMB personnel always avoid certain non-IMB entities (e.g., marketers in illicit or immoral products, CIA, etc.), we remain engaged with as many parties as possible.

Conclusion

Romans 15:5–7 says,

> May the God who gives endurance and encouragement give you a spirit of unity among yourselves as you follow Christ Jesus, so that with one heart

and mouth you may glorify the God and Father of our Lord Jesus Christ. Accept one another, then, just as Christ accepted you, in order to bring praise to God.

This day this Scripture is being fulfilled. But we have a long way to go in order for all of us to accept one another as Christ has accepted us. Let us be like the old lady who testified, "I've only got two teeth in my head, but praise the Lord they meet."

Only God can give us the spirit of unity so that we all can participate in his mission—that with one heart and mouth we may glorify the God and Father of our Lord Jesus Christ.

Romans 15:8-9 adds Christ's part in God's mission and includes the Gentiles:

> For I tell you that Christ has become a servant of the Jews on behalf of God's truth, to confirm the promises made to the patriarchs so that the Gentiles may glorify God for his mercy, as it is written: "Therefore I will praise you among the Gentiles; I will sing hymns to your name."

Circumstances today call for a practical unity focused on the mission—that all peoples will glorify God. We will not come together based on doctrinal distinctives. We will not come together based on organizational models. We will only come together if we are all focused on what is on God's heart—the nations.

Missions can do what all the councils that ever met, all the ecumenicists who ever negotiated, and all the religious authorities who have tried to force unity could not do. It is time to begin the twenty-first century with arms linked together as we march on mission with God to the last peoples on earth who do not know Him so that they can glorify and worship Him with us.

Chapter 12

Assemblies of God Missions: Strategy on the Run

Gary B. McGee

When conducting research on Assemblies of God foreign missions a decade ago, I asked a mission executive where the enterprise would be going in future years. I was somewhat startled when he responded, "What will the Holy Spirit be doing?" If the question were raised today, I would probably receive the same answer. An outside observer might conclude that either the Assemblies of God had successfully recaptured the simplicity of New Testament evangelism or cornered the market on the plans of the Holy Spirit in mission. Neither interpretation accurately reflects Assemblies of God missions.

While Pentecostals have always looked to the Acts of the Apostles as the ideal paradigm for mission, the Assemblies of God adaptation reveals a multifaceted operation, one that stands in sharp contrast to Luke's uncomplicated mapping of the Spirit's work from Jerusalem to Rome. Evidence for this appears in the report for 1998 wherein the Division of Foreign Missions listed 1,819 missionaries and a total budget of $143,713,519.

Working with the permission of fraternally-related national churches, most of which trace their origins to the efforts of Assemblies of God missionaries,[1] the agency supported 821 resident and 588 extension Bible schools. The overseas constituencies numbered 29 million people, conservatively estimated, with 180,217 ministers serving 178,116 churches and preaching points.[2] Although the apostle Paul had little difficulty understanding the summons of the Macedonian man in a vision (Acts 16:9), today he might need all the encouragement Barnabas could give to grasp the underlying complexity of the monthly donor and disbursement statements received by an Assemblies of God missionary in the Republic of Macedonia.

The course of Assemblies of God missions has always been paradoxical. On the one hand, the Division and its personnel have sought to remain faithful to the Pentecostal heritage by seeking to follow the leading of the Holy Spirit as to where evangelism should be done and churches planted, how it can utilize more effective means for sharing the Good News, and what methods it should employ in training ministerial candidates. Rather than presumption or elitism, the posture has generally been one of humility. Mission personnel readily confess their dependence on the divine empowerment and guidance of the Holy Spirit. They believe that Peter's exhortation about the outpouring of the Spirit on the Day of Pentecost has contemporary relevance for mission: "This promise is to you and to your children, and even to the Gentiles, all who have been called by the Lord our God" (Acts 2:39).[3]

In an address to the Evangelical Foreign Missions Association (now the Evangelical Fellowship of Mission Agencies) in 1970, J. Philip Hogan, sometime executive director of the Division of Foreign Missions, went to the heart of the matter when he said, "I am overwhelmed and humbled before the moving of the Spirit's own sovereign presence in the world. Make no mistake, the missionary venture of the church, no matter how well planned, how finely administered and finely supported, would fail like every other vast human enterprise, were it not that where human instrumentality leaves off, a blessed ally takes over. It is the Holy Spirit that calls, it is the Holy Spirit that inspires, it is the Holy Spirit that reveals, and it is the Holy Spirit that administers."[4]

On the other hand, the "stats" reveal a highly structured organization directing its operation from the headquarters in Springfield, Missouri to over 158 nations. While it has often been said that Pentecostal missionaries focus more attention on "doing" rather than "theorizing," it should come as no surprise that within the ranks one will find some of the best mission strategists anywhere. Yet, with the approaching centenary of Assemblies of God missions in 2014, why has an agency of this magnitude not prepared a formal statement on strategy for the next century? In its own way, this absence demonstrates the paradox.

Even though such a document might serve a purpose in some quarters, mission executives exhibit little interest in the preparation of such treatises. To them, the fundamental objectives have not changed. Therefore, given the fast changes taking place around the world, any new statement on strategy would soon be an anachronism. (Nevertheless, they do not discourage the study of missiology or disparage the statements of other agencies.) In contrast, they have proved adept at keeping their supporting constituency aware of the key objectives. The faithful learn about current programs, financial needs, and events abroad through a myriad of publications, newsletters, and itinerating missionaries who are expected to speak in eight congregations every month when home on a year-long furlough. In the locomotion of Assemblies of God foreign missions, the zeal to evangelize, plant churches, and prepare workers for ministry runs the engine. The long line of boxcars that follow are stuffed with "hands on" practical strategies for missions from Santiago to Irkutsk, while missiological declarations are stored in the caboose.

Happily, the many publications of the late Melvin L. Hodges provide valuable insights into the mission policies of the Assemblies of God and the dynamics of Pentecostal missiology for the wider missionary community. Since his death in 1988, historians have traced and interpreted the endeavor for the denomination, the broader church world, and the academic community. My own *This Gospel Shall Be Preached* (1986, 1989) analyzes the growth and development of the Division of Foreign Missions from its beginning in 1914 to 1989. More recently, Everett A. Wilson examined the thirty-year span before 1990 in which the agency realized its greatest growth by writing the biography of a past executive director, published as *Strategy of the Spirit: J. Philip Hogan and the Growth of the Assemblies of God Worldwide, 1960-1990* (1997). Fortunately, an emerging guild of Assemblies of God missiologists has also appeared with some of their contributions appearing in two readily accessible collections of essays: *Called & Empowered: Global Mission in Pentecostal Perspective* (1991) and *The Globalization of Pentecostalism: A Religion Made to Travel* (1999), both edited by Murray W. Dempster, Byron D. Klaus, and Douglas Petersen. Another important monograph appeared with the publication of Douglas Petersen's *Not By Might nor By Power: A Pentecostal Theology of Social Concern in Latin America* (1996).

The easiest way to discover the strategic objectives of the organization is to look at the brief mission statement that frequently appears in full-page ads in the *Pentecostal Evangel*, the denomination's weekly voice:

> **Our Mission**
> ***Reaching.*** We are proclaiming the message of Jesus Christ to the spiritually lost in all the world through every available means.
> ***Planting.*** We are establishing churches in more than 150 nations, following the New Testament pattern.
> ***Training.*** We are training leaders throughout the world to proclaim the message of Jesus Christ to their own people and to other nations.
> ***Touching.*** We are touching poor and suffering people with the compassion of Jesus Christ and inviting them to become His followers.[5]

Despite the lack of explicit references to Pentecostal dynamics in the statement, it demonstrates the evangelical foundation that undergirds Assemblies of God missions. The Pentecostal factor appears in the mention of the "New Testament pattern."

As mentioned earlier, the personnel and programs of the Division of Foreign Missions labor for the above objectives at the invitation of national church bodies. The delegated leaders of "Missionary Field Fellowships" join together with church officers to coordinate a bewildering array of activities. These can include everything from planning evangelistic crusades and church planting projects in Paraguay, to helping nationals produce their own television and radio programs in West Africa, to synchronizing the work of construction teams from congregations in the United States building a Bible school dormitory in Belgium, to raising money for the Assembly of God Hospital and Research Centre in Calcutta, and to Bible distribution in Israel. Along with the efforts of missionaries are those of hundreds of "Missionary Associates," lay and ministerial volunteers who provide indispensable assistance for a variety of projects. One of the remarkable successes of the Assemblies of God has been the welding together of professional and lay participation in ministries at home and abroad.

The Center for Ministry to Muslims, Global University, HealthCare Ministries, International Media Ministries, and Life Publishers represent transnational ventures. To these can be added many more regional ministries such as Africa Tabernacle Evangelism, Asia's Little Ones, Latin America Theological Seminary, Latin American ChildCare, Project Rescue!, Royal Rangers, and Africa Assemblies of God Commission, which among other things, publishes the "Edward the Elephant" comic book series for AIDS awareness and evangelism.

Obviously, given the enormous scope of activities and the energies required to make them happen in other cultures and political settings, the partnership of missionaries with indigenous church leaders functions best when the fruit of the Spirit is in bloom.

Four factors continue to shape the course of Assemblies of God missions: evangelical doctrine, Pentecostal doctrine and spirituality, the implementation of indigenous church principles concomitant with training leaders, and pragmatism in choosing delivery systems. First, like the larger Pentecostal movement, the Assemblies of God finds its heritage in the family photo album of evangelical pietism, the nineteenth-century holiness movement, and premillennialism with its vision of world evangelization in the "last days" before the imminent return of Jesus Christ. The theological frames include belief in the Trinity, the inspiration and infallibility of the Bible, the lostness of humankind, redemption through the substitutionary atonement of Jesus Christ, the resurrection of Christ, Spirit-baptism as a postconversionary empowerment for Christian witness, and the "Blessed Hope." This commitment has prevented the incursion of various forms of universalism.

The evangelical bond also makes possible participation in the World Evangelical Fellowship, the Lausanne Movement, and an assortment of formal and informal regional and local links in many countries. Yet, despite these connections, evangelical and Pentecostal cooperation has not moved beyond the threshold of its potential, due in part to lingering criticisms of Pentecostal spirituality. At the same time, Assemblies of God mission leaders have centered their energies on networking with national churches.

Second, Pentecostal spirituality with its emphasis on baptism in the Holy Spirit accompanied by tongues-speech, prayer for the sick, anticipation of the gifts of the Spirit in the life and mission of the church, and the personal guidance of the Spirit hallmarks the Assemblies of God. This distinguishing orientation unites it with other Pentecostals through memberships in the Pentecostal World Conference and the World Assemblies of God Fellowship.

Prayerful confidence that the Spirit will direct where efforts and resources should be concentrated shows the ethos of Pentecostal missions. In an insightful appraisal, Russell P. Spittler, notes that "the history of Pentecostal missions can be told through stories of persons who sensed the guidance of the Holy Spirit and accordingly took bold, venturesome—some would say foolish—steps of faith."[6] Nevertheless, the arthritis of institutionalism sometimes threatens the creative callings of the Holy Spirit.

Naturally, mistakes have been made. As Paul wrote, "this precious treasure—this light and power that now shine within us—is held in perishable containers, that is, in our weak bodies" (2 Cor. 4:7). Given the human factor, a former field director for Africa once sighed, "It's a miracle that anything gets done!"[7] Still, when one examines the big picture, the successes have outdistanced the failures.

In his examination of post-war Assemblies of God missions, Everett Wilson writes:

> The Pentecostal missionary movement, the result of the remarkable motivation, vision, and initiative of mainly unknown believers in the developing nations, ultimately must be attributed to that which is inherent to Pentecostalism—a personally satisfying, transforming religious experience and its accompanying values and world-view, which in turn have produced cell-like congregations that readily identify with aspiring peoples and extend the message of the gospel with considerable energy and enthusiasm.[8]

Third, from the beginning, Assemblies of God missions have been committed to following "New Testament methods" in planting churches on the mission fields. Regardless of this high-sounding goal, few missionaries knew how to put such methods into practice. When the Lord didn't return according to the expected timetable, they looked to other Protestant missionaries to see how to conserve their work. Consequently, many became skilled in the art of controlling the activities of mission churches and aspiring leaders. Ironically for Pentecostals, while encouraging their converts to seek for the gifts of the Spirit, they often limited them in the exercise of their leadership gifts (Rom. 12:8). Notwithstanding, the vision of Alice E. Luce (the first Assemblies of God theoretician of mission), Ralph D. Williams, and Melvin L. Hodges, all of them skilled practitioners who adapted Pentecostal spirituality to Roland Allen's missiological perspectives, led to the seismic shift in mission policy from paternalism to partnership in the post-war period.[9] From the 1950s onward, the number of ministerial training institutions overseas skyrocketed. As missionaries turned the reins of leadership over to national leaders, church growth accelerated in many countries.

Fourth, from the beginning of the Pentecostal movement at the turn of the twentieth century, the focus on being baptized in the Holy Spirit, along with the "zero-hour" eschatology of dispensational premillennialism that left little time to evangelize, engendered a pragmatism about how missions should be conducted. Before the Pentecostal revival, radical evangelicals like J. Hudson Taylor of the China Inland Mission and A. B. Simpson of the Christian and Missionary Alliance had become dissatisfied with the methods of mainstream Protestant missions with their postmillennial compass and institutional direction. Instead, they searched for new creative ways to fulfill the Great Commission. Some radicals even suggested that God might confer the "gift of tongues" (Mark 16:17) on missionaries who had sufficient faith in order to save them from the time-consuming task of formal language study so they could preach immediately upon arriving on their fields of ministry.[10]

Pentecostals have followed in the wake of radical evangelicals restless to find more successful means of evangelizing the lost. Nonetheless, Assemblies of God mission leaders have not endorsed an unbridled pragmatism.

For example, they have steered away from many of the controversial aspects of the current (and formula driven) "strategic-level spiritual warfare" movement. Leading an agency whose missionaries have had a long hitch of combat duty in spiritual warfare, they suspect that the new proponents have sometimes exceeded what the biblical text warrants when confronting satanic forces.[11]

In conclusion, the words of A. B. Simpson in his famous missionary hymn, "The Regions Beyond," still speak forcefully a century later to non-Pentecostal and Pentecostal evangelicals alike:

> There are other "lost sheep" that the Master must bring,
> And they must the message be told;
> He sends me to gather them out of all lands,
> And welcome them back to His fold.
> To the regions beyond,
> I must go, I must go,
> Till the world, all the world,
> His salvation shall know.[12]

For Assemblies of God missionaries that means, "strategizing on the run" till Jesus comes.

Endnotes

1. For example, while American missionaries pioneered the Assemblies of God of Burkina Faso in West Africa, the Assemblies of God in Brazil traces its origins to the labors of two Swedes, Daniel Berg and Adolf Gunnar Vingren, and the Italian Ligi Francescon. All of them lived in America for a time before they began their ministry in Brazil in 1910, four years before the Assemblies of God (U.S.A.) came into existence. See A.E. Wilson, *Mining Black Diamonds in Upper Ivory Coast* (Springfield, Mo.: Foreign Missions Department, Assemblies of God, 1942); Walter J. Hollenweger, *The Pentecostals* (Peabody, Mass.: Hendrickson Publishers, 1972), 75-93.

2. General Council of the Assemblies of God, U.S.A., Division of Foreign Missions, "1999 Annual Statistics" (For Publication Throughout 1999 as of Dec. 31, 1998), 5-6.

3. All scripture references are taken from the New Living Translation.

4. Cited in Everett A. Wilson, *Strategy of the Spirit: J. Philip Hogan and the Growth of the Assemblies of God Worldwide 1960-1990* (Irvine, Calif.: Regnum Books International, 1997), 136.

5. E.g., "Our Mission," *Pentecostal Evangel*, October 10, 1999, 2.

6. Russell P. Spittler, "Implicit Values in Pentecostal Missions," *Missiology: An International Review* XVI (October, 1988): 415.

7. Quotation taken from a conversation some years ago with the late Morris O. Williams, Assemblies of God field director for Africa (1971-1985).

8. Wilson, *Strategy of the Spirit*, 197.

9. For this development, see my "Legecy of Melvin L. Hodges," *International Bulletin of Missionary Research* 22 (January 1998): 20-24.

10. See my "Looking for a 'Short-cut' to Language Preparation: Radical Evangelicals, Missions, and the Gift of Tongues," *International Bulletin of Missionary Research* (forthcoming).

11. For the perspectives of Assemblies of God missionaries and theologians for "power encounter," see Sobhi Malek, "Islam Encountering Gospel Power," in *Called & Empowered: Global Mission in Pentecostal Perspectives*, ed. Murray W. Dempster, et. al. (Peabody, Mass.: Hendrickson Publishers, 1991), 18-197; and Benny C. Aker and Gary B. McGee, eds., *Signs & Wonders in Ministry Today* (Springfield, Mo.: Gospel Publishing House, 1996).

12. A.B. Simpson and Margaret M. Simpson, "The Regions Beyond," in *Hymns of Christian Life* (Harrisburg, Pa.: Christian Publications, 1936), #454.

Chapter 13

AD2000 and Beyond: Toward a Conceptual Model

Luis Bush

The viability and components of many proposals to work together strategically to advance world evangelization are now being broadly assessed by Christian leaders around the world. Many initiatives to understand the times, the trends, and the vision for the new decade and the new century/ new millennium are in process. Inputs are being solicited.

In dealing with the topic of working together strategically, I would like to propose a conceptual model that builds upon the accomplishments of the past, takes into account the momentum of the present, and is fueled by the inputs of many for the future.

One of the first questions before us is the nature of the vehicle that provides the most effective delivery system for working together strategically. Is it a church or an association of churches? A mission agency or cluster of mission agencies? An organization or group of organizations? A movement or a function?

In considering the most effective means of working together strategically, a movement may well be the best way forward. A movement has been defined as a collective state of mind, a public and common understanding that the future can be created, not simply experienced or endured. A movement is a place to foment harmony, common purpose, innovation, and renewal.

However, the nature of movements is that they often deteriorate into mere organizations: trading off some things, preferring comfort to ambiguity, looking for control rather than challenge, trusting job assignments rather than respecting individual gifts.

This conceptual model is not a stand-alone plan. Rather, it seeks the enhancement of existing efforts and resources. In addition, it strives to catalyze new efforts and resources and to stimulate new ministry— organizational, global, regional, national and local initiatives where they do not currently exist toward a common God-given purpose. It fosters cooperative ventures that will further cultivate coalescing, practical affinity networks and partnerships to advance God's purposes strategically, in a spirit of go-forward cooperation.

The components required to work together strategically include at least the following:

- A compelling vision to galvanize involvement of ministries, mission agencies, churches, associations, networks, and God's people around the world
- A core set of values that serve as a clear basis of understanding for working together
- A network or network-type structure that catalyzes the vision, communicates what God is doing, and coordinates the high level process
- A process that encourages ownership by all the major parties within the global body of Christ which are committed to obeying the mandate of Jesus Christ
- Facilitative, visionary, servant leadership
- A God-given contextualized strategy by which the vision is fulfilled
- An operational network of information that serves the individuals, agencies, and movements committed to the vision

I. A compelling vision: All the Gospel to all Peoples and All Places by All the Church —Christ's Kingdom Come

As we consider a compelling vision for the future we can learn from compelling visions from the past—sometimes referred to as watchwords. For example, the "evangelization of the world in this generation" was one of those.

Recently some people gathered to consider the kind of questions that should be addressed in a compelling vision: Who should be involved in defining the vision? What kind of language should it use, inclusive or limiting? What "governing metaphors" would be most productive in this emerging era, taking into account the spirit of the age, the worldviews it promotes, and the increasing intensification of opposition to the church? Should the vision have a time-target? How does the vision provide continuity and build upon what God has done through his people in the past? How can we ensure that the vision does not truncate the gospel? How can it bring focus to the unfinished task?

For more than 18 months, the viability and components of the vision encompassing all peoples in all places was assessed by Christian leaders around the world. Inputs reflected support for the concept.

For example, the input from Patrick Johnstone, author of *Operation World*, is as follows:

> I am delighted with the initiative and fully endorse the need for such. We had to simplify and focus for these three to five years. We should bequeath to the Church of the twenty-first century the full challenge. I believe we now have the attention, interest and concern of many Christians, and we now also have a commonly agreed set of terms and categorizations to make the complicated analysis more practicable.

In August 1999 three regional consultations throughout Mozambique drew together church and mission leaders intent on completing the unfinished task of the evangelization of all peoples in all places of the country. In the midst of, and parallel to, this process, a group of internationals discussed the matter of a watchword for the next century. The context of internationals meeting together on this topic in the poorest country of the world, having just emerged from a brutal civil war, and surrounded by the reality of devastation from the scourge of AIDS in southern Africa, is nothing short of amazing. The extreme poverty, social injustice, and other social issues undoubtedly influenced the deliberations regarding the unfinished task.

Out of the discussion emerged a compelling vision for the next century that could be expressed as "All the gospel to all peoples in all places by all the Church—Christ's Kingdom Come." Let us consider that vision in detail by asking some key questions:

Why all peoples and all places?

The vision is to network Christians worldwide who are committed to establishing a life-giving congregation of believers among all peoples and in all places, and making the Gospel available to all persons by means of a common purpose, common values, and a common information system.

There exists today among so many of his servants in so many countries the conviction that God is already at work throughout the world, engaged in this process of advancing the gospel among all peoples, in all places, and among all persons. The conviction is strong that God is a sending God, reflected in the compassion of the Father, the commission of the Son, and the compulsion of the Holy Spirit. Many recognize and believe that completing this task is technologically possible. The development of an interactive information system to accommodate pursuit of the vision of all peoples/all persons is already underway.

Why Christ's?

1. Because Christ radically breaks through human history. The world speaks of "before Christ" and "after Christ."

2. Because Christ alone unifies all of Scripture.

3. Because Christ is the very center of the plan of the Father. "God's secret plan has now been revealed to us; it is a plan centered on Christ, designed long ago according to his good pleasure" (Eph. 1:9, The New Living Translation).

4. Because all things will become Christ's. "God's purpose: to bring all things in heaven and on earth together under one head, even Christ" (Eph. 1:10, NIV).

5. Because we are called as servants of God to steward the administration of a divine initiative to exalt Jesus Christ as the Lord of Lords (Eph. 1:10, NASB).

Why Kingdom?

1. Because the message and ministry of Christ are inseparably linked to the Kingdom. The theme of the kingdom as preached by Christ unites biblical truth.

2. Because the world needs it. Just consider the devastating scourge of AIDS, extreme poverty, natural crises such as the recent earthquake in Turkey, human crises such as the war in Kosovo, corruption of all kinds, family dysfunctionality. There is a need for Christ's Lordship and Kingdom principles in each life, in every marriage, in every home, in every church, in every city, and among every people and in every country of the world. Living out "Christ's Kingdom Come" results in transformation—the transformation of the individual, the transformation of the family, the transformation of the church, the transformation of the community, the transformation of the business or school, the transformation of the city, the

transformation of the country, and the transformation of the world.

3. Because the kingdom of heaven breaks into the domain of the evil one. The power of Satan is broken. Jesus possesses and bestows power to trample on the dominion of the enemy. Love finds a way—love toward God, others, self and enemies (Matt. 22:37-40). God's people are to be stewards, risking with God rather than preserving for God (Matt. 25:14-30). Greatness comes by serving (Matt. 20:25-28). Nothing is impossible for those who go forth into the world, invested with Jesus' power, as witnesses of the Kingdom (Luke 10:18f.) to make disciples of the peoples (Matt. 28:19-20).

4. Because it provides a foundation for an administration of the spheres/sectors/domains of life over which the dominion of Christ may be exercised. It calls God's servants to:

• World Evangelization—in all places and among all peoples; all persons are invited to come to the banquet of the king. ("'Come!' Whoever is thirsty, let him come" Rev. 22)

• Personal sanctification
• Dominion of Christ in the home
• Lordship of Christ in the city
• Relief and development in communities among the poor and the needy
• Social justice in countries

5. Because it provides hope for the future for every individual on earth, in this life and the life to come; in the knowledge that Jesus is coming again to set things right that are not right. We have the glorious hope of a place and a time where righteousness dwells. For although it is clearly stated that the Kingdom is manifested here and now in the gospel, so also there will be an ultimate breakthrough of God into human history— an intervention of God's Kingdom still to come.

Why "come"?

1. Because it will bring life to a dying world. Whosoever will may come and have life.

2. Because it will bring abundant life to the person, the family, and the country (John 10:10).

3. Because it is the final cry of God's written revelation. "The Spirit and the bride say, 'Come!' And let him who hears say, 'Come!' Whoever is thirsty, let him come; and whoever wishes, let him take the free gift of the water of life" (Rev. 22:17). "He who testifies to

these things says, 'Yes, I am coming soon.' Amen. Come, Lord Jesus" (Rev. 22:2, NIV).

4. Because the model prayer encourages us to pray: "Thy Kingdom come" (Luke 11:2, KJV).

5. Because Christ's Kingdom is coming to earth anyway sooner or later. It is God's plan at the fullness of time. "... every knee will bow before me; every tongue will confess to God" (Rom. 14:11, NIV).

6. Because the reality of Christ's Kingdom will go on for a long time, so we might as well get used to it. "The whole world has now become the kingdom of our Lord and of his Christ, and he will reign forever and ever" (Rev. 11:15, New Living Translation).

In summary, "all the gospel, to all peoples, in all places, by all the church" seeks to advance the goal of establishing a church planting movement among all peoples, and to present all the gospel to all persons worldwide—a task owned and undertaken by all the church. The coming of Christ's Kingdom involves God's intervention in the course of human history. There is both "kingdom now" and "not yet." God's intervention always brings liberty and a Christ-centered ethic which permeates all of life. Christ's kingdom also comes in a future dimension, which anticipates the consummation of Christ's work when he returns for the final establishment of his kingdom on earth. Missions thus involves the extension of Christ's reign in the world, by the power of the Holy Spirit, to the glory of the Father.

Through God's provision of a "shrinking planet" and the interconnection of his people through multiple technology streams, all God's people can now readily carry the message of the Gospel to all peoples in all places as never before. This happens through a multitude of formal and informal, and structured and non-structured connections.

II. A Core Set of Values that Serve as a Clear Basis of Understanding for Working Together

A Global Evangelism Roundtable was held in Hurdal, Norway from March 21-25, 1999. It included representatives from several global bodies—World Evangelical Fellowship, the AD2000 and Beyond Movement, and the Lausanne Committee for World Evangelization. At that meeting several foundational values were agreed to that provide a basis of understanding for working together:

> We are a people profoundly committed to biblical, historic, Trinitarian Christianity, with particular appreciation for the Lausanne Covenant, as well as our own Evangelical church heritage.
> As we consider the future of world evangelization and the life of the global church, we affirm:
> 1. Our common goal for, and passionate commitment to, world evangelization;
> 2. Our dedication to a life of prayer, and to unleashing the entire Church into global intercession;
> 3. The proclamation of a holistic, transforming Gospel, underscoring the centrality of the church for world evangelization;
> 4. The need for a new, global, relational "wineskin" within a context of continuity, and not based on position nor structure;
> 5. A manifestation of unity grounded in the partnership of equals around the globe;
> 6. The need for a thorough re-examination of a [sic] theology of the church;
> 7. Regional and national networks that also have a global focal point;
> 8. The need for a more representative platform in which all members of the Body of Christ are equal partners (for example: charismatics and non-charismatics, male and female, younger and older, academics and practitioners);
> 9. The need for one cooperative vehicle that supports a plurality of ministries;
> 10. Our obedience to the Holy Spirit for empowerment, guidance, and recognition of leadership;
> 11. Our commitment to a biblical and accountable stewardship of resources;
> 12. Our decision to communicate our unity to every level of our various networks, and to the wider Body of Christ.

III. A Network-of-networks Structure that Catalyzes the Vision, Communicates What God is Doing, and Coordinates Involvement with It

We live in a networked era, an era that has transformed the ways we organize ourselves to get things done. We once were operational entities readily defined, and possessed a keen sense of organizational identity. Everyone else knew who we were as well, and we all pretty much stayed within our own operational boundaries. Time and technology has changed all that!

In the process of networking, we have discovered the principle of working together across these boundaries. This has literally exploded as we approach the new millennium. We have discovered that there are a variety of networks, coalitions, partnerships, and movements. Some are founded on primary unshakable principles, and fairly structured partnerships of one sort or other. Some ride the wave of technological advance with e-mail conference networks. Others are resource-based, seeking to generate and supply greater resources for the task. Some are strategic networks, seeking to advance certain strategic objectives by voluntarily joining together with minimal structure and overhead cost. Their thrust is to achieve a certain multiplying factor by networking together towards a common goal or cause. This is the model proposed here.

The prerequisites, components, and flow of an operational network of networks include the following factors.

- A compelling directional vision exists!
- Organizations/entities identified have a ministry vision portion parallel to that of the compelling vision.
- Organizations "join" movement/retain autonomy.
- A small catalytic communicating and coordinating office is set up with a capable and inspirational leader; staff are energized by relationships and stewardship with integrity of the vision.
- Operational initiatives come forth.
- Coordination and communication items follow.
- God glorifies Himself through it all.

IV. A Process that Encourages Broad Global Ownership Among God's People

Perhaps as important as the vision and values is the strategic process by which these are unveiled. As we prepare to enter the twenty-first century, we need to be wise stewards. We desire to anticipate opportunities, as well as problems, related to these changes. Today there is a maturing Church in the developing world. The center of gravity for Christianity worldwide in terms of growth, energy, and vision is shifting from the North and West to the South and East. The mission field is fast becoming the mission force. Increasing numbers of leaders for the worldwide Christian movement are emerging from the rapidly growing churches of the majority world.

Thus any global vision, value, strategy-developing process must involve the leaders from the global church. It is a listening process through forums or working group consultations regionally/nationally around the globe.

V. A God-Given Contextualized Strategy

The "whole church taking the whole Gospel to the whole world" not only served as a watchword, but also as an effective strategy for world evangelization developed through the Lausanne Movement. Now other emerging strategies are coming forth.

A. National initiatives

In most countries of the world national initiatives are underway. A National Initiative is a strategy focused on mobilizing and deploying the existing churches to penetrate every least evangelized people within their nation, as well as to be significantly involved in reaching the least evangelized throughout the world. The method is aggressive saturation church planting with the ultimate goal of seeing a gathering of Bible-believing Christians established within practical and cultural distance of every person in the nation. This is also called the discipling a whole nation, or DAWN strategy. There are several types of national initiatives, each having various characteristics that respond to national contexts, but each also having several things in common.

At its core a national initiative is a bold undertaking by church leaders in a nation to respond to the Great Commission mandate of our Lord Jesus Christ to "make disciples of all nations." It is a response to the unique opportunity, as we enter this new millennium, to mobilize the Body of Christ in each nation to complete the unfinished task of evangelization in their own country, and make a significant contribution to evangelism and church planting in the least evangelized peoples and countries of the world.

It is an effort to encourage, nurture and facilitate, at a national level, cooperative relationships among existing and developing denominations, congregations, networks, structures, ministries, organizations, etc. that will result in coordinated efforts for completing the task of "filling the earth with the knowledge of the glory of the Lord as the waters cover the sea" (Habakkuk 2:14). The goal is to foster, as a priority and minimum, a pioneer church planting movement within every major ethno-linguistic people in a nation, and every country and megacity of the world.

B. PLUG, PREM, and BE NICE

Many organizations in many places have come together for mutual encouragement and strength in evangelism and church planting efforts. The North India Harvest Network (NIHN) is a prime example. A loosely-organized forum totally managed by volunteers, it has sponsored seminars in 60 of the 200 districts of North India, in order to build networks and mobilize workers for the harvest they truly believe is coming. Their goal is reaching "every people group in every city in every language in every geographic district." Their mission is expressed in the phrase "PLUG, PREM and be NICE," a series of acronyms that describe their focus and their methodology for reaching their goals. The acronyms make more sense when you realize that PREM is the Hindi word "love."

PLUG refers to the different targets their networks are trying to reach: every PEOPLE—in every LANGUAGE—in every URBAN center—in every GEOGRAPHIC division (district, block and PIN code). At the heart of the strategy are 500 groups or units in North India based on this PLUG approach.

200 PEOPLE groups
50 LANGUAGES
50 URBAN areas and
200 GEOGRAPHICAL districts

Each target group serves as a thread woven into a net from a different direction to ensure that every person has a chance to hear, regardless of the language they speak, the cultural grouping of which they are a part, or the city or geographical district in which they reside. These target groups have become the focus of their prayer and mobilization efforts. Through their seminars, the NIHN seeks to identify, prepare and train local leaders who will coordinate the resources and personnel to reach each of these target groups in their area.

PREM and be NICE describe how that work will be done:
- PRAYER must be made;
- RESEARCH into the harvest field must be performed and then utilized;
- EQUIPPING and training those who go out to labor must occur;
- MOBILIZATION must be ongoing.

It is recognized and understood by all concerned that this can only occur by:
- NETWORKING, especially in pioneer situations
- taking INITIATIVE when nothing is happening or a gap is realized;
- being a CATALYST (an agent that provokes or speeds significant change or action);
- ENCOURAGING all the existing ministries and efforts that advance the cause of Jesus Christ.

In so many ways, India is learning to work together to reach its own unreached peoples. The networks of concerned individuals and churches are stretching across the entire country. Perhaps more than any other factor, these networks reveal the growing unity of the Church, without which global evangelization cannot occur.

VI. Transformational Leadership Style

Trends in effective organizational development in the nineties provide a picture of a distinct leadership style appropriate for the new century, the TRANSFORMATIONAL LEADERSHIP STYLE. It emphasizes personal relationship over positional relationship, and it can be characterized by a series of contrasts. The FOCUS OF LOYALTY has shifted from institution to people. The STYLE is less structured and more flexible. THE SOURCE OF ENERGY, but not necessarily stability, comes from change and innovation. Instead of LEADERSHIP being dogmatic and authoritative, it is inspirational, empowering, enabling, and facilitating. The LEADER, rather than giving orders, coaches, and teaches. Instead of QUALITY depending on the affordable best, its standard is excellence.

EXPECTATIONS for associates are not for security, but for personal growth. STATUS does not come from title and rank, but rather from making a difference. RESOURCES are not thought of so much as cash and time, but rather information, people, and networks. This is the wave of the future that lies beyond the year 2000.

VII. A Common Information Sharing System

A common information sharing system with common categories and codes is needed to link the diversity of organizations and ministries working around the globe among the many peoples, and in the many diverse places. The Harvest Information System (HIS) would respond to this need by providing information on the harvest field, the harvest force, and the harvest yield.

A. What is the nature of the Harvest Information System?

1. *Common information:* The coordination of a global effort to collect accurate data regarding all peoples is required so that global, continental, national and local initiatives can all work off the same page.

2. *A Common information system:* The development of an information sharing system is underway through an alliance of Christian entities committed to the stewardship and maintenance of interlinking information sets related to either the harvest field, harvest force, or harvest yield.

3. *A common database:* The communication of non-secured, inter-related, user-friendly information through the preparation of a common information database. This will be distributed by CD-ROM, hard copy, and computer file transfer as appropriate. Security matters will be handled separately.

4. *A common purpose/goal:* The cultivation of a common purpose/goal that expresses the mandate of Jesus Christ and the common conviction of His people throughout the world today is gathering momentum.

B. How will the Harvest Information System work?

1. Summary functions.

• Encompasses all peoples, places, and persons discernible by language, culture, religion and physical location. It identifies who a person is both individually and collectively by languages spoken, country and state/province of residence, religion, and physical location to the level of neighborhood within a community or district within a city.

• Built upon the perception of how people see themselves.

• Based upon the information sets or registries that unite and/or divide people.

• Based on relationships. This is a relationship and relational information system.

• Built upon effectiveness. Changing an item of information once will change that item throughout the entire system.

2. Contents.

• Harvest field—there are five principal descriptors, which cause a people to be seen as the same or different. These are the cultural,

linguistic, religious, political, and spatial.
- Harvest force—including mission organizations and ministries, mission networking capabilities, and individual missions-oriented persons, skills, and products.
- Harvest yield reflects the church in action and in its habitat.

Conclusion

For the first time in history, both the worldwide Body of Christ and nearly instantaneous global communication resources are in place to permit a major advance in working together strategically to advance the cause of Christ throughout the whole world. This is God's work, and it is already happening. There are many precedents upon which to build. Praise God! We must continue to advance this vision, and seek ways to cooperate as never before. We must move forward together.

Leadership Needed for the New Millennium

Chapter 14

Challenging, Nurturing, and Forming Leaders for 2010

Leighton Ford

Not long ago a father and son took a sentimental trip to the father's boyhood hometown. They saw the houses where he grew up, the store his parents owned, the schools he attended, and the park where he played. They went to the civic auditorium, closed for the summer, and persuaded the janitor to open up the locked and darkened theater.

"Here is where we had our youth rallies," the father said to the son as they stood on the stage. "Hundreds of our friends would come. I loved to have the opportunity to emcee the meetings. We saw many kids touched by Christ."

Then he grew reflective. "I remember the night we had a very famous evangelist come. We were sure that most of our friends would accept Christ. The place was packed that night, but I was disappointed. Only one person came forward."

Then the father pointed to the wings at the side of the stage. "I went over and stood there, very discouraged. I remember the evangelist came over, put his arm around me, gave me a hug, and encouraged me. He said he would pray for me and believed God would use me if I stayed humble." The father paused and looked his son in the eyes, "I have never forgotten that arm around my shoulder."

The father in that story is me; the son is my own son, Kevin. The evangelist was Billy Graham, later to be my brother-in-law and Kevin's uncle.

The most important thing that Billy Graham did that night was not the preaching that he did on-stage, but the encouragement he gave off-stage—that arm around the shoulder that I have never forgotten.

My Leadership Journey

That act of affirmation took place fifty years ago this year, January of 1949. That fall, again with Billy's encouragement, I entered Wheaton College as a sophomore transfer from Canada. In September of that year—almost exactly fifty years ago this week—I heard Billy preach a sermon at the Village Church in Western Springs, Illinois. From there he flew directly to Los Angeles to begin the Christ for Greater Los Angeles tent crusade, which launched him into the national spotlight and worldwide ministry.

Tonight I am looking back on a half century of ministry with a sense of deep gratitude for those who encouraged my own leadership, and sense of calling:

• My adopted mother who read to me the biographies of Livingstone and Moffett and Moody, and told me over and over, "Leighton, God is looking for others who will serve him."

• Rowland Bingham, founder of SIM, whom I remember as an unimpressive looking little man, who wore a striped blazer, had a long-jawed face, and prayed for the world from a tower at the Canadian Keswick Conference where we vacationed yearly.

• Evon Hedley, who appointed me president of our hometown fledgling YFC rally, thinking I was 17 because I was tall; he must have had a near stroke when he later found out I was only 14! But he stuck with me, taught me, corrected me when he needed to, and helped me to find my vocation as an evangelist.

After college and seminary, Billy Graham again became my mentor, inviting me to spend a few months in his crusades. This led to my joining his evangelistic team, and made it possible for me to form my own crusade team as part of the Graham organization.

Halfway through this half-century, in 1974, a new chapter opened up for me. That summer the historic Lausanne Congress on World Evangelization was convened in Switzerland. Lausanne brought together evangelists, missiologists, and theologians from church and parachurch, from all parts of the world, from nearly every part of the evangelical spectrum. I was invited by Billy Graham and the planning committee to be program chairman. Having a leadership role in the congress moved me more deeply into the cross-cultural missions world that had been part of my thinking since childhood.

Through the 60s I had preached in crusades around the world. In that turbulent decade of civil rights, the war on poverty, and the

Vietnam agony I had also been forced to think and act more deeply about evangelism and culture, and social issues, and had tried to articulate a biblical theology of evangelism and mission. But in my role as program chairman of Lausanne, I was thrust into new and challenging areas of world evangelization, far beyond my experience. Thankfully, I found not only gifted and informed colleagues to work with, but another mentor, in Bishop A. Jack Dain, the executive chairman of the congress.

An Anglican bishop from Australia, Jack Dain had also been a missionary to India with the Bible and Medical Missionary Fellowship, now Interserve. Out of a lifetime of experience Jack shared with me his wisdom, and guided this 42-year old through the potential minefields of such a complex gathering. And he has continued as a lifelong friend and mentor to me.

As I look back, I am struck by two thoughts: First, that while I have been leading in some capacity for over 50 years, I sense that I am still becoming a leader. And second, that I owe so much to the mentors God brought into my life, who opened doors not only in ministry, but into my own heart.

A New Part of the Journey

In the mid-80s my ministry took a new turn. That "arm around the shoulder" from Billy Graham was a memory that stayed with me, and made me want to do the same for others. But it took a deeply painful loss to show me there was a "new thing" (Isaiah 43:19) that God was doing with and through me.

That loss was the death of our older son, Sandy, during surgery to correct a heart arrhythmia problem in November of 1981. Deep as the loss was, it focused both my wife Jeanie and myself on helping other young leaders to run their race for Christ. We began the Sandy Ford Fund, which since then has been able to give several hundred thousand dollars to help young leaders from twenty-five or more countries with their preparation for service in evangelism or missions.

At the same time I realized that we were going through a major leadership shift. Throughout the world, and in almost every realm of life, leaders had emerged after World War II, and had established strong enterprises in business, and education, and in the church. That era saw the birth of evangelical parachurch movements through leaders like Jim Rayburn (Young Life), Dawson Trotman (Navigators), Bill Bright (Campus Crusade), Bob Pierce (World Vision), Torrey Johnson and Billy Graham (Youth for Christ). Now these veteran leaders were coming toward their retirement from active ministry, and some had already died.

At the same time, I had met in my travels around the world a whole new breed of emerging young leaders, then (in the early and mid-80s) mostly under 40 years of age.

Between the senior leaders who were in their 60s and this emerging crop under 40 there did not seem to be many strong, visionary leaders. There were plenty of managers, who had been called upon to help fulfil their elder's visions, but not many with the vision and courage to strike out themselves in new directions.

In part this was due to the anti-leadership syndrome that developed after Vietnam and the other convulsions of the 60s and early 70s, and the wide cynicism toward all institutional leadership that accompanied it.

But I am convinced it was also in large part due to the "banyan tree" factor. I believe it was Paul Hiebert whom I first heard say that in India "nothing grows under the banyan tree"—those great trees with their spreading branches that do not let enough sunlight through to nurture the seedlings at the base of the trees. And unfortunately, he said, too many big impressive Christian leaders are like banyan trees, taking up so much room that young leaders have no chance to grow in their shadows.

Yet in spite of all this, the Spirit of God was at work, calling up and sending out a whole new generation. I felt deeply the desire to affirm these young women and men in their leadership. Out of that call began Leighton Ford Ministries, aimed at identifying, developing, and networking the next generation of leaders in evangelism—men and women who I prayed would be kingdom seekers and not empire builders.

Tonight We Share a Biblical Vision

I am delighted tonight that you have made the challenges of nurturing and forming leaders for 2010 a major part of your program. Clearly, you do not want to be banyan tree leaders! You seek to follow in the path of those biblical leaders who had a vision for the next generation...like Moses with Joshua.

To my mind, the most poignant and powerful leadership moment for Moses may have been not his defiance of Pharaoh, nor the brave crossing of the Red sea, nor the long grueling trek through the wilderness, nor even his legacy of the Ten Commandments, but that holy moment when he stood alone with God on Mount Nebo. There he surveyed the land of promise which he would never enter, and died knowing another would lead where he could never go (Deuteronomy 32:48ff).

Moses had already prepared in obedience to step out of the way. At God's command he had taken Joshua, and had him stand before the whole assembly. And laying his hands on him, he commissioned him as the Lord had instructed (Numbers 27:22).

Long years before, Moses had chosen Joshua for special attention. He picked this promising young man and sent him out to do battle while Moses stayed home and prayed for him (Exodus 17:9ff). When Moses went into God's presence in the sacred tent, he took Joshua along and let him stay there after Moses left (Exodus 24:13ff and 33:7-11). He taught Joshua lessons of humility. When Joshua tried to get Moses to stop certain unauthorized men from prophesying, Moses said, "Are you jealous for my sake? I wish that all the Lord's people were prophets and that the Lord would put his Spirit on them!" (Numbers 11:26-29). He had tested his protege's courage. He chose him to go with Caleb and the other spies to explore Canaan. He learned that Joshua had the courage to stand with Caleb against the majority, and to convince the people that the Lord could lead them to overcome the giants in the land (Numbers 14:9).

Clearly, Moses was not a banyan tree. He was a planter sowing seeds of new leadership. No wonder, then, that when the time came for a leadership transfer, Joshua was "filled with the spirit of wisdom because Moses laid his hands on him. So the Israelites listened to him and did what the Lord had commanded Moses" (Deut. 34:9). Joshua became the new leader, who could carry the past—including Moses' own God-given vision—into the future. But he who would do it in a new way.

Generational Changes

Since mid-century there has been a cycle of four generations, commonly dubbed the GI Generation (veterans of World War II), the Silent Generation (those who became adults in the 50s), the Baby

Boomers, and the Xers (those born roughly in the 60s and 70s).

Generation X, for all the negative press they have gotten, in my mind have terrific potential for ministry leadership.

I had an interesting discussion on developing leaders in different generations this summer with Thena Ayres, a former InterVarsity staff worker in Canada, who is now a dean at Regent College. "I learned from Cathy Nichols, a pioneer in InterVarsity across western Canada," said Thena. "She didn't intentionally mentor me. I just learned by watching her. Then I taught my student leaders what I had learned, the principles, so that they could apply them. Then I found the next generation—those born in the 60s, who were leading in the 80s—wanted to know exactly what to do. They wanted the one, two, three, rather than being creative. There was an insecurity."

"Now," she said, "I am really positive about the 90s students. We went to Europe in the summer on mission trips. They go to Central Asia. They are pioneers again, in another radical situation."

Interestingly, my own Silent Generation and the Gen Xers have a big similarity: both are generations "in the shadow." My generation came of age in the shadow of the GIs, those strong, pioneering types who started so many things. I can recall many times being asked what it was like ministering "in the shadow of your brother-in-law Billy Graham," and answering "It's a mighty big shadow, with lots of room!" Similarly, the Baby Busters grew up in the shadow of the Boomers, who overwhelmed by their sheer numbers.

But there is also a big difference between the two. Where the Silent generation were more focused on institutions, the Gen Xers are much more strongly concerned with relationships.

Again, I believe there is tremendous potential in the Xers for leadership. I challenge you who are looking for future leaders in your mission to invest in them. I can't put it too strongly: pour your life into them! But keep this in mind: leadership development with the Xers will take relational skills.

An anonymous Xer said to me recently: "I can't tell you how many older people have been ready to teach me, but they were not able to have the relationship which would make the teaching effective."

I asked a number of younger leaders what they would say if they had the chance to say one thing to you, about how you can best encourage the next generation of missions leaders? Here is a sampling of their responses:

- Bill, a professor at a missions-oriented seminary: "The 'younger' generation is looking for relationships...mentoring is a great 'how to' for leadership development."
- Ken, an Asian-Canadian pastor who has led his aging congregation in a turnaround, says: "Have the faith and courage to 'let go' and give the responsibility to a new generation.... When older leaders speak of 'passing the baton to a new generation' and 'taking risks' it's often just rhetoric. It's confusing when organizational rhetoric is contradicted by action... when senior leaders delegate and then seek to control."
- Mike, a young but experienced regional leader for his mission: "Make a fundamental commitment to being developmental as a leader and an organization.... Begin now to develop young leaders who show promise. Bring younger leaders (30s) into positions of leadership with a commitment to mentor them for a specified period of time."
- Alison, an Episcopal rector who works with the Anglican church of Uganda in developing leaders, says it is "important for future leaders to have a servant's heart, especially when working in partnership missions where there is already an established church and a leadership structure. It's important for future leaders to have joy in living a sacrificial life."
- Dan, a former field missionary now at headquarters says: "Young leaders need to be discipled by someone who cares for them personally. They are very uncomfortable with leaders who 'impose a vision' on them."

Brothers and sisters, listen to these voices!

If you want to be really serious about raising up new leaders, ask yourself:

—Am I prepared to take risks on them?

—Am I ready to build relationships with them?

If you want to help develop Xers, you will need to develop that part of yourself which may have been the most underdeveloped: the relational skills. The starting place may be that you are willing to learn from them. And if so, there would be a two-way benefit.

The Relational Difference

Ilya Prigogine, the Nobel laureate scientist, used to write in his lectures on a blackboard the simple formula: one and one is two.

Then he would ask his audiences: what do you need to know in order to understand that? Predictably the responses would be: "You have to know what one is" or "what two is." "Yes," he would answer. "But you also have to know what 'and' is. In reality, relationships are everything."

If we are going to grow leaders as Jesus did, certainly relationships are key. How many times do you suppose the gospels speak of "Jesus and the disciples," or "Jesus and the twelve?"

In *Transforming Leadership* I sought to portray Jesus as the model leader:

• the Son whose leadership grew out of a deep secure relationship with the Father
• the Seer whose vision focused on people rather than projects
• the Storyteller who taught through everyday stories
• the Servant who gave himself away in empowering others
• and the Shepherd-maker, who was concerned not only to rescue lost sheep, but to turn them into undershepherds too.

I wrote that "Jesus' leadership development was not so much a course or a curriculum, as a shared life.... He divested himself of ownership and invested all he was and had in his close associates. With them—especially with his twelve, and most especially his inner three—he shared all things. They ate and traveled, walked, and slept together. If he had not place to lay his head, they shared in his deprivation. But if he had plenty, so did they. He did not hold back from them his deepest feelings, whether anger, joy, sadness, or temptation.... How did Jesus 'deploy himself'...? ...by his shared life—shared vision and goals, shared partnership and time, shared learning and risks, a shared future, and shared power."

Some Underlying Assumptions

Based on my reading of Jesus, and the experience of these past years of seeking to empower younger leaders, I would like to suggest to you some underlying assumptions about leadership development, and also a few proposals.

The assumptions are these:

• That God is at work already raising up and developing younger leaders. We may be "mid-wives" to help, but God has started the process.

- That Jesus is the ultimate model, and we seek to lead like him and to him.
- That emerging young leaders benefit most from leadership guidance when they are at transition points—growth spurts, times of stress and change.
- That leaders grow best in a highly personalized way. Relationships are more important than programs.
- That character and spiritual development are more important even than competency.
- That growth takes place best in a learning community, not a hierarchical structure. Every leader is also a learner, and older and younger leaders learn from God together.
- That growth requires one-on-one mentoring to facilitate character development.
- That people learn from their peers as well as from more experienced leaders.
- That experience is needed to fully learn any character trait or skill. "Experience it, learn it."

A Modest Proposal: To Pay Attention

I like the definition of love as "focused attention." In fact, paying attention is at the heart of our spiritual lives. If there is a central secret to developing leaders, it is to focus attention on them, to pay attention to who they are, and to help them to pay attention to what God is doing in their lives.

There was a student in a seminary module we were teaching on evangelism leadership who said, "My teachers teach me Hebrew, and theology, and church history, but no one ever looked at me before and said that I was a leader!"

Let me share a few ways that I have tried to pay attention in my own ministry, particularly these last dozen years. Perhaps some of them might confirm or stimulate your own nurturing of leaders.

You can be attentive and available at the moment. I believe deeply that the God who is raising up his own leaders will have them cross our paths at the right time. It's up to us to be watching and ready...and available to listen and talk. Often at a seminar or large conference I have prayed, "Lord, I can't meet everyone. Make me open to discern the right moment and the right persons to be with." More often than not, a connection will be made—after a talk, or on the way to the airport. Be alert to God-given moments.

You can learn to listen and ask good questions. Peter Drucker has said that one of the top two qualities of a good leader is being able to listen. Young leaders are hungry for someone who is genuinely interested in them. They will be amazingly responsive if we ask about them, their stories and dreams, rather than looking for the first chance in the conversation to tell them what we think they ought to do.

I remember in the early years of my ministry how excited I was when I got to spend some time with senior leaders I had admired from a distance. Some of these conversations were tremendously affirming. But often, when it was over, I realized I knew almost everything about them and what they did, but they had not asked one question about me and my vision.

One practice I have had since Sandy died is to ask almost every young man or woman who is seeking direction, "What is your vision?" If they don't know I'll ask "Well, if you did have a vision what might it be?" And usually they are genuinely moved that someone thinks their vision is important enough to talk about.

You can teach to observe, reflect, and act. Often I tell young leaders about a Roman Catholic bishop in Belgium who built a strong youth movement through World War II orphans. He taught them to read the Bible and pray, but never told them what to do. Based on his practice, I encourage the young leader seeking a vision to observe, reflect, and act. To observe carefully what God is doing in them and in the world, until they are drawn to some particular need or opportunity, like spotting a plane on a radar screen. Then to reflect in prayer and Bible reading, thought, and learning all they can about this area of need. And then to act, even if it is in some small way, on what it seems God is showing to them.

You can keep a "GGTW" list. Some years ago I heard that Oswald Sanders, the late president of OMF (the Overseas Missionary Fellowship) kept a list of what he called "Blokes to Watch." He would write down the names of promising young missionaries in whom he spotted the potential for leadership. I tried to emulate this fine leader by making my own "GGTW" list—of Guys and Gals to Watch. When I met, or heard, or was told of a young leader with outstanding potential I would add their name. From time to time I would review the list prayerfully, and perhaps give them a call just to see how they were doing, or invite them to some special training opportunity, or ministry.

You can open up doors for ministry. Look for ways to involve them in ministry which will stretch them, and widen their networks. Billy Graham did this for me. When I was 24 years old and only a year out of seminary he asked Jeanie and me to go to New York City for a year, and for me to be in charge of mobilizing the churches in the metropolitan area for his first major NYC crusade. It was a tremendous growth experience, meeting churches and pastors of all sorts—various denominations, different theological persuasions, diverse ethnic groups. I look back and wonder, "If that had been me, going into the biggest crusade of my ministry to date, would I have asked a youngster to be in charge of that crucial part of the crusade planning?" And I'm not certain. To be sure, I was at that age fairly mature and experienced, but still, Billy took a chance that many would not have taken.

Some years ago, Dr. Michael Green wrote asking if I would invite a young unknown British evangelist to spend some time with me in evangelism. It happened that I was going to Lake Avenue Church in Pasadena, California, to pioneer a new "affinity group evangelism" approach to proclamation evangelism in a large urban church. So I invited J. John to come along for the week, and asked Pastor Paul Cedar to let J. speak at some of the key affinity meetings, and at the large Sunday night service. He did great, and I later invited him to become part of a special mentoring group. Today, J. is by all accounts the most effective mass evangelist in the UK, and also a long-term friend to me.

You can hold up the vision of the leader as a polished arrow. It helps to have a symbol that visualizes leadership. For me that has been the arrow, growing from Isaiah's picture of the servant of the Lord as a "polished arrow" (Isaiah 49:2). After I had spoken at the Duke Divinity School chapel, I was asked how I had seen Billy Graham change across the years. It was the first time I had been asked that, and I made a few comments. Then as I was thinking what else to say, the picture of an arrowhead came to my mind. "Billy Graham has been like an arrowhead," I said. "He has always kept the sharp cutting edge of the gospel, like the point of an arrow. But he has grown broader in seeing how that gospel speaks to all of life, whether race relations, or concern for the poor, or nuclear war, or relations between nations and churches."

The arrow metaphor speaks powerfully to young leaders about the godly leader being sharp in vision, broad in understanding, and deep in character. It also calls one to continual growth. Some leaders across the years learn much, but lose the cutting edge and grow flat. Others get more and more narrow and tiresome. But transforming leaders are constantly open to being refocused and stretched, and deepened in their knowledge of themselves and of God.

You can bring together a "Point Group." Isaiah's picture of God as arrow-maker is that of a master craftsman at work, not of a mass production process.

This came home to me strongly about ten years ago, and, ironically, right after Hurricane Hugo came through our home town at the same time as I had invited a group of counselors to work with me in a strategy planning session. In the aftermath of that storm damage (we lost twenty-five trees in our yard and Charlotte was out of power for up to two weeks) we sensed that God was calling us to have an impact on world evangelization through identifying and helping young leaders.

Shortly after, on a quiet day at the lake, I wrote in my journal that such an impact would not likely happen through multiplying programs, but rather through investing in people. That same day I wrote down a list of about ten outstanding young leaders I had met in recent years, many from my GGTW list.

The next spring I invited them to meet with me for a week in Callaway Gardens, Georgia. I shared with them my growing vision for young leaders, including them, and asked if they would join with me, become a group I might intentionally mentor. I also asked if they would, through their own ministries, commit to the vision of developing younger leaders themselves. It was, frankly, not an easy week. They challenged me. They asked if I was really serious, or whether I would succumb to the malady of middle-age and meander, and whether I would really run with the vision. I got irritated. After all, I had called the meeting. But the challenge was a good one, and led me to sharpen my own vision, and to launch into our major Arrow Leadership Program.

However, this group did become what we call the "Point Group," key young leaders from around the world who are the "point" of the arrow. Each year for a decade we have met together for a week, reporting in on our lives, and teaching one another. Often we e-mail or talk on the phone. Sometimes we minister together. In many ways it is very casual, and very informal. But relationships have deepened over the years, and vision has been sustained.

Many of the original Point Group have now emerged into major leadership roles in the evangelical world. J. John, the British evangelist I referred to earlier. Bob Reccord, then a pastor, now is president of the Southern Baptist North American Mission Board. Lon Allison is the newly appointed director of the Billy Graham Center at Wheaton. Doug Birdsall joined the group as a career missionary in Japan and now heads LIFE Ministries. He has also just been appointed chairman of the international Lausanne Emerging Leaders Committee. Carson Pue, who when we first met was an associate at First Baptist Church, Vancouver, recently took over from me as president of the Arrow Leadership Ministries.

I am far from claiming that being part of the Point Group accounts for their leadership. Obviously each was gifted, and all were being used by God significantly before we met. But I do believe each of them would say that taking part in such a peer group with a senior mentor sharpened, broadened, and deepened each of them for growing leadership roles.

Is there anyone here who could not bring together that kind of "point group" of young leaders with potential from your own ministry context?

You can aspire to be a spiritual mentor. Parker Palmer gives one of the best definitions of a leader I have ever heard: "A leader," says Palmer, "is someone who has an unusual ability to project his or her light, or his or her shadow on others." He also suggests that "Great leadership comes from people who have made (the) downward journey" into the deep places of their lives.

All of us can name leaders we have known who cast light, and others who cast shadow. And we all have light and shadow in our own lives. Young leaders know this, and it's been my experience that many of them are looking not only for a mentor to give them practical advice and counsel about ministry (though they welcome that), but long for an older man or woman who will be a spiritual guide, to help them on that downward and inward journey, that spiritual exploration out of which great leadership comes.

The ancient term for this, of course, is "spiritual direction."

Across the centuries, from the old desert fathers through the Reformers there has been a discipline of going to a spiritual guide or director to whom one opens fully and honestly one's inner life with God. The ancient Celts sought spiritual friends for the journey—the "anamchara" they called them. Their practice of spiritual direction was quite informal, and women as well as men, lay persons as well as clergy, could be spiritual guides to one another. In the Roman Catholic and Anglican traditions, spiritual direction was normally a part of the spiritual life of the clergy, and often more formal and institutionalized. Nevertheless, it was a key element for spiritual growth.

Henri Nouwen defined spiritual direction as an art: "It is helping a person to discern the movements of the Holy Spirit in one's life, assisting in the difficult task of obedience to these movements, and offering support in the crucial life decisions that our faithfulness requires." Thus spiritual direction is the work of an artist, not a mechanic.

Spiritual mentoring means paying attention to people, listening to them, and helping them to pay attention to what God is already doing in their lives. It usually involves an ongoing relationship of openness and trust, in which the mentor and mentoree meet regularly, perhaps every month or two, for several hours. The mentoree brings to the meeting a report of what is happening in his or her life as a whole, physically, emotionally, spiritually, relationally. In an atmosphere of sharing and listening, of silence and prayer, the mentor seeks to help the mentoree to discern what God is doing and saying in his or her life. He/she also seeks to help the mentoree to commit to those steps and disciplines which would seem to lead to personal spiritual growth, in knowing and serving God.

While discipleship has been important in our evangelical, Protestant tradition, spiritual mentoring or direction has had very little place, until recently. More and more young evangelical leaders are seeking a spiritual mentor, and if my observations are right, they are more often finding one in the Catholic or Anglican traditions.

I heartily recommend that senior or more experienced leaders explore the ministry of spiritual mentoring, learning what is involved in it from those who are already engaged in it. And if they feel so called, I encourage them to be open to establishing relationships of spiritual friendship with younger leaders.

There is an excellent new book, *Spiritual Mentoring: A Guide for Seeking and Giving Direction*, newly published by InterVarsity Press. The authors are Keith Anderson, campus pastor and associate professor at Bethel College, and Randy Reese, who is a vice president at North American Baptist Seminary and teaches leadership formation. Anderson and Reese have taken the best of the historic practice of spiritual direction, and placed it in a fine biblical and evangelical context. They provide many very helpful practical hints and suggestions for those who wish either to find, or provide, spiritual mentoring.

And what about you?

The very fact you are here says that you are committed in your life to the Lord, to the gospel, to kingdom ministry until Christ comes. So I assume that you want to be a seed-planter and nurturer, not a banyan tree.

Please don't hold back from opening your life as a mentor to the Joshuas and Elishas and Timothys and Deborahs and Phoebes that God has brought into your life. They are longing for senior leaders who will be available and vulnerable with them.

You have much to give to them...and much to receive. We are in a time when older leaders have so much to learn from younger leaders about the changes in our world, and when younger leaders so desperately need wisdom from older leaders about the constants in God's kingdom.

I have found simply hanging with younger people has kept me young! They have gotten me on-line—though e-mail sometimes seems as much a burden as a blessing. At sixty years of age I learned to rappel, and I have always been scared of heights. Our leadership program took a class out to rappel and rock climb. I went along as a cheerleader and then had to strap on the harness and go over an eighty-foot cliff when one of the guides insisted that I needed to take part. It was scary and exhilarating, and I loved it. These young women and men, with their fresh passion for the lost and hurting, have rekindled my own passion again and again.

And, I have made new, young friends who respond and care with an affection that is deep and touching, and who have been there for me through some very tough times. They have become for me "anamcharas," friends on the journey.

Jesus again is the model: the Jesus who on the road to Emmaus came to two disciples, heartbroken over his death, and made his risen presence known to them—in conversation, opening the Scriptures, eating a meal, and breaking bread with them...the Friend on the Journey.

Across the years I have found that the transforming moments for young leaders are often not in the lectures, but in the walks and talks...perhaps by a mountain stream, when our guard comes down and our hearts are deeply open to God and one another.

I took a walk one day with a young African-American man who works with gangs and drug dealers in the inner city. We walked down by a mountain stream, across a bridge, and sat there talking. He rolled up his pant's leg and showed me the scars from a cancer which almost took his life, but also brought him close to God. We both like to paint, and we talked about what drew our attention. I spoke to him about getting older, wondering what the future of the ministry I founded would be. He asked me if I had ever read Herman Hesse's story of the riverboat captain who, after many years, learned to listen to the river speak. And then we sat in silence and listened to the waterfalls, and to God.

Afterward, this is the poem I wrote:

River Speak
I walked this river many
times before,
but never quite so far
or quite so deep.

I've followed down its
darkened banks
this quiet, hidden, winding
ribbon
so close to tourist traffic
yet so far
removed.

But I had never listened for
the river's voice.

Today, I heard the river speak.

I took along a man,
a young, black man
to show the river to him
and the way.
But he showed me to see the way
and how to let
the river speak.

With him I went down
further
deeper
than I'd ever gone before.
A bridge was there I'd
never seen, or
never found, or
was not there
last year.
Across it was another
side, another
path that went down
where I'd never been
and showed me things
I'd never seen.

He showed me tenderness.
Reached out an unselfconscious
youthful arm
that touched my shoulders
and my soul.
I wondered for a moment
what would a watcher
think who saw a
young man hug
an old man
in the woods?
It was a holy touch.

He showed me woundedness.
Pulling up a pant's leg

he let me see on
one dark limb
the foot-long scarry flesh
where doctors poured
the poison to kill
a carcinoma, but left
him one bone short,
with tendons knitted by a stapled knot.
In his Jacob's twisted beauty
I saw the healing
hand of God.

He showed me artfulness.
Below cascades we
tried to frame a view
we'd like to paint.
"We'd want," I said, "the
rocks, the yellows and the
greens, the bridge, the falls."
"If it were me," he said,
"I'd let myself fall down
the bank, be bruised
a bit, and at the bottom
see what I would see."

He showed me guidedness.
Siddhartha, so he said.
And this I did not know,
after many years
of plying his trade
as a boatsman learned
to listen to the river.

And so, at last, we found a ledge
beneath the bridge and
sat a while and listened
to the white noise
of falling sheets
to rushing hiss

on polished rocks
to liquid grunts like
bullfrogs in the hollows
as the river spoke.

And—this is what it said—
"God started me before you came
this way.
He'll keep me going past your longest day.
I'll shape the earth yet deeper
to the falls.
I take my playful course
because He calls."

Like that the river spoke.

I heard my call
to walk the river as He
makes it flow
to take along those hearts
who want to go
and with them find the paths
I long to know.

This, then, is the calling that God the Great Friend gives to you and me...to be spiritual mentors to young leaders as we journey together on the way he is leading.

Epilogue

Kenneth B. Mulholland

As a young pastor, only an unexpected death in the congregation kept me from being present in Washington, D.C. to hear Martin Luther King's "I have a dream" speech. In his Pentecost speech, the apostle Peter also spoke of dreams. He cited Joel's prophecy that "Your young men shall dream dreams...."

This book contains the challenging presentations which emerged from the 1999 Triennial Consultation "Working Together to Shape the New Millennium." You can ignore the challenges presented on the assumption that the future will be like the past. You can retreat into splendid isolation or panic into an institutional survival mode. Or you can dream about the opportunities that the new millennium makes possible and work toward the realization of those dreams.

I have chosen to do the latter. As president of the Evangelical Misisological Society, I, too, have a dream.

A church for every people. As the new millennium dawns, my greatest dream and earnest hope is that the vision of a vital church movement for every people group and the gospel for every person will not be diminished and that the momentum gained in the closing years of this century will not be lost. All of my other hopes are subsidiary to this grand vision that at some point during this next century every person born everywhere in the world will have an opportunity to:

1. Hear, understand, and respond to the gospel message during his or her lifetime;

2. Be incorporated into a local congregation, and experience intimacy with the Father;

3. Be empowered to exhibit his or her Spirit fruitfulness in salt and light witness, as well as exercise Spirit giftedness in significant ministry.

The realization of this hope depends upon increased cooperation and undimmed focus. The distinction between access and lostness must not be blurred, but retained and even sharpened. Lost people are everywhere, but some lost people have access to the gospel and others do not. Some of the lost live next door to church buildings, go shopping in malls that have a Christian bookstore, listen to radios that carry gospel broadcasts, sleep in motels with Bibles in the bedside drawer, and labor with Christian people in the workplace. They may even attend Christian worship on Christmas or Easter and have Christian relatives. Their people group has been reached, but they are lost because they have not yet appropriated the gospel message.

Others who are equally lost have no such access. To them the gospel is unknown because there is no church in their geographic area, language group, or cultural frame of reference. Someone from outside will have to penetrate their world and establish a Christian movement in their midst or they will never hear. Thus, the goal of missions is to create access for the gospel among every segment of the human mosaic by initiating a vital church movement appropriate to each.

Evangelical unity. I dream of great unity and of the increased cooperation and coordination necessary to accelerate this process, not only at the formal and symbolic levels, but at the grass roots as well. Amid the bitter ethnic fragmentation characteristic of our time, reconciliation and the example of unity are essential to maintain the credibility of the gospel.

Already, I see many signs of evangelicals coming together to reflect the God-given unity of the Body of Christ: the Lausanne Movement, with its challenge for the whole church to take the whole gospel to the whole world; the AD2000 Movement, with its multiple networks; the DAWN Movement, with its emphasis on national mobilization; and the World Evangelical Fellowship, with its clarion call for solidarity with the persecuted church around the globe. Associations of missions such as the EFMA, IFMA, and AIMS are working hard at working together to expand their membership, coordinate strategy, eliminate duplication, and increase efficiency. The pacesetting stance of the International Mission Board of the Southern Baptist Convention with its expressed desire to cooperate with all Great Commission Christians is creating new paradigms for denominations intent on maximizing their global impact. And then there are the multiple national partnerships focusing together on completing the missionary task. I dream, too, of greater understanding and increased cooperation between charismatic and non-charismatic Christians as called for and outlined in David Shibley's watershed book, *A Force in the Earth*.

Further, I dare to dream of deeper relationships among evangelicals found in the various branches of Christendom. While I personally could not be a signatory to the "Evangelicals and Catholics Together" document, I recognize the importance of supporting the witness of our brothers and sisters in the faith, whatever their ecclesiastical affiliation. I do not know what shape this will take in order to preserve doctrinal integrity while furthering biblical witness, but I desperately want it to happen.

Compassionate witness. I dream of witness driven by compassion and aimed at the whole person. I believe that mission consists of all that God has called the church, as a pilot project of the kingdom of God, to accomplish among humanity. This includes both the cultural and evangelical mandates (doing justice and loving mercy while preaching grace). While I recognize the dynamic interplay between the two mandates, I continue to assign priority to the evangelistic mandate. Relief, development, and service ministries in the name of Christ, and accompanied by verbal witness where possible, bear witness to the Christ who not only died for our sins and rose for our justification, but by his earthly ministry illumined darkened minds, healed sick bodies, fed hungry people, and released tormented souls from the grip of the evil one.

Mission at the heart of scholarship. Some may call this the impossible dream, but, nevertheless, I dream that evangelical scholars on every continent and in every theological discipline will place "a church for every people and the gospel for every person" at the heart of their academic endeavor and personal lives.

Because of the great desire to work together with evangelical scholars of all disciplines, the EMS regularly conducts its regional and national meetings parallel to the Evangelical Theological Society. No more significant document emerged from the 1997 Global Consultation on World Evangelization in Pretoria than the "PAD Declaration," produced by 256 presidents and deans of training institutions, ranging from Bible schools to theological seminaries, representing 53 nations. (PAD stands for Presidents and Academic Deans.) I long to see those 10 theses implemented, and have committed myself to make this happen at Columbia, the school where currently I exercise leadership.

Adequate preparation. I dream that when religious liberty comes to China, missionary endeavors will not repeat the mistakes committed in the enthusiastic days following the raising of the Iron Curtain. Anticipatory strategy, serious language and culture learning, as well as ministries sensitive to the presence and witness of the existing churches need to characterize the foreign response to open doors.

Partnership. Finally, I dream of using the resources of the whole church so that emerging missions and national evangelism are enhanced without becoming mired in the kind of dependency from which mission agencies have been trying to extricate themselves for the past century. Perhaps we need to employ imagery that reflects not so much the world of contractual agreements and corporate management but more the organic imagery of the various systems of the body working together.

In his likely-to-become-a-classic, *The Church is Bigger Than You Think*, Patrick Johnstone calls churches, mission agencies, and training schools to work together in the kind of mutually accountable synergism that advances God's kingdom and brings glory to his name. I hope and dream that this vision, so well articulated by Johnstone, gives birth to an ecclessiology that understands schools and mission agencies as part of the church, rather than limiting the church to congregational structures. The New Testament is clear that apostolic bands, as well as local congregations, were part of Christ's Body.

How desperately we need churches and pastors with a global vision who, in keeping with Acts 1:8, are determined to make a global impact. For this to happen, pastors must lead their congregations to assume responsibility (either as an individual congregation or as coordinated networks of congregational, educational, and mission structures) for the evangelization of every person in a local geographical area. Then that circle of accountability must be projected to geographical, ethnological, or sociological circles distant from the local church.

Concerns. I am concerned about doctrinal integrity, as well as turf wars and kingdom building, and the human arrogance that tries to go it alone. And I'm concerned about schools and mission agencies that heap financial burdens upon the shoulders of would-be candidates, as well as agencies that permit missionaries to bypass tough language and culture learning for short-term gains. I'm concerned about spiritual flabbiness that substitutes consumerism for godliness, and exalts self-love above self-denial. And I'm concerned about the collapse of the global economy, the implosion of Russia and Central Asia, the appeal of Islamic fundamentalism, and the relativism endemic to the West.

Present momentum, future hope. My hopes outweigh my concerns. During this century, we've seen the ratio of Christians to non-Christians in Asia decline from one in 177 to one in 12, and in Africa south of the Sahara from one in 20 to one in three. We've seen the number of evangelicals in Latin America grow from 50,000 to more than 50 million, and the population of evangelical Christians in China, India, and Brazil rival the number in the United States. The evangelical segment of the Christian church continues to expand more rapidly than either the global population, or Islam. Each day sees an estimated 78,000 new Christians; each week, 1,600 new congregations are established. Most of the world's evangelical Christians now live in Asia, Africa, and Latin America. And most of the Christian world leadership doesn't come from the North Atlantic, but from the Two-Thirds world.

Within the next few years, I'll be passing the baton. When I do, I'll say, "Look ahead to the goal. The future is as bright as the promises of God. Run for all you're worth, but remember, it's a team effort."

Yes! Let's work together to shape the New Millennium.

www.ingramcontent.com/pod-product-compliance
Lightning Source LLC
Chambersburg PA
CBHW071236070526
44583CB00017B/2202